W0225462

RIVER TALES OF IDAHO

Geographic locations of River Tales

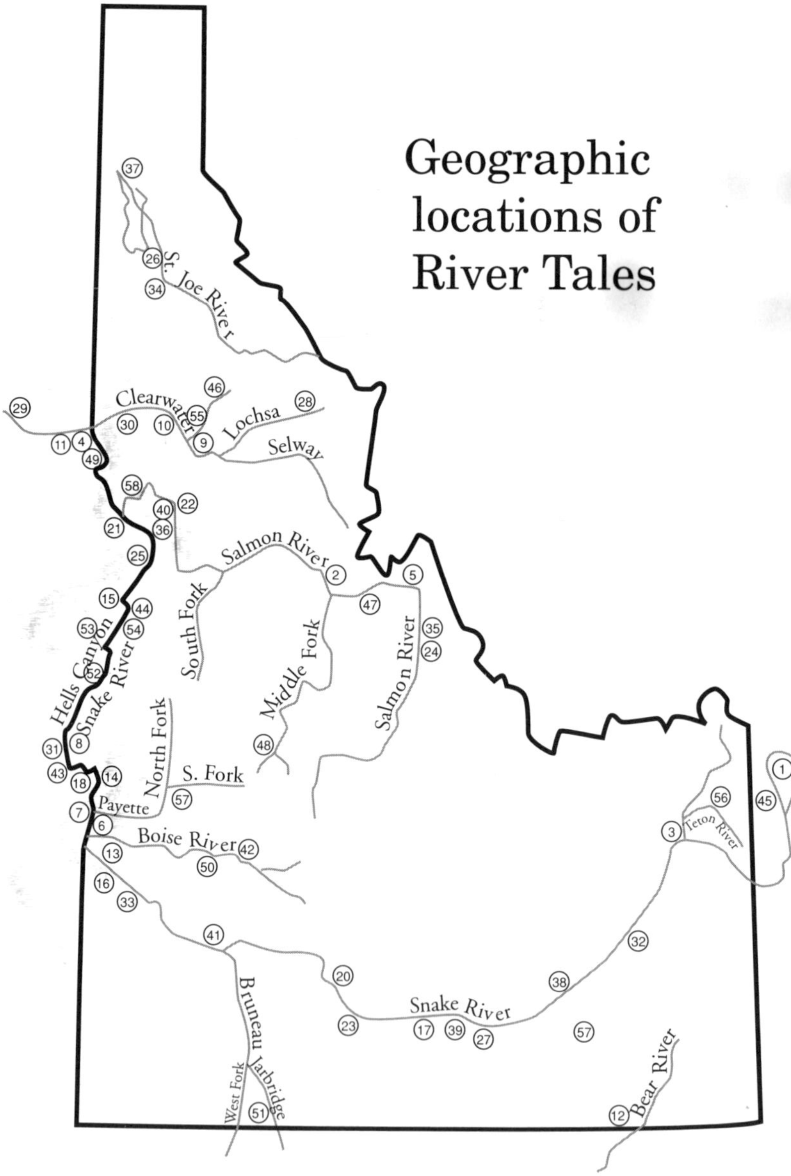

RIVER TALES OF IDAHO

By

Darcy Williamson

Illustrated by Jim Paxton

Cover Painting of the
Wilson Price Hunt Party
by Larry Milligan

The CAXTON PRINTERS, Ltd.
Caldwell, Idaho
1997

Library of Congress Cataloging-in-Publication Data

Williamson, Darcy -
River Tales of Idaho / by Darcy Williamson ;
illustrated by Jim Paxton
p. cm.
Includes bibliographical references and index.
ISBN 0-87004-378-1
1. Rivers -- Idaho -- History -- Anecdotes.
2. Idaho -- History -- Anecdotes. I. Title
F752.A17W55 1997
979.6'009693--dc21 97-12072
CIP

Lithographed and bound in the United States of America by
The CAXTON PRINTERS, Ltd.
Caldwell, ID 83605
162290

Dedication

To my friend, Steven Shephard, of Salmon River Outfitters, who introduced me to Idaho's whitewater.

To guides B.J., Daniel, Kimberly, Erin, Jenny and Dave, who have shared their oars with me over the years — and not scolded too harshly when I bumped into rocks.

To Barry Dow for the grand adventure of rafting on the Colorado.

To Rob Dow for piloting our raft and mastering Lava.

To Don and Connie McClaran for the generous loan of their Havasu.

To Scottie for his guidance. X0X0!

To Brenna, Dave, Neil, Patrick and Valli for the companionship and laughter shared on the Colorado.

CONTENTS

ILLUSTRATIONS

Introduction

This is the story of Idaho's rivers. These waterways have challenged and humbled man since the beginning of recorded history. It also is the story of how those rivers were conquered and eventually harnessed.

This compilation of historical accounts reaches back to the time when all of Idaho's rivers flowed free — unmapped and unchallenged. It documents the changes brought by trappers and explorers who tried to run the white water in bullboats and canoes.

Native Americans and early settlers harvested fish from the waters. Steamboats labored up and downstream through treacherous rapids. "Log Hogs" risked their lives herding timber to sawmills.

Some men and women challenged the rivers for no other reason than the thrill of adventure. Deserts blossomed under irrigation. Dams provided flood control and energy resources, at the sacrifice of steelhead and salmon migrations. Stretches of untamed water now are preserved for recreational uses by legislation.

As each story unfolds, there is one continuous thread. Of all the natural resources that have contributed to the economic growth of Idaho, its rivers have made the largest contribution — and paid the greatest price.

ONE

Snake River

Creation: A Shoshoni Telling

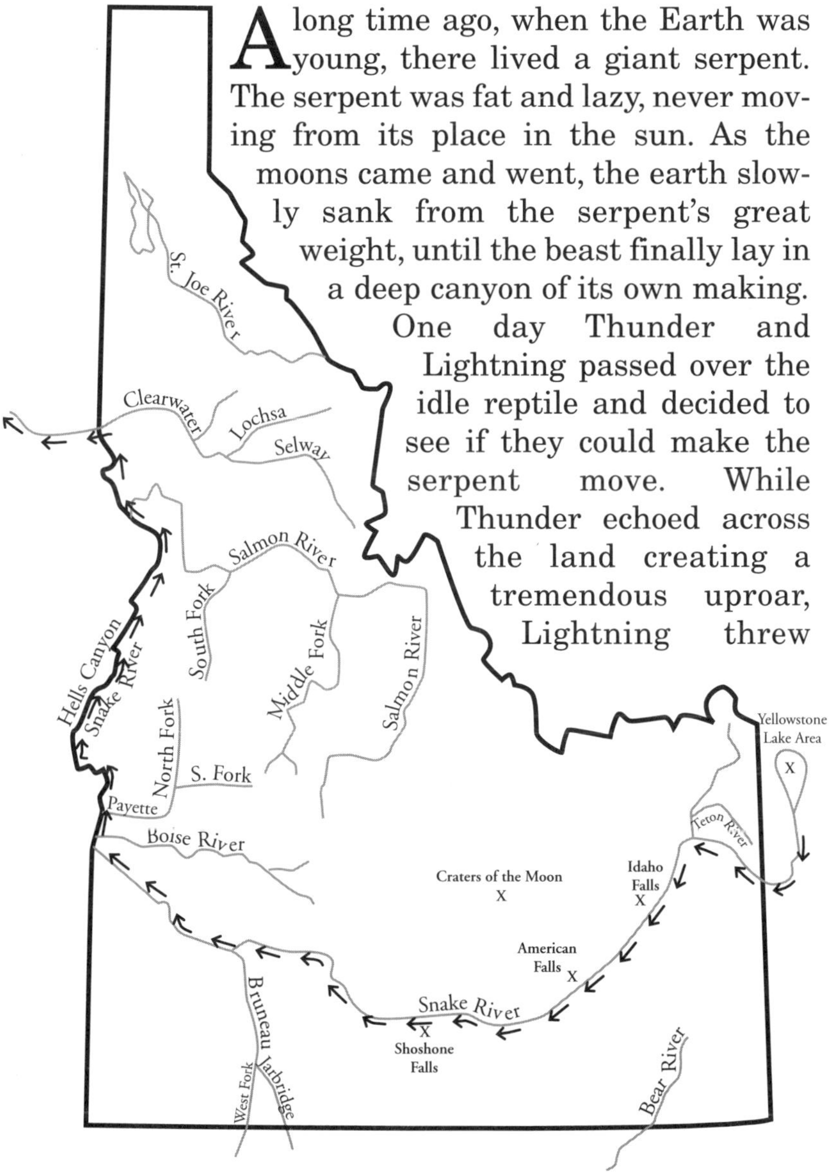

A long time ago, when the Earth was young, there lived a giant serpent. The serpent was fat and lazy, never moving from its place in the sun. As the moons came and went, the earth slowly sank from the serpent's great weight, until the beast finally lay in a deep canyon of its own making. One day Thunder and Lightning passed over the idle reptile and decided to see if they could make the serpent move. While Thunder echoed across the land creating a tremendous uproar, Lightning threw spears that burned small holes in the giant's scales. The serpent began to writhe with anger, striking at Thunder and Lightning with its long white fangs. But Thunder and Lightning remained just beyond the serpent's striking distance. Spying a nearby mountain, the angry reptile coiled around it to get closer to its tormentors.

The two teasers, however, stayed at a safe distance while worrying the serpent. As the reptile became increasingly aggravated, it squeezed the mountain more tightly with its coils, causing the peak to become so hot that it exploded and melted away across the land. Being fat and lazy, the serpent could not escape the melting mountain. Its bones forever lay where the mountain once stood, covered by melted stone cooled to solid rock. If you go to this place, now called Craters of the Moon, you will see the snake's skeleton outlined in the cooled lava.

For many years the great canyon left by the serpent lay empty and dry.

Near the upper end of this canyon lived an old woman who had a very large basket in which lived many salmon. The old woman took good care of her fish, providing special things to eat and stroking their scaly backs. The salmon liked the old woman very much and thrived on her attention.

Coyote also liked the salmon. But the old woman thought he might like them too much and eat one for his supper. She told Coyote to stay away from her basket and leave her salmon alone. Still, Coyote skulked around the fish.

One time the old woman caught Coyote with his paws on the edge of the basket looking in. It was beginning to tip and some of the water almost spilled out. She became very angry with Coyote and scolded him as he slunk into the bushes. But soon Coyote forgot his scolding and again became curious about the salmon. He waited until the old woman went to gather food for her fish and crept up to the basket to peek in. The salmon were swimming around and around in big circles. Coyote liked their pink color and the way they smelled. He climbed a little farther onto the basket to get a better look and a better sniff. But he went too far this time, tipping the basket over so all the salmon spilled out. The water that remained in the basket became Yellowstone Lake.

The escaping water flowed into the canyon left by the serpent, carrying the salmon along as it rushed down the gorge.

Coyote was in a panic. He did not want another scolding from the old woman. Racing ahead, he tried to stop the water before it flowed away to the sea. Coyote built a big dam to hold back the flow, but it was not big enough. The first dam is now called Idaho Falls.

Coyote again raced ahead of the water and built an even better dam. It also failed to stop the flood. The second dam became known as American Falls.

Once more Coyote raced ahead of the water and used all of his might to build the biggest dam possible. The dam held, but only briefly. Suddenly the water reared up and leaped over the dam, carrying with it all the old woman's salmon. That is why the Shoshoni people call the place Pahchulaka, which means "hurling waters leaping." White men call this place Shoshone Falls.

The water carried the salmon all the way to the sea. They liked the ocean, but every year would begin to miss the old woman and the basket. The salmon gathered together and tried to return home. They swam hundreds of miles upstream but were always stopped at Pahchulaka. The falls was so high they could not leap over it. They believed Coyote would someday right the wrong he had done, and tear down the big dams.

The Shoshoni heard about the great dams and knew the salmon would try to return home to the basket. The people gathered each year below Pahchulaka to wait for the salmon to arrive.

When the first salmon was caught, all fishing stopped while they roasted the catch. Each member of the tribe took one bite, giving thanks to the salmon for its nourishment. Fishing resumed the next day, with much feasting and dancing. The Shoshoni fished in the pools below the falls for weeks, drying the salmon so they would have food for winter.

Coyote, being father of all Shoshoni, refused to tear down his dams. He knew his children needed the salmon to sustain themselves through the long seasons of the snowy moons.

TWO

Salmon River — 1805

Lewis and Clark Turned Back

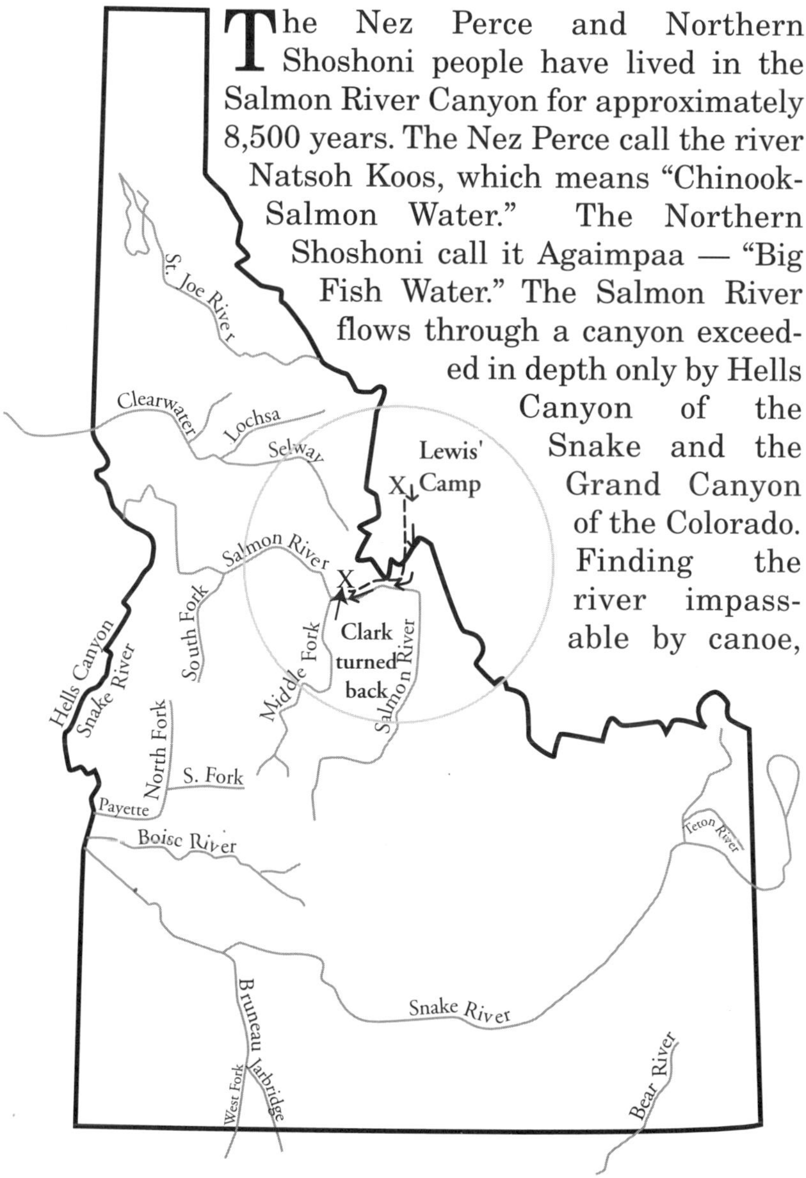

The Nez Perce and Northern Shoshoni people have lived in the Salmon River Canyon for approximately 8,500 years. The Nez Perce call the river Natsoh Koos, which means "Chinook-Salmon Water." The Northern Shoshoni call it Agaimpaa — "Big Fish Water." The Salmon River flows through a canyon exceeded in depth only by Hells Canyon of the Snake and the Grand Canyon of the Colorado. Finding the river impassable by canoe, the Indians reached its banks by making trails down tributary streams.

The first white men to test the Salmon were members of the Lewis and Clark Expedition, during late summer 1805. The explorers planned to build canoes and float down the river, avoiding an arduous journey through the mountains. Although the Shoshoni told them canoes could not descend the river, Captain William Clark had to see for himself. Leaving Captain Meriwether Lewis to do some horse-trading with the Shoshoni, Clark took eleven men, tools for making canoes, and horses for transporting supplies, and headed downstream along the Salmon River.

On August 18, the first campsite was established at Red Butte, eight miles west of present-day Grant, Montana. The next morning, the men proceeded down the valley to Trail Creek, following the gradual slope west of Lemhi Pass. The trail steepened, enroute to Horseshoe Bend Creek. From there, Clark and his group traveled another eight miles, making camp at Pattee Creek.

The next morning the party arrived at an Indian camp near Kenny Creek. Clark hired an elderly Indian man, who they called Toby, to act as guide. The group proceeded to the river, traveling eight miles before camping in the vicinity of Withington Creek.

On August 21, the party crossed the Lemhi River, passed over a hill and struck the Salmon River. They had to stay on the canyon rim because the shoreline was too narrow for passage. Clark and his men traveled twenty miles that day.

On the fifth day of their journey, the explorers began to realize that a river route might be impossible. After passing Boyle Creek, the mountains came so close to the river that the travelers could not get through. The men climbed four steep slopes before dropping down into a small bottom land at the mouth of the North Fork of the Salmon. From the trail above the river they saw long stretches of white water.

Finding three Shoshoni lodges, they rested among the Indians for a few hours before setting up camp three miles farther downstream. The next morning, they proceeded with great difficulty. There was no path. Four miles beyond their last camp, they found it impossible to continue with their horses. Most of the party was left at a small flat on the north side of the river, approximately one mile below the mouth of Little Moose Creek. They were instructed to hunt for game, since supplies were running low.

With the Indian guide Toby and three men, Clark continued, following game trails and climbing over rock slides, until the party came to Indian Creek, twelve miles from where they had left the eight men and horses. Able to travel only a short distance along the narrow shoreline, Clark described the Salmon as "one continued rapid."

The river was five hundred feet wide at that point. Toby led Clark and his three companions up Squaw Creek along a well-worn Indian path, bypassing a bend of the river. Standing on a mountain peak three miles upstream from the present-day community of Shoup, Clark viewed the Salmon while Toby made a wide, sweeping gesture indicating the difficulties the party would experience if it attempted to canoe down through the boulder-strewn rapids.

It was clear the expedition could not navigate the river and would have to cross the mountains by another route. Clark was dejected. Never before on the westward journey had the party turned back because of a natural obstacle.

Clark started back the next morning. Breakfast consisted of chokecherries and hawthorn berries found growing near the water. Exhausted, Clark and his men reached the bivouac about 4 P.M. The hunters had found no game. They packed up camp and moved three miles farther upstream. There was no supper that night.

The following day, the men reached the North Fork of the Salmon, where the Indians gave them some dried salmon. Four days later, Clark and his followers rejoined Lewis and the main party.

After giving Lewis the bad news, Clark tried to add a note of celebration to the reunion by writing in his journal:

"I shall in justice to Capt. Lewis, who was the first white man ever on this fork of the Columbia, call this Lewis's River. . ."

But the name did not stick. By 1810, maps of the area called the wild river by the name it is known today – the Salmon.

THREE

Snake River — 1811

The Wilson Price Hunt Party

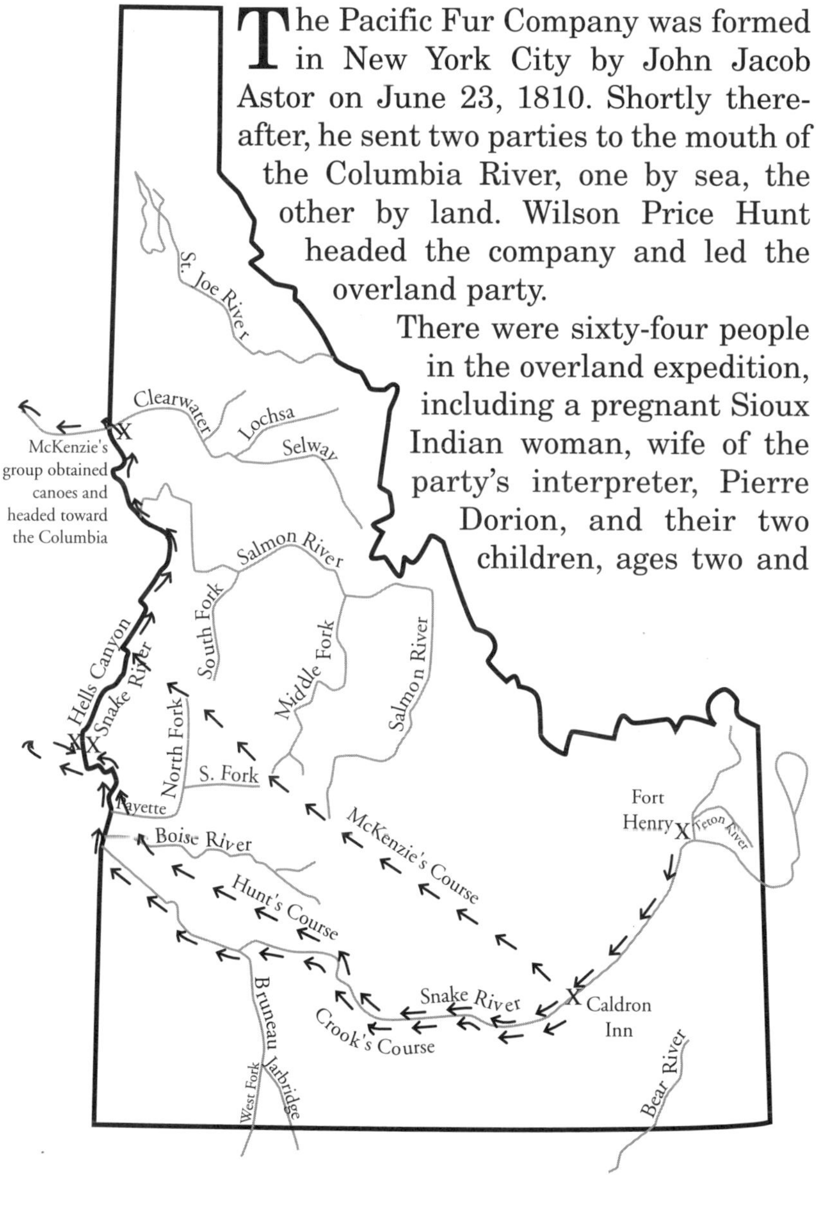

The Pacific Fur Company was formed in New York City by John Jacob Astor on June 23, 1810. Shortly thereafter, he sent two parties to the mouth of the Columbia River, one by sea, the other by land. Wilson Price Hunt headed the company and led the overland party.

There were sixty-four people in the overland expedition, including a pregnant Sioux Indian woman, wife of the party's interpreter, Pierre Dorion, and their two children, ages two and five. The journey was uneventful until they reached Idaho's Snake River.

On October 7, 1811, the overland party arrived at a trading post on the North Fork of the Snake. Called Henry's Fort, the first American post west of the main ridge of the Rockies had been built the previous summer. But its founder, Andrew Henry, and his employees, abandoned the fort after almost starving during a bitter first winter.

Weary of traveling by horseback, the members of the Hunt party decided to use the large cottonwoods growing along the river to build canoes to float down the Snake to the Columbia River. Wilson Price Hunt negotiated with two local Shoshoni Indians to watch the party's horses, numbering more than 100 head, until his planned return the following year. The natives warned Hunt that river travel on the Snake was not possible. But because a member of the party was suffering from an ailment that made "riding a horse a torture . . .," the warning went unheeded.

Four men were left in the vicinity of Henry's Fort to trap beaver. The rest of the party loaded the fifteen new canoes with supplies and resumed their journey toward the Columbia.

The voyage down the Snake began smoothly. The day was clear and cold, but the landscape was warmed by golden leaves still clinging to the cottonwoods lining the river, the rust-orange of hawthorn, and the barren red twigs of Osier Dogwood.

When the party reached the junction of the Snake and Mad rivers, the channel widened and the water took on a pea-green hue. The current became stronger, moving the canoes along at a swift pace.

The first major rapid was encountered October 21, near present-day Idaho Falls. The hand-hewn canoes were rigged with ropes. Then, with all the men ashore, the craft were eased down the rapids. Several capsized, spilling their cargo into the river. Below the rapids, the river ran smoothly, so the men got back into the canoes. Geese and ducks and beaver were abundant. Two days of traveling on placid waters brought the Hunt expedition to the mouth of the Portneuf.

But October 28, river travel came to an end. Temperatures dropped below freezing and ice crusted the river's edge. In the distance, the Teton Mountains stood white against a dark, gray sky. The hiss of wind-driven sleet covered the ominous roar of a rapid downstream.

When the danger became apparent, there was no time to get the canoes ashore. The first canoe survived the rapid. But the second vessel, manned by Ramsey Crooks, hit a large boulder and flipped over. Crooks and three of his boatmen clung to a rock and were rescued. The fifth occupant of the canoe, Antonine Clappine, disappeared into the dark, whirling vortex below. Hunt named the spot Caldron Linn.

The river narrowed and more white frothing water was visible in the distance. Although the travelers considered themselves finished with the Snake River, the river wasn't finished with them.

The defeated trappers hauled their supplies up the icy banks of the Snake. With no horses to carry the stores, they had to cache the lot. Most of the goods were trade items such as knives, mirrors, cloth and paint. The river had swallowed most of the food, leaving the group with rations for only five days.

Realizing the situation was desperate, Hunt divided the party into four groups. He sent Ramsey Crooks with five men to Henry's Fort to retrieve the horses and rejoin the main party. Robert McClellan was sent to scout downriver with three companions. Donald McKenzie and four men went north toward some distant mountains to search for a pass to the Columbia.

Hunt, left with about thirty people, began digging the caches. Nine large pits were dug, then lined with sticks, dried grass and sage. Nine canoes, loaded with supplies, were lowered into the pits. The sandy soil was carefully smoothed and clumps of grass and sage were planted to help erase evidence of the pits. The process took several days.

Before the caches were finished, Ramsey Crooks and his men returned. The exhausted men had been forced to turn back before reaching Henry's Fort.

Robert McClellan, fearing that Hunt's desperate situation might tempt him to again take to the river, sent two messengers upstream to report that the Snake was impassable.

The trappers couldn't stay in the river camp without provisions. They only had a small reserve of corn, dried meat, grease and bouillon tablets. Hunt again divided the group. Nineteen men, led by Ramsey, crossed to the south bank of the Snake. Nineteen others, including the Sioux woman and two children, stayed on the north bank with Hunt.

Two days later, Hunt found a trail and fresh horse tracks which he followed to a Shoshoni encampment. The Indians had few provisions to spare. But the trappers were able to trade for a few bits of food and some horses, one for the woman and children to ride.

The party left the river bank and struck out across the desert. The trek through the bleak land covered with rock, sand and sage took nearly three weeks. Water was scarce. On the frosty morning of November 21 they saw the Boise River in the distance, bordered by cottonwoods and willows. They followed the stream through flat, easily-traveled country until the Boise joined the Snake River.

The Snake River flowed smooth and rapid before dropping through a narrow canyon with steep slopes caped in the brown grasses of winter. Travel in the canyon appeared impossible so the explorers continued north. Soon they were in snow. Scouts reported they could see great pine clad mountains covered with snow ahead. It was the roughest country the travelers had seen.

The trappers headed back toward the Snake River. The snow got deeper. All the horses except the one ridden by the woman were killed for food. They melted snow for drinking water.

Finally Hunt's party made it back to the edge of the river, below the snow line. They traveled the slippery, treacherous banks for six miles before making camp.

The next morning, Dec. 6, they heard shouting from the opposite river bank. It was Ransey Crooks and his band. Hunt ordered a bullboat built from willows and the fresh horse hides. Some meat was sent to men on the far bank. One of Crook's men, demented by the sight of the food in the approaching boat, tried to swim out to the vessel and drowned.

Ramsey Crooks, John Day and Fracois Le Clerc returned to Hunt's camp in the bullboat. The men were gaunt and near starvation. During their month and a half ordeal they had survived on one beaver, the carcass of a dog, a few dried chokecherries and the soles of worn-out moccasins.

Crooks told Hunt there were impassable cliffs downriver and mountains blocked by snow. They had no choice but to leave the river.

The rest of Crooks party came across the river in the bullboat. Some of Hunt's men wanted to forge ahead without the feeble new arrivals. When Hunt refused, several members of the group set out alone.

The reunited trappers persuaded some reluctant Indians to guide them up the Burnt River and across the mountains to the Columbia River. The Sioux woman's baby was born Dec. 30, but died nine days later. There was no way to protect one so new to the world from the harsh elements and winter winds. Although the explorers needed food, they spared the last horse for the sorrowing woman and her children to ride.

On February 15, 1812, the Hunt Party arrived at the newly-constructed Fort Astoria. Some stragglers did not reach the post until several months later.

Robert McClellan was at Astoria to greet Hunt, having arrived a couple of months earlier. Donald McKenzie and his group had come in January 12.

After leaving Hunt at Caldron Linn, McKenzie's party of five cut north, then northwest, struggling through some of the West's most rugged country. When they ran out of rations, they lived for a time on strips of boiled beaver pelts. They nearly died of thirst while traveling the east rim of Hells Canyon, more than a mile above the winding stream.

In the high reaches of the canyon, a member of the party shot a mountain sheep. The spirits and strength of the men were revived by the feast of fresh meat.

When McKenzie reached the Clearwater River, he obtained canoes from the Nez Perce Indians. They followed the river to the Columbia, then floated on to Fort Astoria.

The Hunt party's attempt to navigate the Snake River was the first on record, as was their crossing of southern Idaho.

In 1938, rusty traps and guns were found in the Snake River near Cauldron Linn. They were the type used by early trappers and are believed to be from the doomed canoe. The items are on display at the Idaho State Historical Museum in Boise.

At 1,038 miles, the Snake River is the third longest river in the lower 48 states.

FOUR

Snake River — 1819

Donald McKenzie — Perpetual Motion Upstream

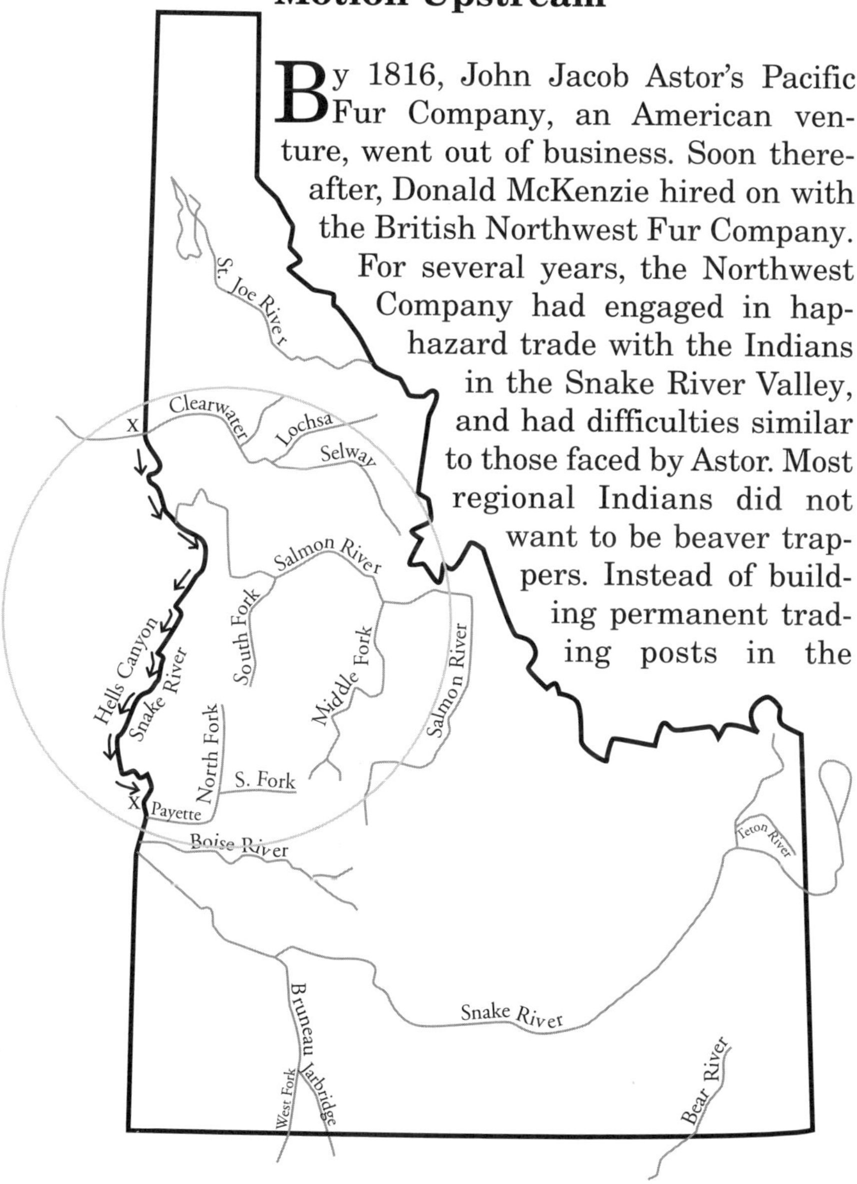

By 1816, John Jacob Astor's Pacific Fur Company, an American venture, went out of business. Soon thereafter, Donald McKenzie hired on with the British Northwest Fur Company. For several years, the Northwest Company had engaged in haphazard trade with the Indians in the Snake River Valley, and had difficulties similar to those faced by Astor. Most regional Indians did not want to be beaver trappers. Instead of building permanent trading posts in the midst of uncooperative natives, large parties of white or French-Canadian trappers were sent out to collect the pelts. The first expedition was headed by Donald McKenzie.

A Canadian native of Scottish descent, McKenzie was red-headed, stood six feet three inches tall, and weighed more than 300 pounds. Fearless in the face of adversity, he was described by Washington Irving in his book, *Astoria* as a man with "...a frame seasoned to toil and hardships, a spirit not to be intimidated, and the reputation of being a remarkable shot."

So intense was the man's energy that another ex-Astorian, Alexander Ross, nicknamed McKenzie "Perpetual Motion." Soon he was known throughout the trapping community as Perpetual Motion McKenzie.

Establishing Fort Nez Perce (later Fort Walla Walla) in 1819, as a staging place for his trapping expeditions, he set about expanding the company's territory. McKenzie marched his "Nor'Westers" as far east as present day Utah, discovering the beaver-rich Bear River area. And he always was looking for ways to use the rivers for transportation.

McKenzie's experiences with the Hunt Party on the upper Snake ruled out that part of the river for travel. But the section through Hells Canyon (known as Box Canyon in the early 1800s) remained unexplored. Even with his boundless strength, McKenzie did not regard himself so indestructible that he could canoe down through Hells Canyon in his quest for short-cuts. But going up the river was a challenge he was willing to undertake.

During late February 1819, McKenzie selected six Canadians from his brigade at Fort Nez Perce, loaded a bateau with supplies and headed through snow and ice to the mouth of the Clearwater. From there, he proceeded up the Snake. In spots where the river was still frozen, the barge easily glided along on improvised skids. But there were long stretches where the river flowed free. The men battled up through ice-choked rapids. By April 15, the explorers reached Burnt River, near present-day Farewell Bend.

McKenzie and his Nor'Westers were the first white men to pass all the way through Hells Canyon. To ordinary human beings, such an expedition seemed an amazing feat. To Perpetual Motion McKenzie, it was a routine achievement to be taken in stride. The only record of his astonishing achievement was in a note sent to Alexander Ross:

> "Point Successful, head of narrows, April 15, 1819...The passage by water is now proved to be safe and practicable for loaded boats with one single carrying place or portage. Therefore, the doubtful question is now set to rest forever. Yet from the force of the current and frequency of rapids, it may still be advisable and perhaps preferable to continue the land transportation while the business in this quarter is carried on upon a small scale... We had often recourse to the line. There are two places with bold cut rocks on either side of the river where the great body of water is compressed within a narrow compass, which may render those parts doubtful during the floods, owing to rocks and

whirlpools, but there are only two and neither of them are long."

McKenzie's declaration of a "safe and practicable" passage did not result in an onslaught of river runners through Hells Canyon. In fact, it was not until 1852 that the next adventurers attempted to travel that section of river in anything resembling a boat.

FIVE

Salmon River — 1832

Disaster of 1832

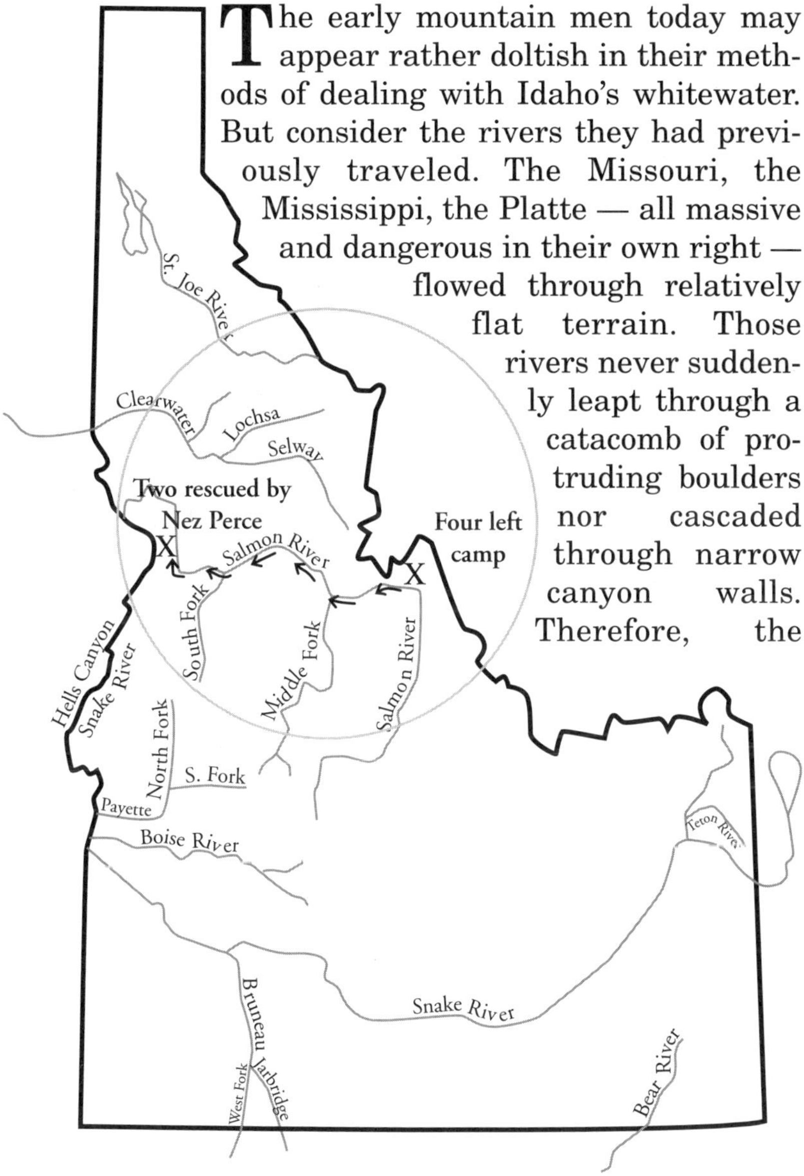

The early mountain men today may appear rather doltish in their methods of dealing with Idaho's whitewater. But consider the rivers they had previously traveled. The Missouri, the Mississippi, the Platte — all massive and dangerous in their own right — flowed through relatively flat terrain. Those rivers never suddenly leapt through a catacomb of protruding boulders nor cascaded through narrow canyon walls. Therefore, the journey of four men down the Salmon River in 1832, the first recorded, was not an act of stupidity nor an attempt at suicide. It was merely an adventure into uncharted territory, as the trappers sought new sources of beaver pelts.

The four men, L. Boisdnt, A. Dumaris, H. Plante, and J. Laurin, were members of a Hudson's Bay Company expedition led by John Work. They volunteered to venture into a territory never before trapped by white men, floating down virgin waters hopefully teeming with thick-coated beaver.

Sunday morning, March 25, 1832, was blessed with unseasonably warm weather. Having never seen that area of the Salmon River before, the four men mistook the unseasonable weather for the arrival of spring. They were in high spirits as they built their hide-covered vessel — a contraption commonly referred to as a bullboat.

A bullboat was a circular craft approximately three feet in depth. It was an ungainly vessel that required considerable skill to maneuver through rough water. The boat was most manageable when loaded with at least 250 pounds of cargo. Fresh hides, preferably elk, were stretched over a frame. When the hides began to dry, the seams were sealed with generous amounts of tree sap applied with a wooden paddle.

Monday morning dawned bright and clear. The four men waved a cheery farewell to their well-wishing comrades lining the shore, as their primitive craft caught the current and floated off down what would later be called "The River of No Return."

The first few rapids were choppy and rough. Each bend in the river brought new horrors as the river narrowed. The bullboat was continuously swamped with icy water. Rocks and boulders jutted out of the river, stabbing at the vessel as it spun dangerously out of control. The men finally managed to work the craft to shore. Supplies were unloaded and the boat inverted to drain accumulated water.

The men reasoned that the boat would swamp less if two of them walked along the shoreline, while the other pair manned the craft. Each man took a turn ashore.

The weather turned cold. Sleet, rain, then sleet again slashed their faces. The men walking the shore had to scramble along game trails, zigzagging up and down the steep canyon walls to bypass obstacles along the river's edge. Although the climbing was exhausting, the men ashore considered themselves fortunate. By walking, they avoided the bone-chilling water and the heart-stopping rapids of the Salmon River.

For thirty days, the four men worked their way down the river, sometimes lining the boat, sometimes carrying it around the more dangerous spots. They were not surprised that they found no beaver. No beaver could dam such a damnable river. Although the mountain slopes high above them were golden with arrow-leaf balsam, they found few plant foods and little game along the Salmon's steep, treacherous shores.

While the boat was being manned by Dumaris and Plante one afternoon, it disappeared around a bend in the river as Boisdnt and Laurin were struggling around a steep canyon out-cropping. The two men on shore walked until dark, but found no sign of the boatmen. After a cold night without bedding or supplies, the two afoot continued their trek. At midmorning, they found a paddle from their boat caught between some rocks near shore. Farther downriver, they discovered the scattered remains of their supplies. Neither of the bodies of their drowned companions nor their bullboat ever were found.

With no weapons or gear, Boisdnt and Laurin continued on. Several days later, some Nez Perce Indians found the cold, starving, nearly naked men trudging along the banks of the river, took them to their camp, clothed, warmed, and fed them.

Continuing their trapping expedition through central Idaho, John Work and his party expected the four men to appear at any time, loaded with pelts and tales of their float adventure. Months passed with no word of the men's fate other than rumors circulating among the Shoshoni that two of the trappers had met with mishap and drowned. On July 19, Boisdnt and Laurin finally rejoined the expedition.

Not until 1886 did a boat make a successful run down that stretch of the Salmon River.

SIX

Snake River — 1843

The Fort Boise Ferry

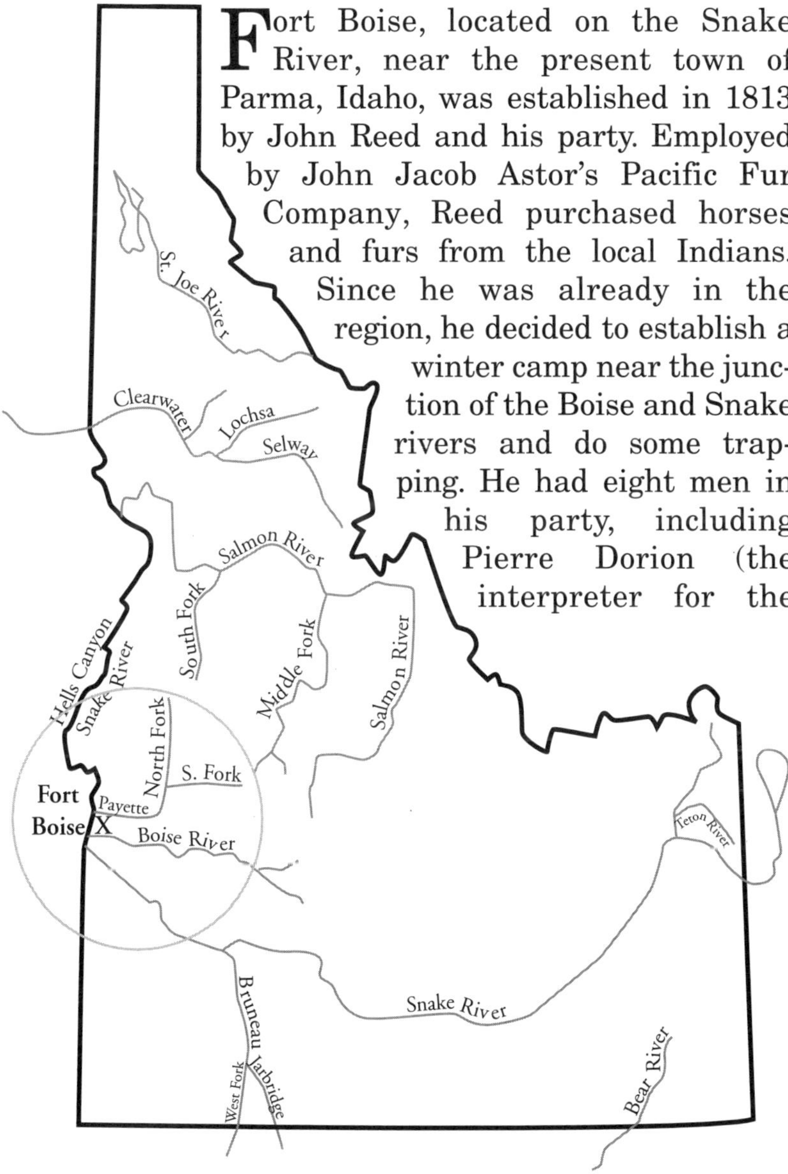

Fort Boise, located on the Snake River, near the present town of Parma, Idaho, was established in 1813 by John Reed and his party. Employed by John Jacob Astor's Pacific Fur Company, Reed purchased horses and furs from the local Indians. Since he was already in the region, he decided to establish a winter camp near the junction of the Boise and Snake rivers and do some trapping. He had eight men in his party, including Pierre Dorion (the interpreter for the

William Price Hunt Party), Dorion's Sioux wife and their two children.

A temporary fort was built that autumn. In January 1814, while trapping along the Boise River, the Reed party was attacked by Bannock Indians and all nine men were killed. Dorion's wife, tending camp, had been forewarned by friendly Indians, and escaped to the Columbia River with the two children. After spending a cold winter hiding, they were rescued in April by Donald McKenzie and his Northwest Fur Company brigade. Many years later, the Sons and Daughters of the Idaho Pioneers erected a monument, located near the Fort Boise site, in honor of the Sioux woman.

For several years after the massacre, the Boise River was known as the Reed River.

In 1819, "Perpetual Motion" McKenzie, established a Northwest Fur Company post near the site of Reed's post. Again, the Bannocks attacked. McKenzie and his men barely escaped the fate of the Reed party.

In 1834, Thomas McKay built a Hudson's Bay Company fort on the east bank of the Snake, north of Reed's site. Francois Payette, for whom the nearby river and town of Payette are named, joined McKay in 1835, Payette was in charge of the fort for the next nine years. After 1836, the adobe structure was known as Fort Boise.

In 1836, the Whitman and Spaulding families, who were missionaries, reached the fort in a two-wheeled cart. It was the first vehicle to cross the Snake River on a ferry at that location. The ferry was built from cattail rushes attached to a frame made of willows. It was pulled across the river by Indians on horseback, one positioned at each corner of the crude boat.

By 1843, the fort was well established and crossings were common. The structure was of adobe and log, surrounded by an adobe wall twelve and a half feet high and 400 feet long – 100 feet per side. The fort was entered from the side facing the Snake River.

At that time, the ferry was a large wooden canoe. The contents of the wagon to be ferried were loaded into the hull, then the wagon was balanced across the canoe. Depending on the water level of the river, the ferry was either rowed or pulled across by riders on horseback.

In 1844, Francois Payette retired and was succeeded by James Craigie. Craigie retired in 1852. By that time, large numbers of Oregon emigrants frequented the fort. Some paid the fees for crossing in a primitive canoe ferry, a slow, costly process. Others caulked their wagon beds and floated across.

In spring of 1853, floods washed away much of the adobe structure and the fort was abandoned. Later that summer, two men, H.P. Issac and Orlando Humason, took over the site and built a tavern and a ferry. Business went well for the partners until the Ward Party Massacre in August 1854, just twenty miles from the thriving establishment. With the Indians clearly hostile, the two men poured their liquor into the river, cut the ferry free to drift downstream, and fled to The Dalles, Oregon from whence they had come.

During the great flood of 1862, the river swallowed the remaining ruins of the fort and abandoned tavern.

Jonathan Keeney and two partners, John Duval and J. B. McLaughlin, established a windlass, wire-rope ferry at the Old Fort Boise site in 1863. An advertisement announcing the new business ran in the *Idaho Tri-Weekly Statesman* in Boise the following year:

> "The traveling public are invited to take notice that the ferry is now completed and furnished with good new boats and careful attendants. This ferry is located at the most eligible crossing on the Snake River for travel.....Being furnished with buoy lines, and the largest boats, it is believed to be the safest ferry on the Snake River."

The Idaho Territorial Legislature approved the application for ferry operation on December 14, 1864:

> "...Authorizes Jonathan Keeney, J.B. McLaughlin, and John Duval to establish a ferry across Snake River at Old Fort Boise. Parties are to have exclusive rights 2 1/2 miles above and below ferry site for 10 years. Rates of toll to be:
>
> One Wagon and one span of animals, and one ton of freight $2.50
> Each additional ton of freight $1.00
> Each additional span of animals . . . .$ .50
> Each pack animal, loaded . . . .$ .50

Man and Horse	$ .75
Loose Animals	$ .25
Footman	$ .25
Sheep and Hogs, per head	$ .05"

Jonathan Keeney erected a small log wayside inn in 1864 on the Oregon side of the river to accommodate travelers, locating it near a hot springs which provided heated bath water for trail-weary customers.

McLaughlin sold his share to Keeney, so the business became known as Keeney's Ferry. On September 16, 1865, John Duval sold his one-third interest in the ferry to W.C. Boreau for the sum of $1,600.

In 1866, the Oregon Steam Navigation Company built the steamboat *Shoshone* one-quarter of a mile above Keeney's Ferry, with plans to run the boat the ninety miles between Farewell Bend and Owyhee Crossing. On May 17, the *Shoshone* made her first journey downriver to Farewell Bend, forcing Keeney to remove his cable and build a horse-powered ferry. It is believed that W.C. Boreau sold his share to Keeney at that time, due in part to the extra cost of horse ferry operation over that of the less expensive windlass and wire-rope.

The horse ferry was powered by two paddle wheels, one attached to each side of the boat. Each wheel was turned by a horse walking on a treadmill. The horses were enclosed in separate wooden corrals to help keep the animals steady and for the safety of the passengers. Keeney's horse ferry was the only one of its kind on the Snake River.

When the mission of the *Shoshone* failed a short time later, Keeney converted his ferry back to the windlass, wire-rope system.

Jonathan Keeney attempted to sell his ferry in 1870, due to ill health, running the following ad in Boise's *Statesman* on August 11, 1870:

> "I have become so infirm that I am compelled to give up my business, and I now offer my beautiful farm and ferry at old Fort Boise for sale or lease. Will not be leased for less than three years, bond and security required of the leasor; and if sold the money will be expected, or approved security with a reasonable interest until paid. Persons desiring to buy or lease would do well to call and examine the property. No trade will be closed before the 11th. day of October, 1870.
>
> "All proposals will be made to J. Keeney, at Lower Boise post office, in Ada county, Idaho territory, and I shall claim the right or privilege of accepting the most favorable proposition."

The ferry business consisted of one ferry boat, one wire-rope across the nearby Owyhee River, another wire-rope 150 yards long, all the machinery, bolts and equipment for a horse ferry, plus land on each side of the river that contained the landing or loading platforms. However, it wasn't until seven years later that a buyer was found for the ferry. Samuel McDowell purchased Keeney's Ferry for $2,000.

Over the next twenty-five years, the ferry changed hands numerous times. McDowell made a hefty profit when he sold the ferry five years later to Loring A. Sevey and Albert Fouch for $5,475. A year later Fouch sold Sevey his share for $3,000, took his money downstream and invested in a competing ferry.

In October 1885, two years after buying out his partner's share, Loring Sevey sold his crippled business to Abner Packard for $500. The business consisted of two ferry boats, two small boats, and the ferry landing.

A year later, Packard sold half of his business to Andrew Lackey for $700. By then, ferry competition up and down the river had forced rates to drop. Sheep now crossed at a penny-a-head, cattle, a dime. There were many more sheep and cows in the area than in previous years and their crossings made up the bulk of ferry revenue, sometimes exceeding $900-a-month.

After three years in business, the partners sold the ferry to William S. Geary for $3,000. Geary made a nice profit when he talked Thomas J. Huff into buying the business in 1890 for $3,600.

Huff had the business for twelve years. In 1902, the interstate bridge was built across the Snake River nearby and Huff's ferry business became obsolete.

Upper and Lower Mesa Falls, on the Snake River in Eastern Idaho, are the last free flowing major waterfalls in the Columbia River watershed.

SEVEN

Snake River — 1852

Ezra Meeker's Ferry Service.

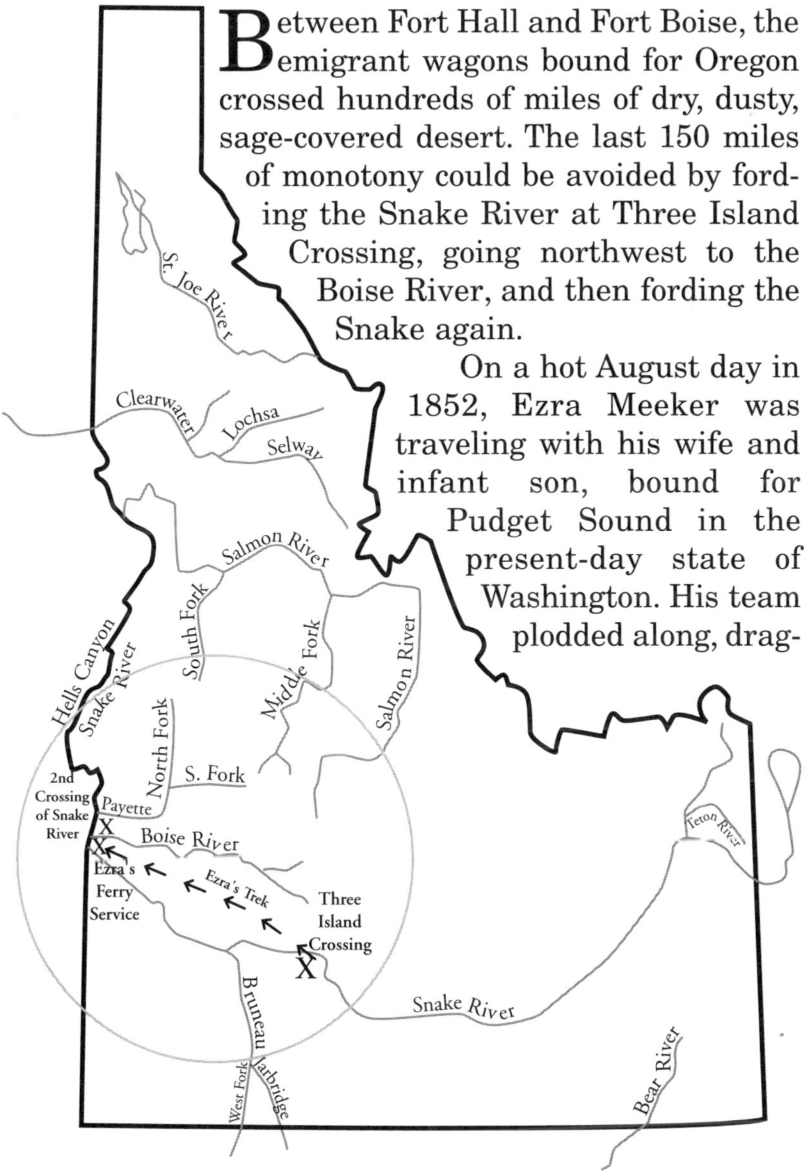

Between Fort Hall and Fort Boise, the emigrant wagons bound for Oregon crossed hundreds of miles of dry, dusty, sage-covered desert. The last 150 miles of monotony could be avoided by fording the Snake River at Three Island Crossing, going northwest to the Boise River, and then fording the Snake again.

On a hot August day in 1852, Ezra Meeker was traveling with his wife and infant son, bound for Pudget Sound in the present-day state of Washington. His team plodded along, dragging the dust-shrouded wagon. Fort Hall lay four days behind and Fort Boise was still several days ahead. Although crossing the rivers would cost two or more days, the wagon train members decided to do it in order to avoid a long stretch of dry trail.

Although there was a ferry at Three Island Crossing, Meeker and a majority of the members of the wagon train did not have enough money to pay for the service. Lining up along the banks of the Snake, they caulked the seams of their wagon beds with tar carried in wooden kegs. Travelers who had run out of tar used tree sap.

The Snake River ran cool and clear. The fragrant mint that grew along the banks provided a refreshing change from the pungent scent of sage. As each wagon was made river-worthy, it was rowed across the river. Ezra was one of the first to get his wagon across. In the spirit of the moment, he had christened the caulked wagon *Mary Jane*, in honor of his wife. It took several trips to ferry all his belongings but he enjoyed the crossings so much he eagerly looked forward to the next.

Ezra hit upon an idea. He asked the ferry man at Three Island Crossing if there was a ferry service at the Boise River. Upon being told there was only a canoe ferry, which was expensive as well as precarious, Ezra decided to set up a temporary ferry on the Snake. Gathering contributions from other members of his train, he left his wagon, wife and baby in the care of a trusted friend. His plan was to purchase an old wagon bed at Fort Boise, make it river-worthy, then use it to ferry wagons across the river.

Jim Paxton

With only a bundle of food and a blanket, Ezra began the long walk to the next crossing near Fort Boise, 150 miles away.

"All I remember about that tramp is the jackrabbits," Ezra remembered in later years. "Such swarms, as I traveled I had never seen before and I never saw again."

Reaching his destination several days ahead of his party, Ezra found a large wagon bed. He caulked and tarred it until it bobbed like a cork, then began ferrying wagons across. As he suspected, people were eager to pay his fee for a quick, easy crossing. When members of his train arrived, he ferried their wagons across the Boise River at no charge, since they had supported his idea. Because he was having so much fun with his new venture, he stayed with it for several days. When, with great reluctance, he finally walked away from his thriving business to catch up with his wagon train, he had earned $110.

As time passed, Ezra Meeker realized the historic importance of the Oregon Trail. In 1906, at age 77, he journeyed back in time. Starting in Washington, in a covered wagon pulled by oxen, he re-traced the route he followed west fifty-four years earlier. As a result of the publicity generated by his trip, monuments and markers now guide the way for travelers today.

EIGHT

Snake River — 1852

Wagons on the River

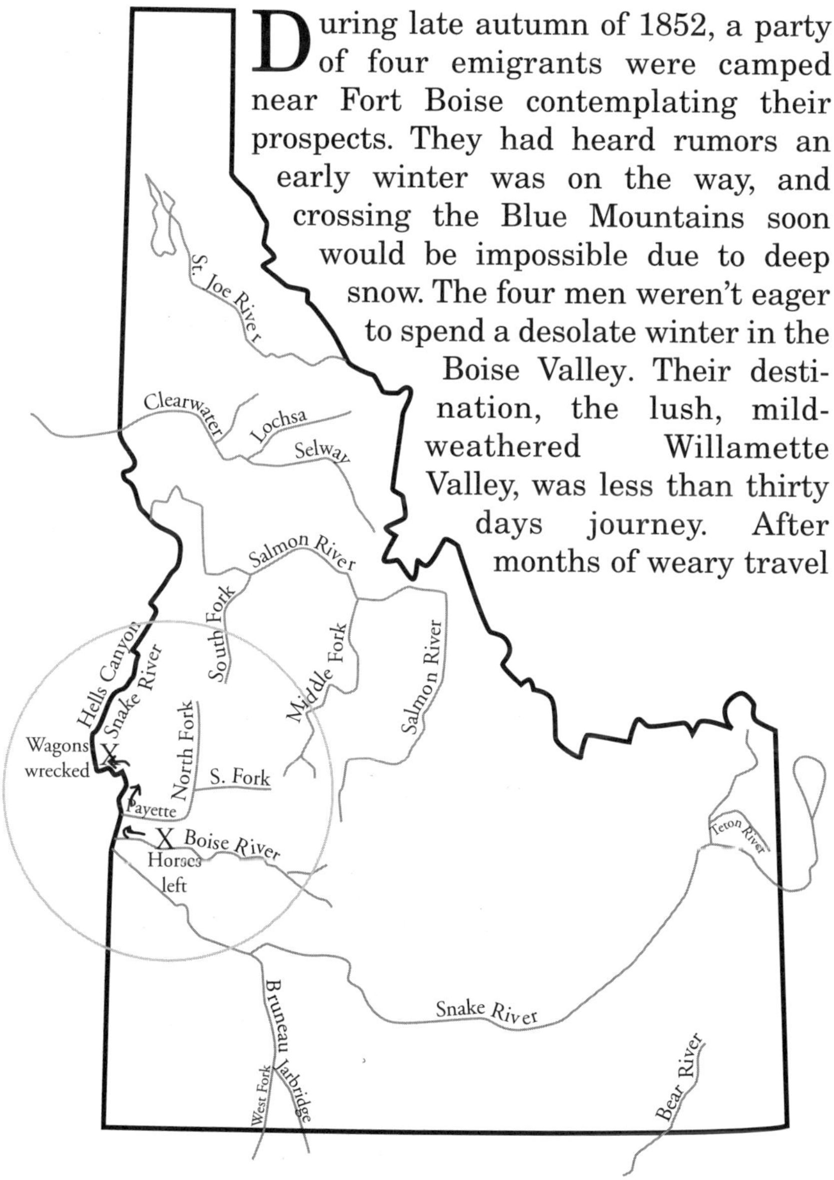

During late autumn of 1852, a party of four emigrants were camped near Fort Boise contemplating their prospects. They had heard rumors an early winter was on the way, and crossing the Blue Mountains soon would be impossible due to deep snow. The four men weren't eager to spend a desolate winter in the Boise Valley. Their destination, the lush, mild-weathered Willamette Valley, was less than thirty days journey. After months of weary travel on the Oregon Trail, it seemed ludicrous to be waylaid by bad weather.

After eyeing the placid stretch of the Boise River, the men rode horseback to where it emptied into the Snake. Since there didn't seem to be any obstructions or heavy currents, they devised what they believed was a brilliant plan. They would caulk their two wagon beds and float down the Boise River, into the Snake — and eventually to the Columbia, avoiding the Blue Mountains altogether.

The men turned their horses loose on Goose Island in the Boise River where there was plenty of grass. Should their plan to float the Boise and Snake Rivers go awry, the wagons could be beached and the men could double back for their horses. If they were successful, the animals could easily ford the river when feed became scarce on the island.

Launching their caulked wagons along a calm stretch of the river, the travelers floated away, praising each other for such an ingenious plan. But sixty miles down the Snake, they heard the sweet singing song of gently moving water turn into a ferocious growl. A strong current took hold of their clumsy craft, pulling them toward a rocky gorge. Clinging to the wagon beds, which were airborne one minute and nearly submerged the next, the men panicked. There was no way to maneuver the makeshift boats through the dangerous entrance to Hells Canyon. The wagon beds soon splintered on the jagged rock outcroppings that lurked midstream like a congregation of malicious trolls. One man, Dugan, was drowned. Another, Masters, managed to reach the shore on the Idaho side of the river. The other two men were swept along some distance downstream before clawing their way to shore and up to the steep banks on the Oregon side of the Snake.

Masters located his companions on the opposite bank. He had to hike several miles up river before he found a stretch of calm water where he could swim across and join them on the Oregon shore.

Of the cargo carried aboard the wagons, only one small trunk was recovered. Since so little was salvaged, the men did not return for their horses, choosing instead to proceed on to the Willamette Valley on foot. Not until the pale green grass of spring blanketed the Oregon valley did the men end their miserable winter of travel.

Idaho has more running water than any other state in the continental U. S.

NINE

Clearwater River — 1861

Greer Ferry

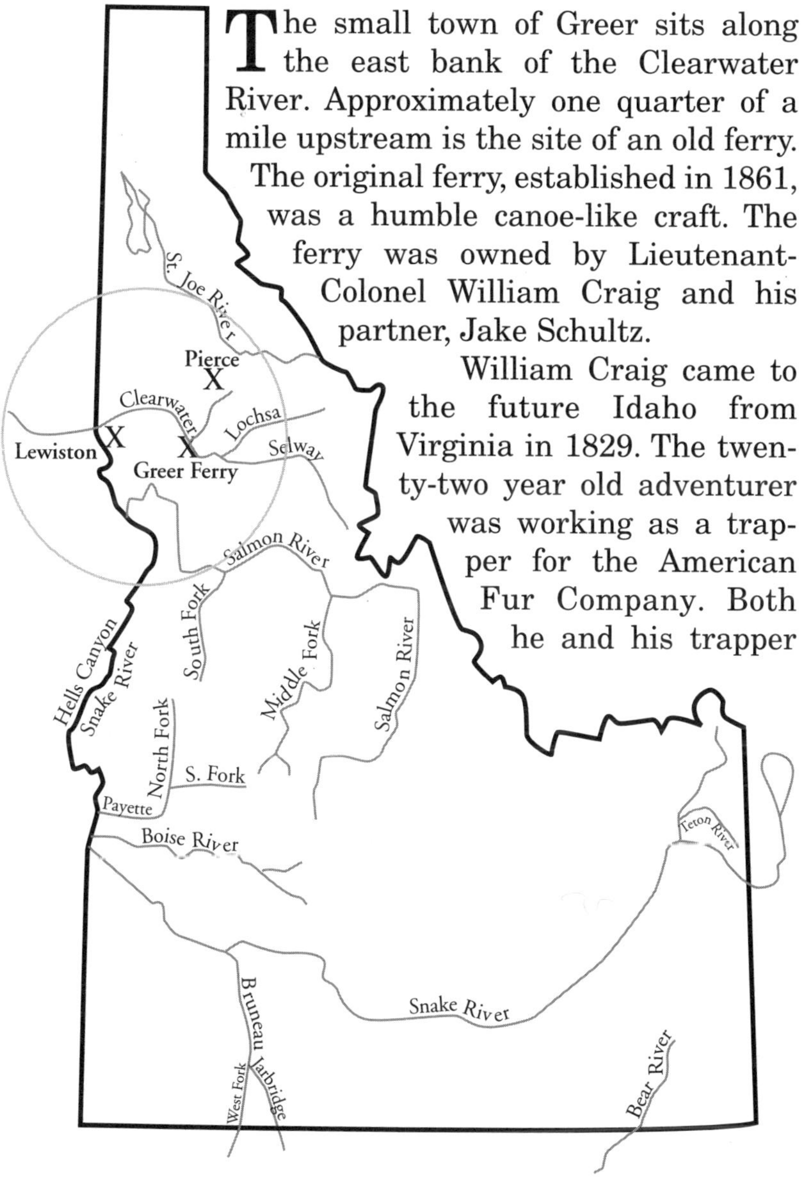

The small town of Greer sits along the east bank of the Clearwater River. Approximately one quarter of a mile upstream is the site of an old ferry.

The original ferry, established in 1861, was a humble canoe-like craft. The ferry was owned by Lieutenant-Colonel William Craig and his partner, Jake Schultz.

William Craig came to the future Idaho from Virginia in 1829. The twenty-two year old adventurer was working as a trapper for the American Fur Company. Both he and his trapper friend, Robert Newell, liked the Clearwater country and spent several years trapping the area. After the American Fur Company dissolved, the two men choose to live among the regional Indians. Both took Nez Perce wives. Craig's wife became known as Isabel.

Newell and his wife moved on west to Oregon, but Craig and Isabel stayed in Idaho, Craig becoming Idaho's first permanent white settler in the fall of 1846. Under the provisions of the Oregon Donation Act of 1850, William and Isabel Craig claimed and patented 640 acres of land at Lapwai.

In 1855-56, as interpreter for Governors I. I. Stevens of Washington Territory and Joel Palmer of Oregon, Craig negotiated the first treaty with the Nez Perce Indians. Working on the tribe's behalf, he helped draw up a document that clearly defined the boundaries of the Nez Perce reservation. Shortly thereafter, he was given the title of Lieutenant Colonel in the Washington Territorial Militia.

During a Christmas celebration in Lapwai, Craig grew better acquainted with a man who later became his partner in the ferry business. John Silcott and wife, Jane, threw a grand party, inviting guests from a fifty-mile radius — twenty people in all. To bolster the Christmas spirit, Silcott had procured all the whiskey in the vicinity.

In the merriment of the moment, Craig invited all the guests attending the Silcott bash to his and Isabel's home for a New Year's dinner. Since the guests didn't begin leaving the Christmas party until all the whiskey was gone, Craig found himself in a bad situation. How could he host a "dry" New Year's Day dinner?

Jake Schultz and another man volunteered to ride to Walla Walla to get some whiskey for Craig's party. After all, it was merely a 200-mile round trip, a journey that could easily be completed before New Year's Day. John Silcott provided funds for ten gallons of whiskey; Colonel Craig provided the horses.

Schultz and his companion returned in plenty of time for the gala dinner party.

As the whiskey flowed, talk turned to the new year. Bragging with a loosened tongue that he owned two thriving ferry businesses in the Lewiston area, John Silcott wondered aloud why no one had built a ferry up the Clearwater to accommodate the miners and packers enroute to Pierce City and Oro Fino? That was where the true gold mine lay. He charged tolls of fifty cents for each foot passenger, seventy-five cents per pack animal and $2.50 per horse and wagon.

As Silcott rambled on about the viability of such a business, Craig eyed Schultz. Certainly a man, who had transported ten gallons of whiskey one hundred miles without taking a single nip, was trust-worthy. At fifty-two years of age, Craig had no interest in ferrying folks across the Clearwater. He would leave that side of the business to someone with youthful vigor. Someone like Schultz.

That spring, Craig financed the ferry business, while Schultz provided the manual labor for the day-to-day operations. The two men even built a ferry house where travelers could stay overnight for a fee.

Business thrived. Soon the canoe was replaced with a proper wire-cable ferry.

In 1869, Craig suffered a stroke, dying during late September that year.

Jack Greer and John Molly bought the business. It became known as Greer Ferry. Things moved along smoothly for the partners until 1877 when the Nez Perce came raging through, enroute to Weippe Prairie, with General O. O. Howard's men hot on their heels. To buy themselves some time, the Indians cut Greer Ferry loose, then torched the ferry house. Greer and Molly later rebuilt their business.

Twenty years later, the railroad came through the area. Jack Greer and a partner, John Dunn, platted the townsite of Greer. Had the whole business been on more equal footing a likely name would have been the Greer Ferry at Dunn Town. Greer's health failed shortly after the establishment of the town and the ferry was sold to Bill and Harry Gamble. This turned out to be a fruitless gamble. A bridge soon replaced the ferry, and the town died.

TEN

Clearwater River — 1861

Slaterville

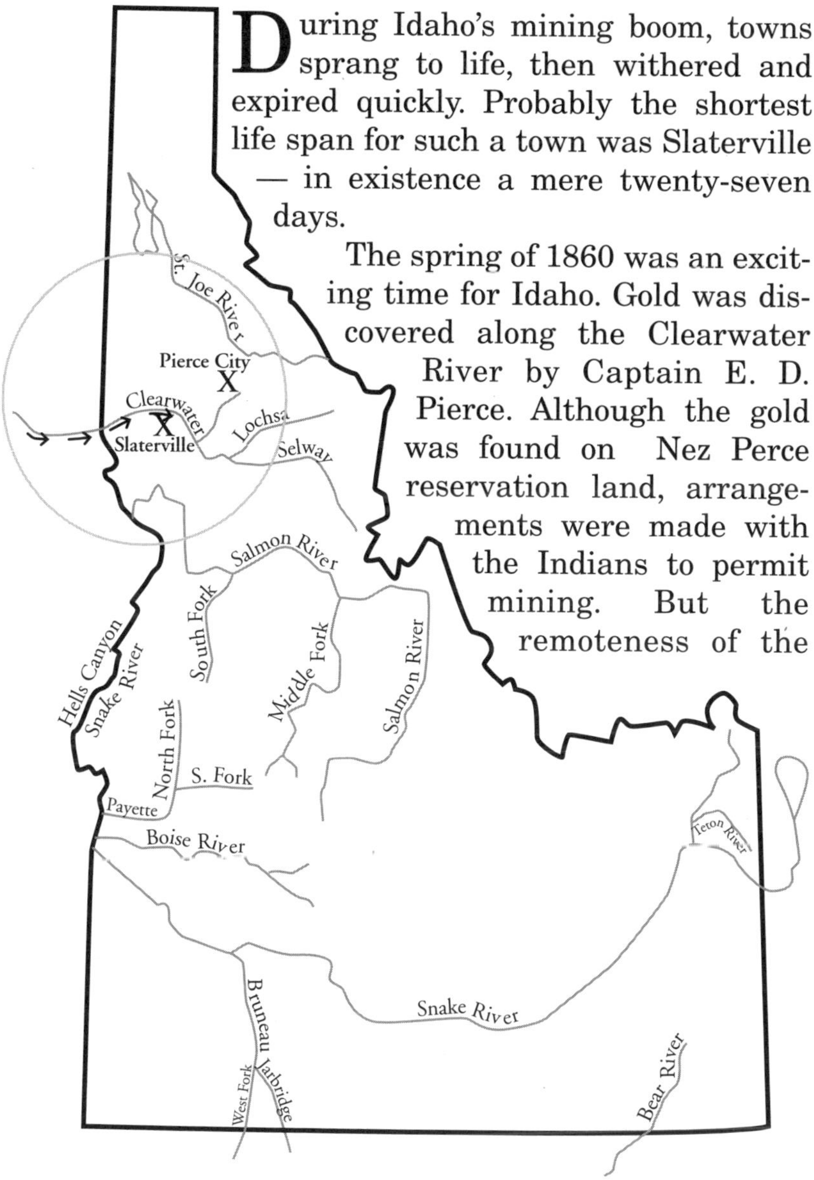

During Idaho's mining boom, towns sprang to life, then withered and expired quickly. Probably the shortest life span for such a town was Slaterville — in existence a mere twenty-seven days.

The spring of 1860 was an exciting time for Idaho. Gold was discovered along the Clearwater River by Captain E. D. Pierce. Although the gold was found on Nez Perce reservation land, arrangements were made with the Indians to permit mining. But the remoteness of the area made it difficult to transport supplies to the new mining town of Pierce City.

The 110-foot sternwheeler, *Colonel Wright*, piloted by Captain Len White, was put into service as a solution to the problem. The plan was for the boat to travel from Portland, up the Columbia, to the uncharted waters of the Snake. From the Snake, it would make its way up the Clearwater, trying to get as near as possible to Pierce City.

Eager to reach the fresh gold fields, 300 people booked passage on the *Colonel Wright*. The boat was also loaded to capacity with flour, canvas, picks, shovels and other materials needed on a new mining frontier.

By the time the *Colonel Wright* reached the Snake in early May, the river was at high flow. The heavily-laden vessel labored through the swift currents. The officers aboard amused themselves by naming every unnamed creek, rapid and landmark as they pushed upriver. Most of the original names remain today.

On May 10, Captain White nosed the steamer's prow into the Clearwater. Here, they were met by Nez Perce warriors on horseback. It was at first thought that the Indians might be hostile toward those aboard the steamer. The *Colonel Wright* was, after all, traveling through the Nez Perce reservation. But the Indians were merely curious about the white man's boat. The Nez Perce also knew of a place upstream, later called Big Eddy, that would provide excitement for the travelers and viewers. According to Indian legend, the mythical Coyote lived in a cave at the bottom of Big Eddy. And the Coyote was always up to mischief. The braves, riding along the shore, followed the *Colonel Wright* upstream thirty miles to Coyote's lair.

The *Colonel Wright* did not have enough power to negotiate the large rapid. Captain White lightened the craft by making all the passengers disembark. A cable from a winch on the boat was attached to a big boulder in order to line the boat past the obstacle. The trickster Coyote entertained those on shore by causing the cable to snap. The *Colonel Wright* swung toward sharp boulders jutting out of the river. The current pulled the bow back into midstream just as Captain White slammed the engine into reverse, sending fountains of water shooting high into the air.

Skillfully backing downstream, the captain safely steered the boat to the riverbank. The performance greatly amused the Nez Perce, who whooped mightily as they raced their mounts back and fourth along the shore to show Coyote how much they appreciated his trick. When the spectacle ended, the Indians, still grinning broadly, headed for home.

One of the passengers on the *Colonel Wright* was a merchant named Seth S. Slater. He had supplies aboard the steamer he intended to sell to the miners. Seeing the boat could go no farther, he unloaded his goods.

Although no permanent structures were allowed on reservation land, necessity made its own laws. Convinced that steamboats would continue to bring supplies up the Clearwater, Slater formed the township of Slaterville.

Slater hastily built four long, wooden, canvas-covered frameworks. Two of the dwellings housed mining equipment and provisions. The others were used as bunk houses for travelers.

The town founder also set up the first saloon in Clearwater Country — an eight-foot-square frame. Since his canvas supply was depleted. Slater roofed the saloon with blankets — two red and one blue. Two boxes served as a bar. With one barrel of whiskey, two bottles and three tumblers, the saloon opened for business.

Slater had grand visions of miners flocking to his establishments. Slaterville could become a hub where supplies and gold dust would change hands. Steamboats could arrive weekly loaded with fresh goods and would-be miners who would need provisions and tools.

On June 1, the steamer *Okanagon* struggled up the Clearwater. The high waters of spring had receded. Now the river was barely wide enough for passage. Boulders and shallow water added to the hazards. Commercial river travel to Slaterville ceased. Lewiston, forty miles downstream, would be as far upstream as steamboats would come in the future.

When the whiskey barrel was empty, Seth Slater disassembled his town.

ELEVEN

Snake River — 1862

Through Hells Canyon in 1862?

In 1862, three men from the Army Corps of Engineers, Charles Clifford, Washington Murray and Joseph Denver, claimed they walked up the Snake River from Lewiston to Fort Boise; then returned down the Snake by raft. Their mission was to determine if the water route was a practical method to reach the new gold fields near Fort Boise.

Beginning their trip in September and concluding it in October, they claimed to be the first white men to navigate Hells Canyon. Since there

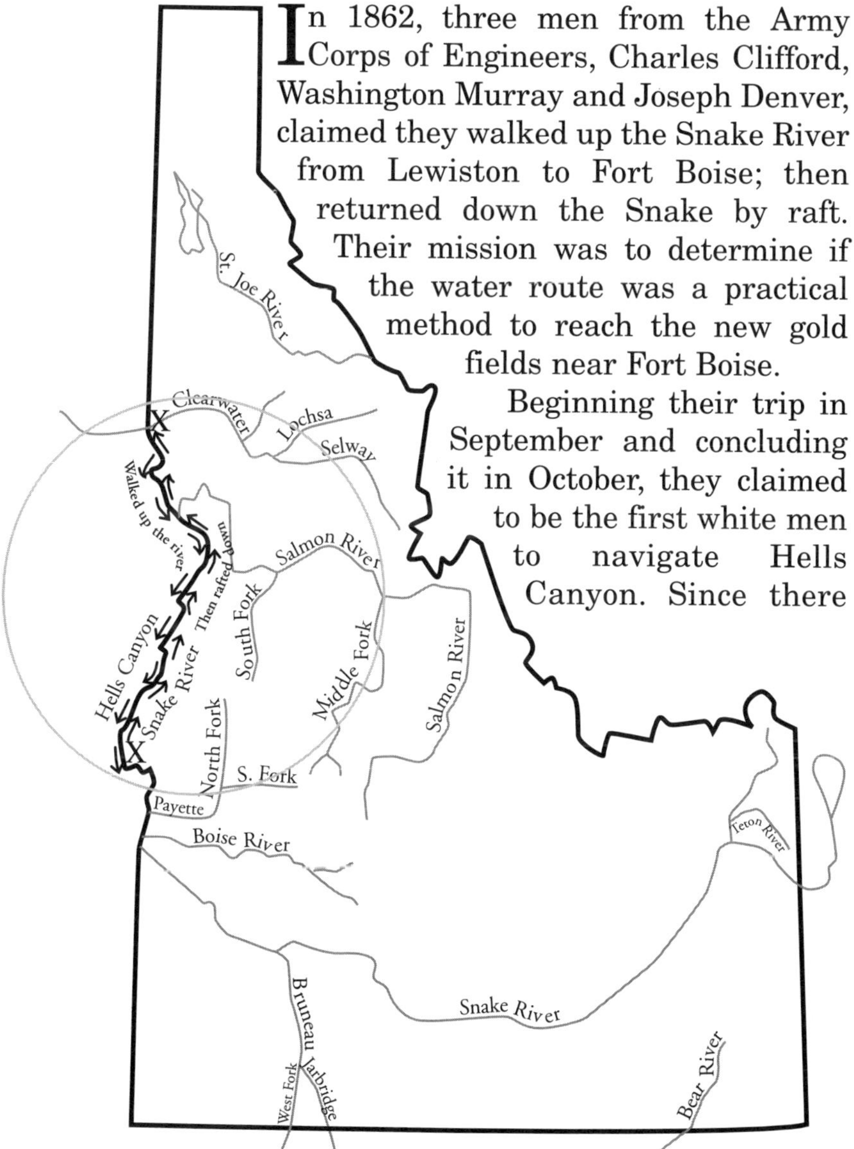

were no witnesses to the alleged fete, no one could repudiate the story.

Hells Canyon, the deepest gorge on Earth, lies in a broken basalt upland known as the Snake River Plateau. It is 7,500 feet deep — a third of a mile greater than the deepest portion of the Grand Canyon. The river drops 1,400 feet during the 200-mile distance that the three men claimed to have rafted. Granite Creek Rapid, one of those the men would have faced, is exceeded nationally in water volume and vertical descent only by Lava Falls on the Colorado River. The men reported that the banks of the canyon showed a water mark sixty feet higher than the September level. Bold, rocky sides towered far above the river, giving way to rolling tablelands interspersed with stands of evergreens. The explorers claimed they were charmed by the country.

Submitting a glowing report to Washington, D.C., the three men stated they found nothing in the river to impede navigation and that it was passable any season of the year unless clogged by ice. The report appeared in the *Official Records of the Union and Confederate Armies in the War of the Rebellion*.

Such an optimistic report naturally caused a lot of excitement in Lewiston. If it was correct, steamboats could go upriver from that city with supplies for miners and homesteaders. Miners could ride the steamboats to new claims, since, the report stated, "gold in all the ravines and gulches." Lewiston's first newspaper, *Golden Age*, added to the excitement of the new avenue of travel by publishing an optimistic editorial:

> "The shrill whistle of the steamer will reverberate along the banks of this noble river and its echo will be heard for ages yet to come, through the ravines, gorges, and canyons, as well as on the mountain tops in our golden land, as a symbol of ambition and perseverance."

A few years later, steamboats did attempt to navigate the Snake between Lewiston and Fort Boise, but they found a route different than the one advertised. After the *Colonel Wright* failed in an attempt to go up river during the summer of 1865, serious doubts arose concerning the accuracy and competency of the Corps of Engineers report.

The Middle Fork of the Salmon River has more than 100 world class rapids.

TWELVE

Bear River — 1863

The Battle of Bear River

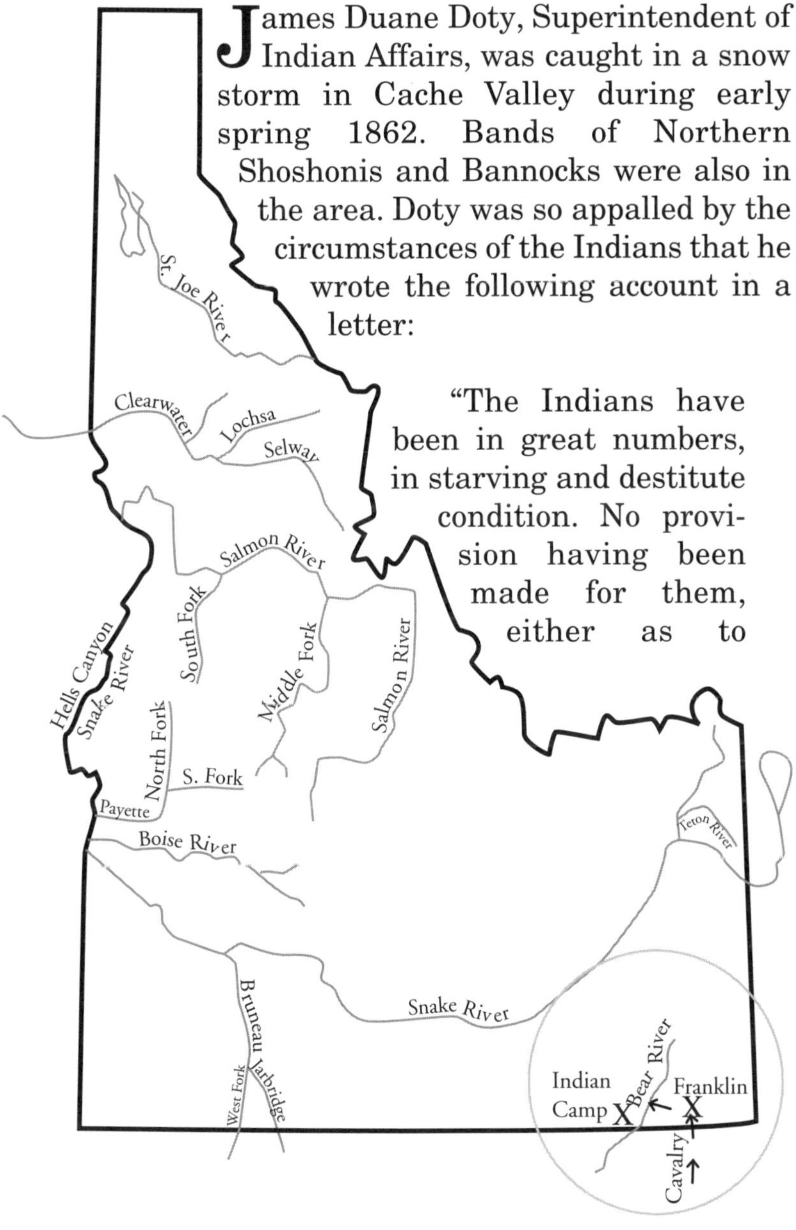

James Duane Doty, Superintendent of Indian Affairs, was caught in a snow storm in Cache Valley during early spring 1862. Bands of Northern Shoshonis and Bannocks were also in the area. Doty was so appalled by the circumstances of the Indians that he wrote the following account in a letter:

"The Indians have been in great numbers, in starving and destitute condition. No provision having been made for them, either as to

> clothing or provisions, by my predecessors. I have been compelled to purchase supplies where they could be best obtained and transport them to the places where the Indians had assembled, and where they are enduring great suffering . . ."

Later that same year, Doty described a similar scene where he saw Indian children laying on their stomachs along the banks of streams, grazing on the tender shoots of grass.

Settlers had invaded the region. Cattle, sheep and horses grazed where herds of elk and deer once roamed. Fields of wheat were planted where the Shoshoni and Bannock previously harvested camas bulbs.

Many of the settlers were Mormons. Their Utah leader, Brigham Young, preached tolerance of the native people, telling the Idaho members of his church, "We exhort you to feed and clothe them so far as lies your power; never turn them away hungry from your door . . ."

The largest Mormon Idaho settlement was Franklin, near the Utah border. Under the leadership of Chiefs Bear Hunter, Pocatello and Sagwitch, a camp of more than 500 Indians was established along the Bear River just north of the town. Abiding by their prophet's words, the Mormons gave what they could to the starving people. As their situation deteriorated, the Indians became more demanding.

By the winter 1862, Franklin residents were afraid of their Indian neighbors. The desperate Shoshoni and Bannock resorted to plunder and mur-

Jim Paxton

der. Although the Indians were blamed for more atrocities against settlers than actually took place, it was evident that the situation had become grave.

In late December 1862, a party of miners came down from the Salmon River mining country for supplies. Enroute to Salt Lake City, having lost their way in a blinding snowstorm, the miners missed the Bear River Ford near Franklin. Following along the Idaho side of the Bear River, the men finally crossed to the Utah side using a boat made from a wagon bed. As they prepared for the final trip across the river, they were attacked by Indians. One man was killed and several others wounded.

When the miners reached Salt Lake City, they appeared before Chief Justice Kinney and filed an affidavit detailing the circumstances of the attack, placing a value of $2,000 on the gold dust, horses and other property stolen by the Indians. The miners also stated ten miners from another group were murdered by Indians three days prior to the attack on their party.

An arrest warrant for the three chiefs was given to Marshal Isaac L. Gibbs. Calling on Colonel Patrick Edward Connor and his California Volunteers, a unit temporarily stationed at Salt Lake City, Marshal Gibbs asked for a military escort to protect him while he served the papers.

On Thursday, January 22, 1863, Colonel Connor sent forty men of Company K, Third California Infantry, under the command of Captain Samuel N. Hoyt, north to Franklin. Two howitzers and a train of fifteen wagons loaded with guns, ammunition and twelve days' supplies was sent with the unit.

Assuming Indian scouts would spot the first company sent out, Colonel Connor departed three days later with Marshal Gibbs, accompanied by companies A, H, K and M, Second California Cavalry. The column traveled at night. Captain Charles H. Hempstead described the march:

> "Those who were there at the time and participated in the events recounted can well remember — how could they forget? — that fearful night march. Clear and brilliant shone the stars upon the dreary earth mantled with deep snow, but bitter and intense was the cold. The shrill north wind swept over the lakes and down the mountain sides freezing with its cold breath every rivulet and stream. The moistened breath freezing as it left the lips, hung in miniature icicles from beards of brave men. The foam from their steeds stood stark and stiff upon each hair and motion only made it possible for them to endure the biting, freezing blast. All that long night the men rode on, facing the wintry wind, and uncomplainingly endured the intensity of cold rarely if ever before experienced even in these mountain regions. Hour after hour passed on, dragging its slow length along, with not a word save that of command at intervals to break upon the monotonous clamp, clamp of the steeds and the clatter of sabres as they rattled in their gleaming sheathes ... The sufferings of that march of 68 miles can never be told in words. Many were frozen and necessarily left behind, but the

> troops after a halt by day, again faced the severity of winter in the mountains and pressed on: the infantry by day and the cavalry by night, to deceive the wily foe."

The infantry reached Franklin the afternoon of January 28. The cavalry arrived late that night. After guides were secured, the infantry began its march toward the Indian camp about 3 A.M. The horsemen followed an hour behind, both reaching the high east bank of the Bear River at dawn.

The Indian encampment was located on the west bank of the river. Willow blinds had been built along the shore, equipped with forked sticks to be used a rifle rests. The Indians rushed forward to engage the troops.

The cavalry was ordered across the river. Horses plunged into a stream forty feet wide, eight to ten feet deep and choked with floating ice. Freezing water poured over the saddles as the steeds swam for the opposite shore, into enemy fire. The swift current swept several horses and riders downriver.

On the far bank, men dismounted, pant legs and boots sheathed in ice. Every fourth man was assigned to hold the horses as the other soldiers formed a skirmish line. The cavalry suffered its heaviest losses during and immediately after the river crossing.

The infantry also attempted to cross, but the river was too deep and swift. Ice floes added to the hazard. Hampered by deep snow, the howitzers had to be abandoned and couldn't be brought into action. Unless the infantry could cross the river, Colonel Connor's battle would be lost. The cavalry horses were forced back across the stream to bring the wet and freezing foot soldiers into battle. The fingers of the men were so numbed by the cold that they fumbled awkwardly trying to load their rifles.

With the addition of the infantry, a flanking movement was executed. Driven into a ravine, the Indians were boxed in on three sides. The trapped warriors, women and children fled in the only direction left open. Charging fiercely, the cavalry closed the gap and hand-to-hand fighting ensued. Many of the Indians, including Chief Sagwitch, broke through the lines and dove into the frigid river. Many were shot in the water.

Chief Sagwitch, wounded and presumed dead, tumbled downriver and floated beneath some brush. After hiding until dark, he joined several other warriors and returned to the battleground. The Indians stole several horses and fled north.

Colonel Connor and his men captured 160 women and children. As the battle raged in the ravine, the noncombatants walked to the rear of the troops and sat down in the snow, "like a lot of sage hens." Since no provision had been made to transport prisoners, they were released. Troops burned the lodges and destroyed the meager food stores.

The bodies of 300 Indians lay on the frozen battleground, ninety of them women and children. There was no time for the fleeing Shoshoni and Bannock to claim their dead. For years, the bleached bones remained scattered about the area, stark, silent testimony of the Battle of Bear River.

Colonel Connor lost twenty-two men in the battle. The troops made the miserable river crossing one last time, taking their dead and wounded with them. Corporal Tuttle eloquently described the conditions:

> "the night of January 29th 1863 I never shal far get (how can I). We camped on the Bank of the Bear River with our dead dieing wounded and frozen 2 feet of snow on the ground nothing for fire but green Willows which would burn about as well as the snow oh! the groans of the frozen it seems to ring in my ears yet the poor fellows some lost their toes some a portion of their feet I worked near all night bringing water from the river to wett cloths to draw frost from their frozen limbs I had not sleep for any two nights befor it was a dreadful night to me but managed to get through the night while some never saw the morning."

THIRTEEN

Snake River — 1863

Footprints in the Sand

According to the storytellers, in midsummer 1863, three men were riding along the Snake River searching for some stray horses.

"Look! Here!" Ben Cook yelled.

John W. Wheeler and Frank Johnson reined their horses around and loped back to the sandbar. The three riders formed a half circle as they stared down at the huge footprints. Twice before Frank Johnson had measured the prints, once along the shoreline of the Payette River and again, several years later, along

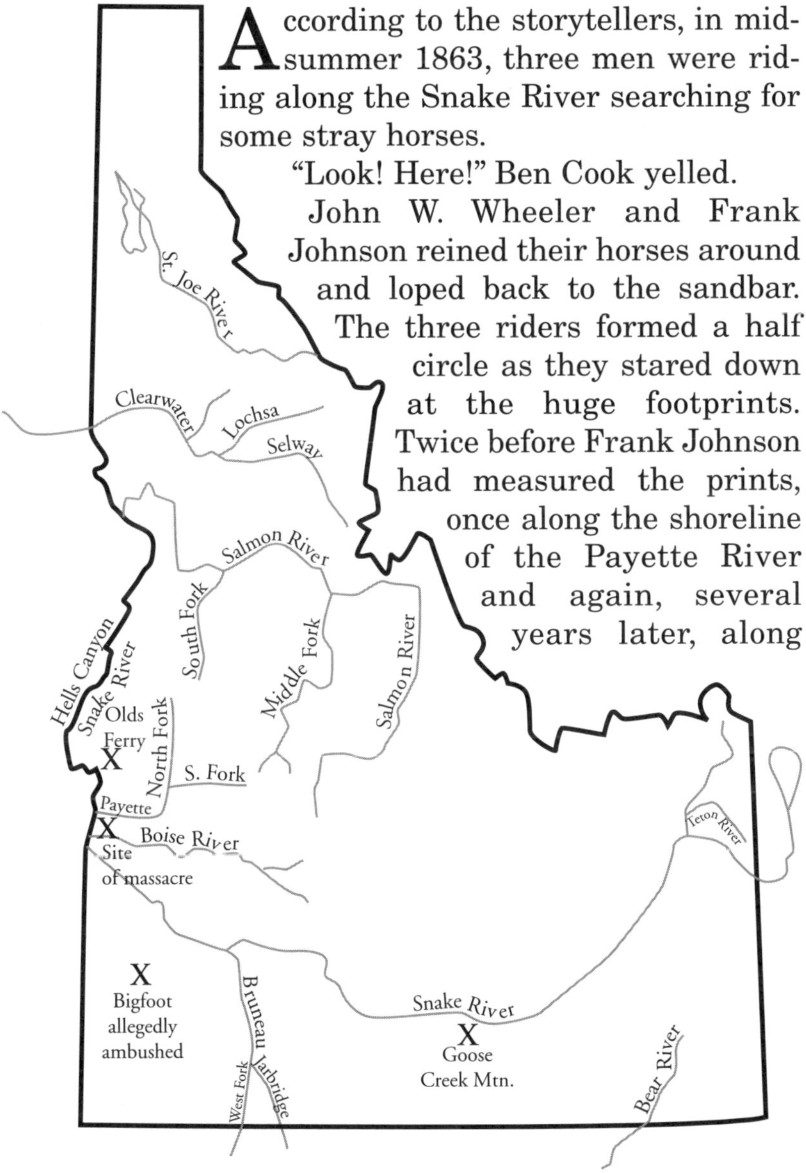

the Boise. Incredibly, they measured 18 inches from heel to toe.

The fresh footprints indicated the legendary Bigfoot was nearby. Each man began calculating his share of the reward money — $1,000 split three ways. Following the tracks downstream, they soon caught sight of the buckskin-clad giant.

To the north lay the entrance to Hells Canyon, an escarpment so steep a mountain sheep had trouble finding a foothold. To the west flowed the Snake River, its treacherous currents, undertows and swift waters made swimming or fording nearly impossible. To the east rose a sagebrush steppe, an area of gentle foothills and easy riding. The riders prepared to chase their quarry across that sector.

Bigfoot heard the riders approaching. But instead of heading for open country, he plunged into the Snake. The three men stared in disbelief as he easily swam through the churning water and climbed the bank on the Oregon shore.

"Olds Ferry," John Wheeler shouted above the roar of the nearby rapids. "We'll head him off there!"

By the time the men raced their horses the five miles to the ferry, their mounts were tired and winded. The $1,000 reward didn't seem such a sure thing now. But they weren't ready to give up the chase. Once across the river, they doubled back along the Oregon bank.

About five miles downstream, they found a smoldering campfire and the skeletons of two large salmon. Bigfoot's prints were clear in the sand, leading from the river. Even fresher prints led back to the water. Stretched out on a sandbar on the Idaho side lay Bigfoot, enjoying the rays of the late afternoon sun.

"He made a fool of us," said Wheeler, as he glared across the torrid Snake. "Just like he made fools of those freighters a couple of years back. Well, he hasn't seen the last of me!"

A group of teamsters driving twenty wagons, allegedly encountered Bigfoot while camped on the Payette River. During the early morning hours, the renegade and two other Indians stole some of the teamster's horses. Five of the freighters mounted the remaining horses and gave chase. They caught the thieves at dawn, north of the site of present-day town of Weiser. In the ensuing battle, the two Indians were killed. Bigfoot escaped on foot. Herding six horses ahead of him, he reached the Snake River, forced the horses into the water, then swam the river himself. When the exhausted horses reach shore, he was waiting for them. The teamsters said he disappeared into the distance herding the horses before him.

Reports of the renegade giant had brought terror to settlers and miners of the region since the spring of 1857. It was the same year a wagon train of emigrants was massacred by Indians on the Boise River. Some residents said Bigfoot was a myth, a handy explanation for any murder or theft. But there were plenty of believers.

According to the standard Bigfoot story, he was born in the Cherokee Nations in Oklahoma, the son of a white man named Archer Wilkinson and a Cherokee-Negro woman. His name was Starr Wilkinson. But because of his size, the other children called him Bigfoot. While Bigfoot was still a boy, his father met his end dangling from a noose. Because Starr was light skinned, he wasn't accepted by his Indian peers.

Starr Wilkinson headed West in 1856 on an Oregon-bound wagon train. Along the way he became infatuated with a young woman who encouraged his attentions. But several weeks later, their wagon train was joined by one from New York that included a young artist named Hart. Hart began courting the woman who was the object of Wilkinson's attention.

By autumn, things began to heat up between the two rivals, climaxing at a place called Goose Creek Mountain, near the Snake River in southeast Idaho. The men met in private to sort out their differences. During the discussion Hart drew his pistol and shot Wilkinson in the shoulder. Enraged, the giant grabbed Hart by the neck and choked him to death. He threw the body into the Snake River, took Hart's rifle, pistol and knife and fled.

Soon the renegade was robbing miners, settlers, stages and wagon trains. He made friends with some Bannock Indians by sharing his booty with them. The result was a loyal group of followers. His Indian friends called him Nampuh or Bigfoot. Some say the city of Nampa, Idaho is named for Bigfoot.

According to the legend, the following spring, while traveling along the Boise River, Bigfoot spotted the wagon train he had left back at Goose Creek Mountain. The group had wintered in the Boise Basin. Bigfoot rounded up about 30 of his Indian friends, plus a French trapper named Joe Louis. The raiders massacred all the members of the wagon train, including the young woman who once had claimed the giant's heart.

When the carnage was discovered along the banks of the Boise, giant footprints were found in the sand. Other bloodbaths followed. Soon Bigfoot had a $1,000 bounty on his head.

In 1868, five years after his near encounter with Bigfoot, John W. Wheeler was appointed to a special force of lawmen dispatched by Governor David M. Ballard, to restore order between the feuding mining companies — the Golden Chariot and the Ida Elmore of Silver City.

There had been a rash of stage robberies between Silver City and Boise City. Despite his law job, Wheeler was considered a suspect.

According to legend, one hot July day, William T. Anderson was driving his two-horse wagon from Silver City to Boise. As he neared Reynolds Creek Canyon, he pulled his team to the side of the road and took cover in a stand of juniper trees. Bigfoot had attacked many stage coaches and other passers-by in the canyon. Anderson didn't want to run the gauntlet alone. He knew a stage wasn't far behind him.

As he waited for the stage, Anderson noticed a movement in the canyon. Bigfoot and two other Indians, all afoot, appeared. Suddenly shots rang out from behind some boulders. Both Indians were killed and Bigfoot was wounded. The shooter kept firing, the bullets hitting Bigfoot again and again until he dropped.

Anderson said a lone man emerged from the boulders and approached the fallen renegade.

Recognizing the man as John Wheeler, Anderson left his place of concealment and joined the ambusher.

Bigfoot was dying. The men promised to bury the fallen giant in the hills and keep his death and the whereabouts of his grave a secret. Some claimed Wheeler kept the killing of Bigfoot a secret because he also was waiting to rob the stage.

Anderson later claimed he counted sixteen bullet wounds before burying Bigfoot. He said the giant was 6'9" tall, 59" around the chest with a foot measuring 18" in length and 18" in circumference.

Later that summer, John Wheeler tried to rob a Blue Mountain Stage. A possee captured him and he was sentenced to 10 years in the Oregon penitentiary.

Ten years later, William Anderson sent a letter to the *Idaho Statesman* newspaper in Boise, detailing the incident on Reynolds Creek. Many historians today believe the Anderson newspaper account was written by Wheeler, using a pen name, in an attempt to improve his public image.

On August 24, 1974, a monument to Bigfoot was dedicated at the Fort Boise site near Parma. Governor Cecil Andrus presided over the dedication ceremony.

Even if Bigfoot is nothing more than the figment of an outlaw's imagination, he has become an important part of the history of the Snake River Valley.

FOURTEEN

Snake River — 1863

The Notorious Washoe Ferry

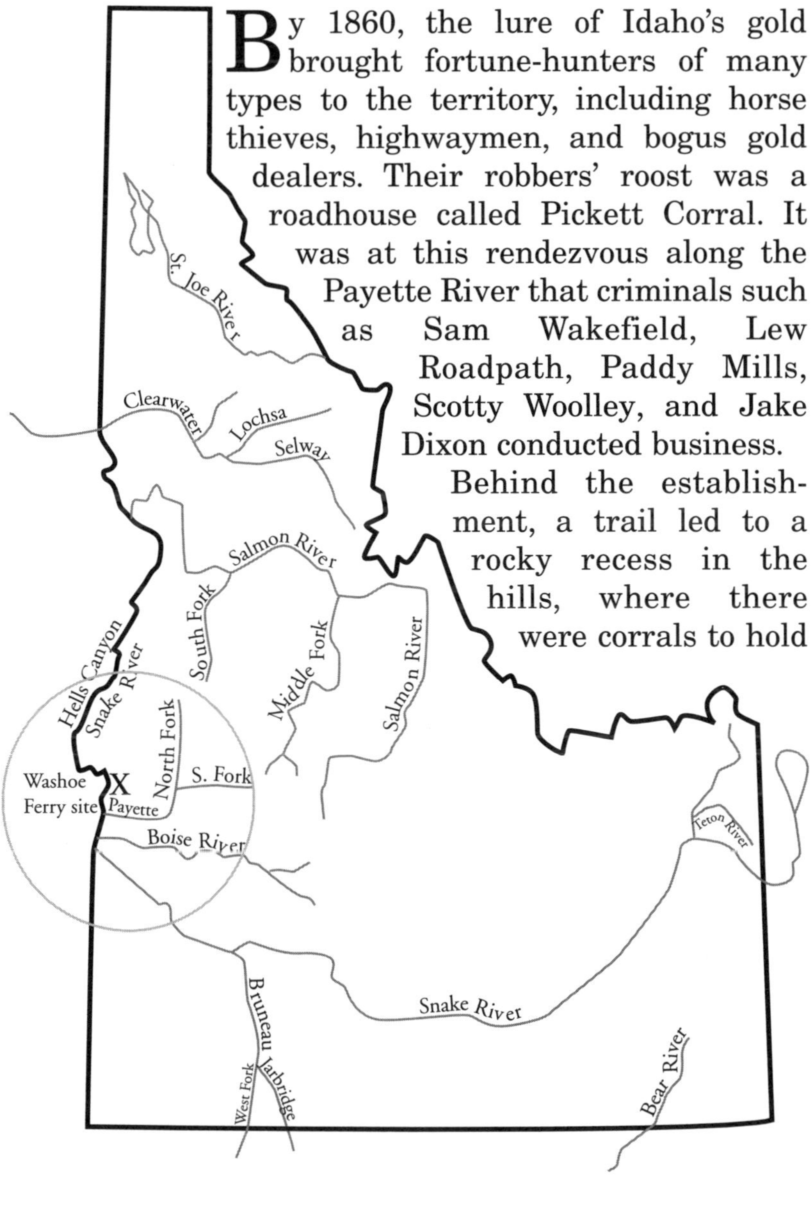

By 1860, the lure of Idaho's gold brought fortune-hunters of many types to the territory, including horse thieves, highwaymen, and bogus gold dealers. Their robbers' roost was a roadhouse called Pickett Corral. It was at this rendezvous along the Payette River that criminals such as Sam Wakefield, Lew Roadpath, Paddy Mills, Scotty Woolley, and Jake Dixon conducted business.

Behind the establishment, a trail led to a rocky recess in the hills, where there were corrals to hold stolen horses and cattle. A similar facility was located in Oregon. Stock stolen from the Payette Valley was herded to the Oregon corrals under cover of night, while animals taken from the Baker City area near the Blue Mountains were brought to Idaho. Area settlers were grateful to have a source of horses or cattle to replace those they assumed had been stolen by Indians.

Gold dust was the accepted method of payment. When settlers did business at the Pickett Corral roadhouse, they received change from their transactions in bogus dust. Since "pure" bogus dust — colored lead cuttings manufactured in San Francisco — could be easily detected by an experienced miner, it was mixed half-and-half with real gold dust.

In 1863, two Canadian brothers named Charles and Alexander Stewart, with their partner, Bryant, established the Washoe Ferry, four miles downriver from Pickett Corral. It was located on the Snake River between the mouth of the Malheur River, on the Oregon side, and the Payette River, which came in from the Idaho side. The ferry was a forty by sixty-foot boat manned by six oarsmen.

The three partners soon succumbed to the easy money spell of bogus gold dust, joining with the notorious men from upriver. They built an unusual ferry house. Twenty feet long by sixteen wide, the building was on the Oregon side of the Snake. It had a dirt floor and a thick sod roof. There was a fireplace at one end with the chimney on the inside. The structure had a heavy wooden door. Instead of windows, numerous small portholes were cut into the walls.

Locals gossiped about the strange building, concluding that the young Canadians feared Indian attacks.

Payette Valley citizens eventually became concerned with all the plundering and pilfering. Until a local rancher spotted one of his stolen horses at Pickett Corral, they didn't know who was responsible. The animal had apparently mixed back in with the Oregon stock and was herded home. Things suddenly began to make sense. Under the guise of honest businessmen, the perpetrators were living and working among their victims. Even worse, the community discovered that their elected sheriff, Dave Updyke, was a member of the gang, too.

The citizens nominated twenty vigilantes to deal with the thieves in their midst. It was the first organization of its kind in southern Idaho. The vigilantes chose Captain William McConnell as their leader. They also appointed a trial jury of seven members. Punishments included banishment, public whipping, or death.

When the gang got wind of the movement, they got the names of the vigilante organizers. Sheriff Updyke issued warrants for the arrests of thirty leading citizens. A posse of thieves, headed by Jake Dixon, was authorized to make the arrests, then murder their captives under the pretense that they had resisted.

Hearing rumors of the plan, the Payette vigilantes and area settlers armed themselves with six-shooters, rifles and double-barreled shotguns. The posse came face-to-face with the armed group. The citizens and their appointed defenders would not surrender their guns. Since the posse was outnumbered three to one, it backed down.

Several days later, Sheriff Updyke was found hanging by the neck from a tree along a lonely stretch of Syrup Creek. Pinned to his body was a note:

> "Dave Updyke — Accessory after the fact to the Port Neuf stage robbery near Boise in 1864, chief conspirator in the burning of property on the Overland Stage Line, guilty of aiding and assisting West Jenkins, the murderer and other criminals to escape while he was sheriff of Ada County, accessory and accomplice to the murder of Raymond, threatening the lives and property of an already outraged and suffering community."

A few miles further downstream the body of Jake Dixon was found dangling at the end of a rope. "Horse thief, counterfeiter, and a bad agent generally. A dupe of Dave Updyke," read the note attached to his body.

The hangings frightened many of the gang members so badly that they took off for parts unknown. But the Washoe Ferry boys were not so easily intimidated. Snug in their small fortress, the Stewart brothers wrote insulting letters to the president of the Payette Vigilante Committee, distributing copies of their taunts to Boise City and mining communities throughout Idaho and Oregon. Mocking the vigilante efforts, the Washoe Ferry boys challenged them to attempt the capture of their citadel, stating that there were not enough vigilantes in Payette Valley to subdue them.

Captain McConnell called his men together in mid-February, 1885. Ice flows choked the river. Surely the Stewart brothers and their partner, Bryant, would not expect an attack during such conditions. Selecting three of his most trusted men, McConnell headed for Central Ferry, three miles downriver from the Washoe, arriving there late in the evening. His remaining men were instructed to stay the night at Bluff Station, on a branch of the main road leading to Washoe Ferry. The main group was then to meet him at Stewart's Ferry at sun-up.

McConnell and his men rested at the Central Ferry. The ferry owner, Eply, was taken into the vigilantes' confidence. Over a hot meal at the ferry house, the men discussed their plan. Eply would ferry McConnell and his men across the river that night, a risky undertaking because of the ice. One of the men would ride up to the Washoe Ferry house and knock on the door. He would say he and a group of fellow travelers had tried to cross on the Old's Ferry upriver, but it had been locked in ice. The group would pay twice the going ferry rate to be taken across on the Washoe. The decoy would then enter the house, cross over to the fireplace and stir the fire, sending sparks up the chimney as a signal that all was going according to plan.

The decoy rode to the ferry house. At three o'clock in the morning, all five occupants of the building were asleep. McDonnell and his men rode down near the ferry, dismounted, and stomped around in the cold, trying to keep warm.

One of the men in the building sleepily unbolted the door. The decoy shivered into the room, babbling about the frozen Old's Ferry and how much his group was willing to pay, as he walked the length of the room to the fireplace. He continued his prattle as he heaped kindling on the dwindling fire, sending a shower of sparks into the night. Before he finished his spiel to the drowsy occupants of the ferry house, his three companions, armed with shotguns, burst through the door. The capture was made without a shot being fired.

When the remainder of the vigilantes arrived, they found Captain McConnell and his three men in possession of the prisoners. Two of the five captives were innocent travelers rooming for the night. They were set free.

The Stewart brothers and Bryant were locked up for the night in a small log cabin to await trial the following morning. Bryant found a nail and picked the lock. Slipping past the snoozing guard, the three men swam the icy river and obtained rifles from the ferry house. Then they split up and high-tailed it out of the valley.

One of the Stewart brothers made his way to Auburn, near Baker City, Oregon to visit an acquaintance, Mr. W. H. Packwood. The young Canadian explained that he could not return to the Washoe Ferry business because of some trouble with the local vigilantes. If Mr. Packwood was interested in taking over the ferry business, he could pay for it at a later date. Packwood said he was interested.

W. H. Packwood came west in 1849 from Kansas to seek gold in California. He later moved to Oregon where he became a founding member of the state constitution of 1858. Five years later, Packwood moved to Eastern Oregon, where he became one of the pioneers of the flourishing mining community of Auburn and the first school superintendent of Baker County.

Traveling to the Washoe Ferry site, Packwood discovered the business had been sold at a sheriff's auction. Seeing the great potential of the ferry, he sought out the new owners and purchased the business, then sent $5,000 to pay off the Stewart brothers and Bryant.

With the gang banished from the area, travel became safer throughout the valley. More stages and freighters used the Washoe Ferry, which was soon converted to a cable operation.

Packwood formed a company with two partners, Ruben P. Olds, operator of Old's Ferry, and John Parton, head of Parton & Company Toll Road along the Burnt River, They called their new venture the Oregon Road, Bridge & Ferry Company, starting with capital stock of $300,000.

The objective of the new operation was to connect all stage roads coming from Walla Walla, Washington and Umatilla, Oregon. A way station was located at the head of the company's toll road, which continued down the Burnt River to the Snake River ferries. The partnership purchased a third business, the Central Ferry, connecting all three ferries with roads leading to the Idaho mining districts. Most freight and express moved over the route. At the height of the gold rush, the company's receipts often exceeded $1,000 per day.

By 1868, the Union Pacific had completed its railroad from Kelton, Utah to the Idaho mines. When the demand for ferry service declined, the Oregon Road, Bridge & Ferry Company disbanded. Packwood retained ownership of the Washoe Ferry, hiring the Emison brothers as ferrymen before returning to Baker, Oregon. William Emison, one of the brothers, purchased the ferry from Packwood about 1872, later selling it to G. W. Brinnon. In 1884, Brinnon sold the ferry to Captain W. W. Payne, a retired Union Army officer from Illinois. The towns of Payette and Ontario were developing on opposite sides of the Snake River, so Payne moved the Washoe Ferry downriver to a more convenient site servicing both communities. The ferry operated until the interstate bridge was completed in 1902.

FIFTEEN

Snake River — 1863

The *Colonel Wright*

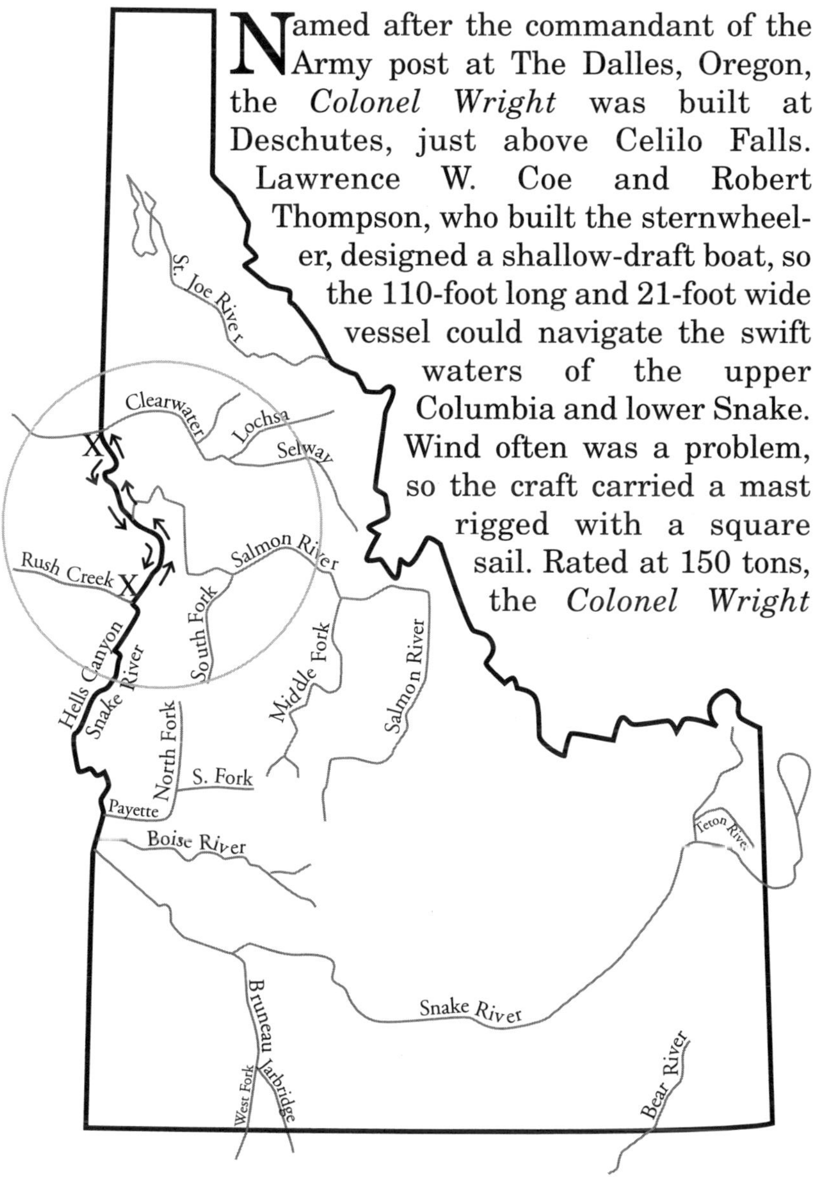

Named after the commandant of the Army post at The Dalles, Oregon, the *Colonel Wright* was built at Deschutes, just above Celilo Falls. Lawrence W. Coe and Robert Thompson, who built the sternwheeler, designed a shallow-draft boat, so the 110-foot long and 21-foot wide vessel could navigate the swift waters of the upper Columbia and lower Snake. Wind often was a problem, so the craft carried a mast rigged with a square sail. Rated at 150 tons, the *Colonel Wright*

could carry supplies and heavy equipment to Idaho's developing mines.

Launched on October 24, 1858, the boat was commanded by Captain Leonard White, with Captain E.W. Baughman as pilot. The craft was the first steamboat to run the rapids of the upper Columbia and the lower Snake. For the first two years of operation, the *Colonel Wright* ran between The Dalles, Umatilla Landing, Wallula and Priest Rapids.

In the spring of 1861, the *Colonel Wright* made its first journey up the Snake, into the Clearwater River After hauling supplies for Idaho's booming mining town of Pierce City to Slaterville, forty miles up the Clearwater, the boat returned to moor at that river's junction with the Snake. The place was called Tsceminicum, a Nez Perce word meaning "where two rivers meet." The site soon was renamed Lewiston, in honor of Meriwether Lewis of the Lewis and Clark Expedition. A tent city, with thousands of occupants, sprang up at the newly-established inland port. Steamboat transport generated a steady flow of commerce to the young town.

In 1860, three Washington businessmen, John Ainsworth, William Ladd and Jacob Kamm, formed the Oregon Steam Navigation Company. The owners had heard of the alleged journey up the Snake River through Hells Canyon by a party from the Army Corps of Engineers. They were determined to be the first company to send a steamboat through that section of water to service the Boise Basin and Idaho City mines. With its shallow draft and carrying capacity, the *Colonel Wright* seemed ideal for the mission. The OSNC purchased the steamboat in autumn 1861.

When John Ainsworth, president of the company, reduced Captain White's salary from $500 to $300 a month, the captain quit. He was replaced by Captain Thomas Stump, a native of Nashville, Tennessee, who had considerable experience on the Sacramento River, but was unfamiliar with Idaho's rugged waters.

Because of previous shipping contracts, the *Colonel Wright* was not free for the upriver adventure until spring 1865. In mid-June of that year, an exuberant Captain Stump and his equally excited assistant, William Polk Gray, left Lewiston and pointed the steamboat upstream. Its crew and two passengers expected to travel through Hells Canyon to the Boise Basin with few problems.

It was slow going for the steamer. The rapids encountered during the first two days were the worst Captain Stump had ever seen. The boat pulled itself through several cataracts, using the steam capstan and heavy cable.

The captain began to suspect the river might be even rougher upstream. But he didn't give up. If he mastered Hells Canyon and brought service to the Boise Basin mines, he would be a hero. It also would open steamboat service to the Salmon and Powder River mining districts.

By the fourth day, travel upriver was nearly impossible. While lining through Mountain Sheep Rapid, three and a half miles above the mouth of the Salmon, the boat nearly capsized. The following afternoon, after traveling seventy-three miles in four and a half days, the journey ended. Near Gold Rush

Rapid, the *Colonel Wright* stalled and turned back. Soon after beginning the return trip, the boat struck a boulder, then slammed into a submerged rock bar. William Polk Gray's journal described the incident:

> ". . . The boat was caught in a bad eddy, thrown into the current from the Idaho shore. It carried away eight feet of her bow, keel and sides to the deck. Things looked desperate for a moment. Captain Stump gave an order from the pilot house to get out a line on shore. You never saw such a universal willingness to get on shore with that line. Every deckhand, the mate, the chief engineer, the fireman and our two passengers, who were standing forward watching the boat, seized the line by both ends, the middle and wherever they could get hold of it and jumped ashore. The only people left on the boat were Captain Stump and myself in the pilot house, and a second engineer, who was below, and old Titus, the cook. Before they could make the line fast the boat was caught by the current and went down river half a mile. Here Captain Stump succeeded in beaching her."

The crew and passengers scrambled down the riverbank and re-boarded the maimed *Colonel Wright*, whose sides had been torn open and were leaking badly. With the paddlewheel nearly destroyed and the rudder cracked, Captain Stump nosed her into the current and let the flow of the river carry the crippled boat home. It took four and a half days to struggle upriver as far as Gold Rush Rapid. It took only three and a half hours for the *Colonel Wright* to return to her Lewiston pier.

The steamboat was so badly damaged from the attempt to master Hells Canyon that only the engines could be salvaged. Captain Stump had proved beyond all doubt that it wasn't practical to navigate the canyon in a steamboat. But it was a bitter blow to the OSNC and all the miners isolated along that rugged stretch of river.

The Lochsa River has more than forty class II-IV rapids.

SIXTEEN

Snake River — 1866

The Steamboat *Shoshone*

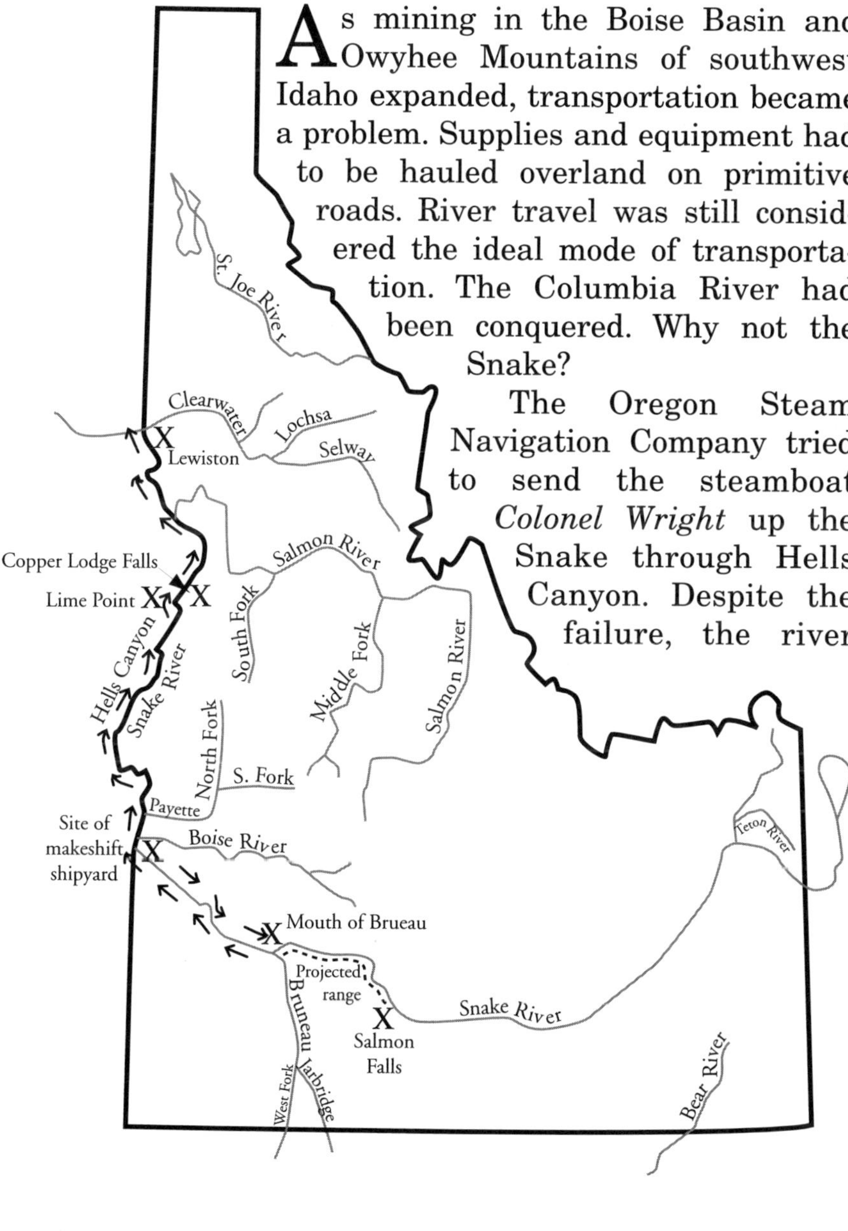

As mining in the Boise Basin and Owyhee Mountains of southwest Idaho expanded, transportation became a problem. Supplies and equipment had to be hauled overland on primitive roads. River travel was still considered the ideal mode of transportation. The Columbia River had been conquered. Why not the Snake?

The Oregon Steam Navigation Company tried to send the steamboat *Colonel Wright* up the Snake through Hells Canyon. Despite the failure, the river travel dream remained firmly embedded in the minds of company owners. Since they couldn't bring a steamboat upstream through the canyon, they decided to build one specifically to serve the region above the natural obstacle.

A temporary shipyard was established at Riverside Ferry near Old Fort Boise, at the junction of the Snake and Boise rivers. The OSNC directors figured that big profits could be made if they could monopolize river transportation between that point and Salmon Falls, about 150 miles upstream.

Work on the new steamboat began in October 1865. The boilers, engines and other pre-assembled machinery were hauled over the Blue Mountains by wagon from company shops at Umatilla, Oregon. Iron also was brought over the mountains by pack train. Since there was no foundry at the improvised shipyard, many metal parts were beaten into shape by hand on an anvil.

With no sawmill, all the lumber for the boat's hull and superstructure had to be hauled to the site, too. A. H. Robie agreed to deliver the timber by December. Mountain pine was whipsawed by hand. Pine, which becomes soft and brittle when seasoned, isn't a good wood for shipbuilding. But it was the only material available within hauling distance. Delivery of the planks began October 20, but storms halted shipments during December.

About January 1, Captain Gates arrived at the shipyard to act as building superintendent. He had the reputation as the best boat-builder on the Columbia. With a crew of twenty men, Gates went to work building the 136-foot sternwheeler. The boat

SHOSHONE
Jim Paxton

had a shallow draft of only 20 inches. It weighed about 300 tons and could haul about 175 tons of freight.

By February 2, 1866, the frame was up and ready for planking. But an early thaw made the primitive roads impassable and held up delivery of the boards. Construction was further hampered because the wagons carrying the last of the machinery from Umatilla bogged down, too, and had to wait for the roads to dry out.

When construction was finally completed in April, the new boat was christened *Shoshone*.

The *Shoshone* wasn't cheap to build. The lumber and 400 cords of firewood for the boilers cost $19,000. Hauling equipment from Umatilla was also expensive. The steamboat company could have built three similar vessels on the Columbia for the cost of the one Snake River craft.

On May 16, under the command of Captain Joshiah Myrick, the steamboat started her maiden voyage. Invitations announced the event. J. S. Reynolds, of the *Idaho Statesman* newspaper, gave his readers a first-hand description of the *Shoshone*:

> "Anticipating the arrival of the boat at Owyhee Ferry, a small party of gentlemen from Ruby City and another from Boise City, came over on the stages this morning just in time to hear the music of the steam whistle reverberate for the first time along the sage brush solitude of the Snake. It was pleasant music to the ears of us who have for two years heard no other than whoa-haw, driver's whip or the

Jehu's horn. First taking a good dinner at the hospitable invitation of Captain Myrick, we started down the river at half past one o'clock, running down to the Boise Ferry in five hours, including time to wood and other delays. The wind several times blew a gale as it generally does on the Snake and Columbia. The boat being entirely light it was difficult to keep her head in the wind. Two or three times it turned her completely around in spite of helm and stern."

The voyage to Salmon Falls was a failure. The *Shoshone* could not navigate above the mouth of the Bruneau River, a little over halfway between her Riverside shipyard and Salmon Falls.

The *Shoshone* lost money from the beginning. Cargoes were scarce and the boat cost more to run than anticipated. Its boilers quickly consumed the original 400 cords of wood. Coal deposits known to be near the river proved too low grade to be used as fuel.

After three years of sporadic service, the upper Snake runs were abandoned and the *Shoshone* was docked at Owyhee Ferry.

During the spring of 1869, OSNC directors decided to have the *Shoshone* taken through Hells Canyon so it could operate between Lewiston and The Dalles. Captain Silas Smith was hired to bring the steamboat to the Columbia or wreck her in the attempt.

It was early June when Captain Smith cast off and headed the *Shoshone* downstream, past Jacob's Ladder, around Oxbow and through Kern and Cattle rapids to Lime Point, above Copper Ledge Falls. After scouting the roaring whitewater chute with its bed of boulders, Smith returned to the sternwheeler and tied her to a lone pine tree. Leaving two of his men, Livingston and Smith, to watch the boat, the captain climbed out of the canyon with the rest of the crew. He contacted OSNC's chief, John Ainsworth.

"It's folly to take a ship the size of the *Shoshone* any further," Smith told Ainsworth. "I quit!"

Smith's statement enraged Ainsworth. Within days he dispatched a new captain, Sebastain E. Miller, to Lime Point with explicit instructions: "If Copper Ledge Falls can be run, then run it! If not, burn the *Shoshone* and sink her remains."

Enlisting the services of engineer Dan Buchanan, Captain Miller left Portland on March 21, 1870. After traveling by steamboat to Umatilla Landing, the two men continued the journey via buckboard, sled, horseback and on foot. Arriving at Lime Point April 8, Miller and Buchanan were amazed to find the two watchmen were still with the *Shoshone*, having spent ten months guarding her.

Following a winter of boredom, the guards were eager for excitement and glad to accept Miller's employment offer. Livingston was hired as mate and Smith as fireman. A third man, W. F. Hedges, who had kept the guards company, was hired as deck hand.

The *Shoshone's* engines received an overhaul. Long months of disuse had badly weathered her hull, opening large cracks between the planks. Since it would have taken weeks to chaulk the gaps, Engineer Buchanan attached a hose to the bilge pumps and sprayed the hull until the wood swelled, closing the seams. Extra bulkheads were built into the hull as reinforcement. Lighted candles were placed in the hull so leaks could be detected and stopped.

On April 20, 1870, the refurbished *Shoshone* headed for the brink of Copper Ledge Falls. The plan was to drift through the rapid with the engines backing. Unfortunately, the boat caught an eddy above the falls. It spun completely around three times like a stick of driftwood, before being spat out crossways in the current. Captain Miller fought to get the boat straightened out before it reached the falls. Scraping a gravel bar near shore, the bow swung around and nosed over the cataract, with the paddle wheel fanning the air. Then the *Shoshone* belly-flopped into a hole below the falls.

Above the roar of the rapids, the sound of the splintering of wood was heard. Eight feet of the bow floated off down the Snake. The *Shoshone's* jackstaff and flag washed after it.

As water flooded into the boat, Captain Miller wrestled the wheel, guiding the craft through the remaining rapids to quiet water. Once the steamer was beached, men made repairs while standing waist deep in frigid water. They worked through the night, around the clock, using makeshift tools and materials.

After an encounter with some of the river's worst rapids, the next day the boat was jockeyed back to shore. Two days were spent repairing the paddle wheel. A patch was fashioned from planks and pieces of broken lumber.

When the *Shoshone* returned to the river, there was another delay as the wind whipped through the narrow canyon with such fury that headings could not be maintained.

On April 24, a large stand of pine trees was spotted on the bank. Miller ordered a layover while the crew cut the trees for fuel. While the captain was strolling along the shore, one of the felled trees bounced down the mountain and rolled over him. Although he was bloodied and bruised, the leader of the expedition escaped without any broken bones. He was carried to the boat and put to bed for a couple of days rest before resuming his duties.

Still nursing his injuries, Miller piloted to boat on downriver. On April 26, it passed the mouth of the Salmon River, which flowed into the Snake from the east. They moored that night at the mouth of the Grande Ronde River on the west bank.

The following day, the *Shoshone* nosed in at the Lewiston pier. Her arrival was greeted by a cheering throng of surprised residents. Four days earlier, her bow section and flag had been fished out of the Columbia River near Umatilla. The boat and crew had been given up as lost.

From Lewiston, Captain Holmes steered the *Shoshone* down the Snake and Columbia to The Dalles, where she received extensive repairs. She operated in the upper Columbia until 1873, when Captain John Ainsworth took her to the lower river, then up the Willamette, where she was sold to the Willamette River Transportation Company.

Late in 1874, the *Shoshone* struck a rock near Salem and sank. The machinery was salvaged in November. In January 1875, the hull surfaced and floated downstream to Lincoln where is was pulled ashore and converted into a chicken coop.

SEVENTEEN

Snake River — 1868

Niagara of the West

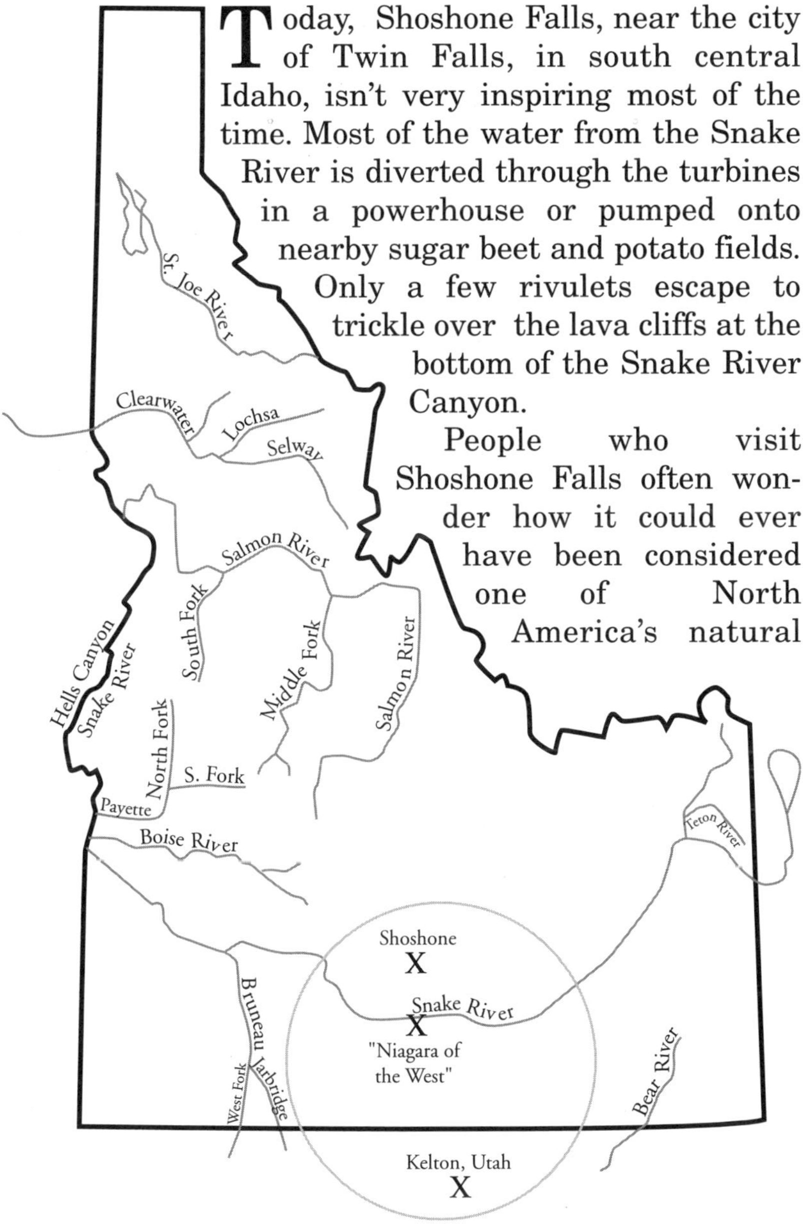

Today, Shoshone Falls, near the city of Twin Falls, in south central Idaho, isn't very inspiring most of the time. Most of the water from the Snake River is diverted through the turbines in a powerhouse or pumped onto nearby sugar beet and potato fields. Only a few rivulets escape to trickle over the lava cliffs at the bottom of the Snake River Canyon.

People who visit Shoshone Falls often wonder how it could ever have been considered one of North America's natural wonders, often referred to by nineteenth century writers as the "Niagara of the West." But there was a time when even that description didn't do justice to the landmark.

When Hudson's Bay Company trappers entered the area in the early 1830s, men stood in awe at the magnificent quivering wall of water that made an impressive 250-foot plunge. In honor of their homeland, they named the cataract Canadian Falls.

In 1849, a regiment of mounted riflemen, lead by Major Osborne Cross, came upon the spectacle while on an expedition from Ft. Leavenworth to Ft. Vancouver. Cross proclaimed the falls one of nature's greatest wonders. Although he knew the Hudson's Bay men had previously named the site, Cross renamed it Great Shoshone Falls.

In 1857, Albert D. Richardson began a ten-year tour of the West, doing research for his book *Beyond the Mississippi From the Great River to the Great Ocean, 1857-1867*. Though he had heard of the Great Shoshone Falls of the Snake River, he had difficulty finding someone who could guide him to the spot. He finally persuaded a soldier from a detachment camped near a new stage station in the area to escort him to the falls. On first viewing the falls, the author was impressed.

> "The world how far it seemed and God how near!" Richardson wrote. "Under the deafening roar, how the firm-set earth quaked and vibrated. How deep the chasm from which rose pearly mist... Long I lay upon the rock-shelf,

gazing over the brink, riveted by the great white cataract."

Richardson's book was published in 1867. By 1868 the publicity it generated drew many visitors from the East, eager to view this splendid, newly-discovered natural phenomena — "Niagara of the West."

One year later, the U. S. Geological Survey of the Fortieth Parallel Expedition examined the area. Its photographer, Timothy O'Sullivan, described the falls as "one of the most sublime of the Rocky Mountain scenes."

Charles Walgamott visited Great Shoshone Falls in 1875. An enterprising individual, he immediately recognized the commercial potential, filed on the land above the falls, and built a dugout shelter at the site.

Tom Bell placer-mined the back eddies around the islands above the falls during the early 1880s. Building a cabin along one of the sandbars, the Scotch miner used a flat-bottomed boat for transport back and fourth across the river. During high water, one June day, Bell and two Chinese miners attempted to cross. One of the oars snapped from the strain of moving against the current, the craft was swept over the falls and all three men perished. Shoshone Falls had claimed its first victims.

In 1883, when the Oregon Short Line Railroad reached the town of Shoshone, twenty-five miles away, Charles Walgamott swung into action. Purchasing an aging Deadwood coach with an interior lined with faded red plush, he went into the tourist business. Soon, so many travelers flocked to the attraction that Walgamott found himself ill prepared to handle them.

After a long, bumpy, dusty ride across the listless landscape, the coach pulled up to a lone juniper tree standing amid dark lava formations. Below lay the Snake River Canyon — and just beyond, the falls. A rough trail down the north wall of the canyon led to a smooth, wide, deep stretch of river. Once the passengers made their way down the trail, they came to a small sandbar and Walgamott's dugout. A rickety rowboat was tied nearby so that guests could cross the river, to get a different view of the resplendent cataract. Camp was prepared for the night.

Although Walgamott had enough bedding for a dozen people, he often had twice that number of visitors. At first he tried to rent hammocks for an additional dollar. When customers showed a preference for sleeping on the ground, he had his partner tell tales around the campfire about warmth-seeking rattlesnakes crawling into bedding. The scare tactic worked and the hammocks were rented.

Charles Dewey purchased Walgamott's river holding and established a ferry on the north side of the river. The ferry was a flat-bottomed boat guided by a wire cable and worked by a windlass. The trail down the north wall of the canyon was widened so wagons could descend to the ferry. On the south bank, atop a high bluff, overlooking Great Shoshone Falls, Dewey built a small hotel. Walgamott continued his stage service to the site; food and lodging was provided by the Dewey Hotel.

In 1884, another book, *The Pacific Tourist*, gave details on how to reach the falls. Passengers from the

East arrived at Kelton, Utah, on the transcontinental railroad at 10:00 P.M., while those from the West arrived at 2:00 A.M. The following morning, they booked in at the Northwestern Stage Company for a 100-mile, twelve-hour coach ride to Rock Creek Station. After an overnight stay there, a stage carried them ten miles to the rim above the falls.

Edwards Roberts' book *Shoshone and Other Western Wonders*, was released in 1888. It included beautiful pen and ink sketches as well as graphic descriptions of the falls:

> "The Great Fall of Shoshone is crescent-shaped, and is two hundred and twenty-five feet high by nine hundred and fifty feet wide. The plunge is unbroken. Facing it one sees a quivering wall of water that stretches from one side of the canyon to the other. The roar is deafening, and its force is so great that the displaced air is as fierce as a tornado. The earth trembles from the blow it receives. You yourself are drenched with spray; and the rising mist is like a fog at sea, blown hither and thither, and so catching the sun's rays as to form arch upon arch of glorious color...
>
> "... In the cliffs at the foot of the Great Falls are curiously fashioned caves. In one the roar of the waters reverberates in sound like the paddle-wheels of a steamer run at full speed; in another — an ear-shaped grotto two hundred feet high, and named 'Diana's Bath-room'— cold drops of water trickle from the ceiling

> walls, and are caught by a stone-rimmed basin set in the floor of the vaulted chamber...
>
> "You should see the river gather itself together for its leap into the lower depths of the canyon; should listen to the roar it makes; should feel the earth tremble with the shock; should watch the rising mists, ghost-like in the moonlight; should give days to the isolated place, to know the fascinations of Shoshone Falls. Telling one how high the Falls are, how deep the canyon is, gives no idea of the place itself, of its coloring, and its weirdness."

Visitors continued to flock to the falls. In the 1890s, the Union Pacific Railroad joined in promoting the tourist attraction. The company sponsored special excursions to the town of Shoshone, where passengers boarded a stage that took them to the falls. In August 1891, Jay Gould, the eastern magnate and principal investor in the Union Pacific Railroad Company, arrived at Shoshone in his private Pullman car, curious to see what all the excitement was about. Gould was so impressed that he commissioned Charles Walgamott to make photographs of the area for promotional purposes.

The newspaper, *Shoshone Journal*, reported in July 1892 that 200 visitors had registered at the Dewey Hotel during the months of May and June.

In 1893, a painting of Shoshone Falls displayed at the Chicago World's Fair, drew crowds of admirers.

Soon, tourists no longer went to Shoshone. A new town, Twin Falls, was established in the late 1890's. Visitors took the train to Twin Falls, then boarded a battery-powered Edison Electric Railway car for a comfortable ride to the new, grand, Shoshone Falls Hotel which had replaced the modest Dewey Hotel.

As interest in the area continued to grow, a petition to establish a preserve was filed. Idaho's Senator Shoup was notified that an inspector would be sent to tour the area for possible national park status. In 1901, a congressional bill was introduced to designate a Snake River Canyon National Park which would include the Shoshone Falls. But with special interest groups working against the bill, it died.

That same year, Bert Perrine and H. L. Hollister attempted to harness the power of the falls to generate electricity. The partners began tunneling 200 feet up through the rock to the brink, but ran out of money before the project was completed. Shoshone Falls Power Company took over the effort, but it, too, failed. That company was purchased by another local concern. Soon a power plant situated at the base of the falls, was producing 500 kilowatts — enough energy to supply the nearby towns.

Idaho Power Company acquired the facility in 1915. Six years later, the company built an additional plant alongside the first. Output was increased to 12,000 kilowatts. In 1929, a diversion dam was built for water storage during peak use.

Even though hydroelectric power had become the new wonder of the day, the once Great Shoshone Falls power plant failed to draw tourists. The man-made structure scarred the beauty of the site. Half the river flow had been dammed upriver, to be consumed by the turbines of another power plant.

In an effort to revive public interest in Shoshone Falls, the Twin Falls post of the American Legion hired Al Faussett, a lumberjack from Monroe, Washington, to perform an attention-getting stunt by going over the falls in an orange, canvas-covered torpedo-shaped, twelve-foot canoe on July 28, 1929.

Faussett's fee for going over the falls was half the proceeds. At thirty cents per person, ticket takers admitted nearly 5,000 spectators. Idaho Power supported the stunt by interrupting its water diversion to the reservoir long enough to raise the river to a level close to its normal flow. The American Electric Company provided radio music which blared out of loudspeakers. Dynamite explosions marked the count-down.

At the designated hour, Faussett was zipped into his canvas boat. In order to direct his craft over the south edge of the falls, a wire cable was run from a large boulder, through a three inch ring on his craft, then down to a man in a boat at the base of the falls.

Shortly after the craft was shoved out into the river, it snagged on a rock at the brink of the falls. Two men waded out with long poles and worked the boat free. The orange craft then slid down the falls and plunged into a pool below. When it popped to the surface, it was upside down. Two motorboats chugged out to the bobbing craft and towed it ashore. There were no dramatic drum rolls, but one of the rescuers produced a large hunting knife to cut the canvas open. Out jumped an exuberant daredevil. After claiming his share of the take, he went on his way.

Perhaps the event failed to produce the desired enthusiasm. Perhaps people who came to ogle or speculate on the fate of a man foolish enough to challenge the falls, walked away shamed or unsatisfied. Whatever their reasons, the side-show brainstorm fizzled.

What remains of the Great Shoshone Falls retains some grace. And in high water years, people flock to the falls in the spring. When the Snake River is at full cry, one can see why the falls was once known as the "Niagara of the West."

The 425-mile Salmon River is the longest free flowing river in the lower 48 states.

EIGHTEEN

Snake River — 1870

James Henoty's Salmon Fishery

Mining camps sprang up in many areas of the Idaho Territory in Idaho during the 1860s. Men came from afar to stake their claims. The newcomers were not always successful, however. Many lived off ever-present optimism and their firm trust in "tomorrow."

One bachelor, swept into Idaho by the winds of promise, quickly sized up the silver and gold situation and decided there was a more reliable natural resource — fish! James Henoty was the first

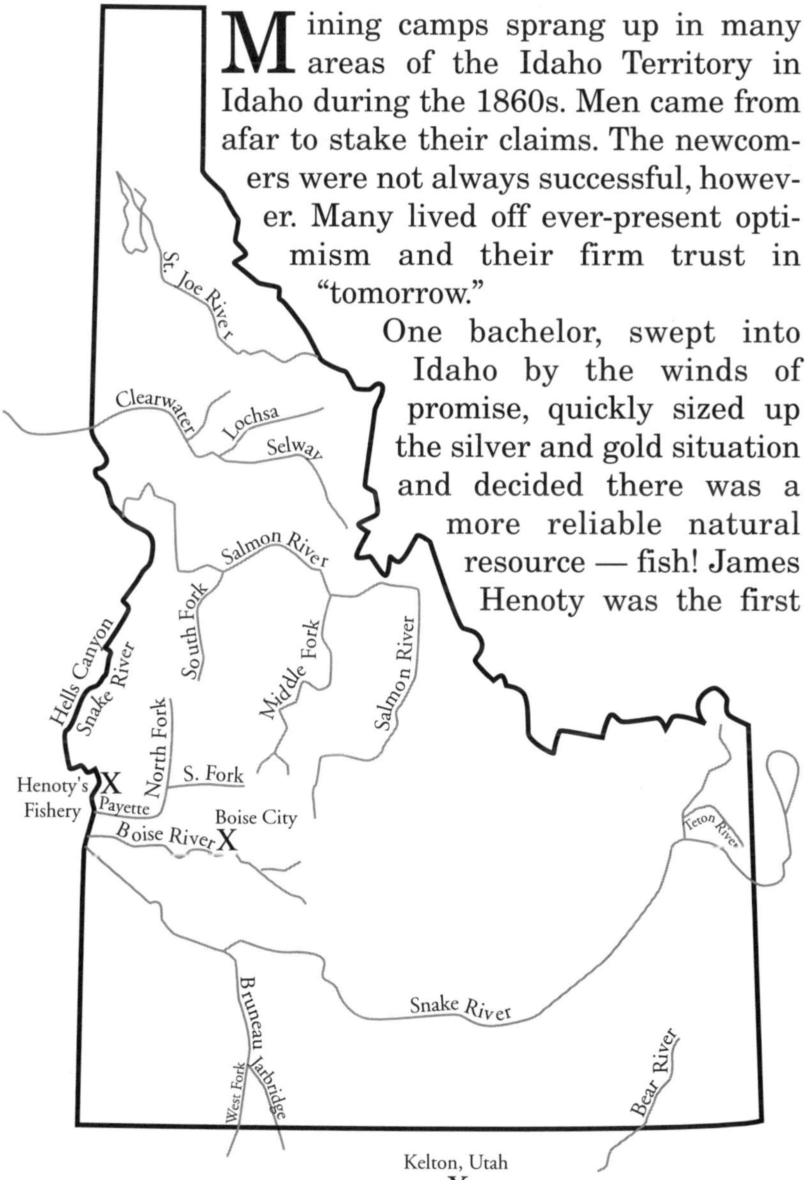

white man to operate a salmon fishery on the Snake River.

Before the building of the Columbia and Snake River dams, one of the Snake's greatest assets was the Chinook salmon and Pacific steelhead. The Snake River system was the world's second largest producer of the fish, exceeded only by Canada's Fraser River. Each year more than 200,000 three to four-foot-long fish migrated upstream from the Pacific Ocean to spawn.

Henoty figured that if the Nez Perce, Shoshoni and Bannock Indians could harvest the protein-rich fish, he could, too.

Henoty located his fishery on the Idaho side of the Snake near the Washoe Ferry. He built a double-log cabin, the first home in the Washoe Bottoms. His two hired men, Andy McGuern and Dick Luce, lived in the cabin with Henoty.

A large seine, about 300 feet long and five feet wide, was used to catch the fish. The net was rigged with corks and sinkers and carefully folded so it wouldn't tangle while unwinding. The rigged net was placed on a platform at the rear of a skiff. A long rope, attached to one end of the seine, was fastened to metal rings mounted on the platform. Another long rope was tied to the opposite end of the net before being tossed ashore to a man on horseback. The rider tied the rope to his saddlehorn.

An oarsman rowed the skiff to midstream, then turned the boat and rowed downstream as swiftly as possible, muscles straining. The net unfolded from the platform and sank into the water as the man on shore rode downriver keeping pace with the skiff.

After rowing about 200 yards, the man in the boat rowed ashore. The two men then pulled the seine to the bank.

Sometimes the net would be so full of fish it was difficult to pull in. Other times they would get a "water haul" — not a single fish. The haul the men dreaded the most was when a sturgeon, sometimes weighing 400 pounds, charged through the net releasing the entire catch. Fishing halted while the net was repaired.

A few fish were marketed fresh. But the majority were cleaned, salted and laid in the sun to dry. When sun drying wasn't possible because of rain or snow, fish were cured in a smoke house.

James Henoty's fishery proved so profitable that in 1873 he decided it was time to reward himself by taking a wife.

Finding a woman willing to live with the constant smell of fish was no simple fete. Through mail order, Henoty managed to locate a willing lass in Cincinnati, Ohio. It was a nervous bachelor who drove his wagon to the nearest train station at Kelton, Utah to meet his bride. He waited more than an hour for the train with his hair slicked down and hat in hand.

When Miss Bridgett Morgan stepped down from that train, James Henoty thought she was the loveliest woman he had ever seen. They were married at the Catholic Church in Boise enroute to the Washoe fishery. James built his wife a frame house a hundred yards north of his original cabin.

For the next eleven years the couple made a decent living from the fishery.

In 1884, while trying to ford the swift Payette River near Falk's Store, Henoty's horse lost its footing. His body was later found floating in an eddy downstream. His wife, Bridgett, sold their home to Jacob Stroup and returned to Cincinnati.

William O'Brion and G. W. Brinnon operated the fishery until 1887. It then passed on to F. M. Draper and W. J. Mink, who managed it for about a year. After that, James Henoty's fishery vanished.

NINETEEN

Payette River — 1876

Payette River Log Drives

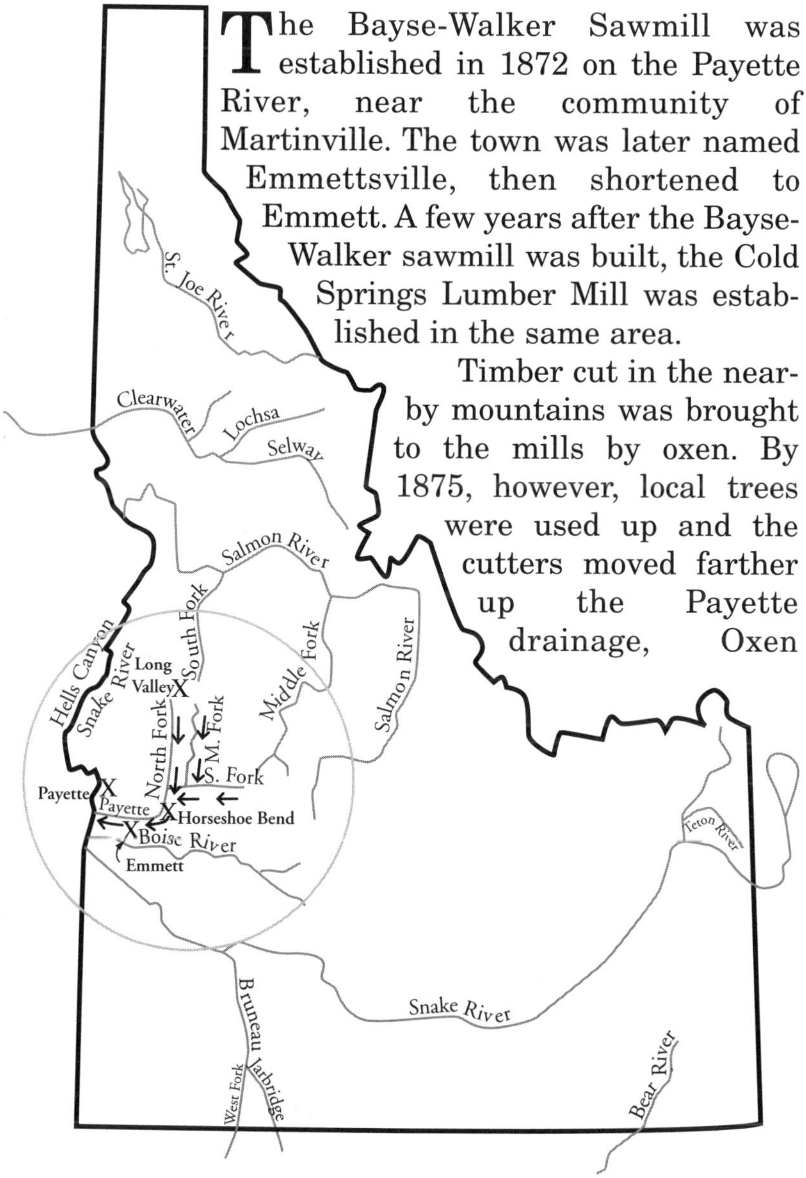

The Bayse-Walker Sawmill was established in 1872 on the Payette River, near the community of Martinville. The town was later named Emmettsville, then shortened to Emmett. A few years after the Bayse-Walker sawmill was built, the Cold Springs Lumber Mill was established in the same area.

Timber cut in the nearby mountains was brought to the mills by oxen. By 1875, however, local trees were used up and the cutters moved farther up the Payette drainage, Oxen hauled logging equipment over the Boise Basin trail to the South and North Fork logging areas in the autumn. Crews worked in those areas throughout the winter.

Trees were felled with broadaxes and crosscut saws. The limbed timber was dragged through the snow by oxen and stacked on decks built along the Payette River. During the spring runoff, from mid May through mid June, logs were released from the decks to float downstream to the mills.

Loggers followed pack trails along the river, watching the logs. Jams often formed at bends or on gravel bars. Men leaped onto the jams and pried the jammed logs loose with Peavey hooks. When the logs broke loose it wasn't always possible to return to shore, so the loggers rode logs downriver until they could jump to safety.

Sometimes logs lodged on gravel bars and workers couldn't get them loose. Teams of large draft horses were used in such situations. Cables were looped around the ends of the logs and tied to the horses. The horses strained against the cables and worked the logs loose. The loggers quickly released the cables before the current carried the logs and the horses downstream.

One of the earliest log drive fatalities occurred on June 28, 1876. Walter Dingley was driving logs for the Cold Springs Lumber Company when some timber jammed against boulders in the middle of a frothing rapid. Dingley jumped onto the jam and pried loose a large log lodged between the rocks. When the log popped free, it stood on end and knocked Dingley into the river. The logger was trapped in the moving mass of timber and drowned.

In 1883, the Oregon Short Line Railroad needed ties while building a section of track across southern Idaho. The firm of Coe and Carter, from Omaha, Nebraska, was hired to furnish 300,000 ties. It sent its own logging crew, a group of men from Maine, Minnesota and Michigan, to the North Fork drainage. They were a different breed, known as "Log Hogs."

Log Hogs didn't follow the drives from the shore. They floated behind the logs in narrow, deep-hulled wooden boats called bateaux. Each bateau carried six to eight men. The craft was steered by men in the bow and stern using long poles. The other occupants rowed. Cables were used to lower the craft over hazardous rapids. But the boats, designed for less turbulent Eastern rivers, frequently swamped or flipped in the wild Payette. With Log Hogs floating the river with the logs, deaths became an annual occurrence. The rough and rugged men considered drowning an occupational hazard and refused to give up their boats.

The clannish group of log drivers had their own dress code. They wore denim pants cut off just above the knee, hob nail boots, red woolen shirts, gray wool mittens and short-brimmed black felt hats. They hit the mill towns at the end of a drive ready to celebrate. They tossed back glasses of Red Top whiskey, got in street fights and danced holes in saloon floors with their hob nail boots. Log Hogs spent money freely and were welcome additions to the local economy.

In 1890, an attempt to float logs down the upper South Fork of the Payette to the Horseshoe Bend mill claimed seven Log Hogs at Big Falls. The falls, located in South Fork Canyon, is one of the most challenging sections of the Payette River. During high water there is a long wave train leading to the twenty-five-foot waterfall. The bateaux were always lowered through the falls. The ill-fated men either decided to challenge the falls or failed to spot landmarks in time to avoid the cataract.

The spring of 1894 brought flooding along the Payette River. Although the logs moved quickly downriver with the high water, the Log Hogs faced an unusual problem when they reached the Central Lumber Company mill in Emmett. The mill was gone!

The river current had been cutting away at the northeast corner of the mill for a week before the penstock, housing the big turbine wheels, broke loose. It was carried downstream until it stuck on a gravel bar. Within two days, the river washed away twelve feet under the corner of the mill foundation. Because it was only a matter of time before the entire structure would topple into the river, mill employees removed all the machinery. Then the building was disassembled board-by-board and stacked a safe distance from the river. The mill was rebuilt and back in operation later that summer.

Flooding occurred again in 1904. The Payette River Basin had a heavy snowpack and the river was swollen and extremely dangerous. On May 26, four Log Hogs flipped their bateau in the rapids where the South and Middle forks join. The men were part of a crew bringing a large log drive to Prestel's Sawmill in Payette. The cataract was called Hell's Half Acre. Today it is known as Staircase Rapids. The river narrows and makes a steep drop through a labyrinth of boulders, holes and logs. By today's river running standards, Staircase is a Class V rapid. The bodies of the men were recovered several miles downstream.

In 1915, the Idaho Northern Railroad built a line up the North Fork of the Payette. Trees were cut in Long Valley and hand hewn into ties. The ties were floated downriver and collected at strategic points. The completion of the railroad eliminated the need for log drives. Timber now rides the rails, rather than rapids.

The Salmon River Canyon, which effectively splits Idaho in half, is the second deepest canyon in North America.

TWENTY

Snake River — 1876

Stagecoach Overboard

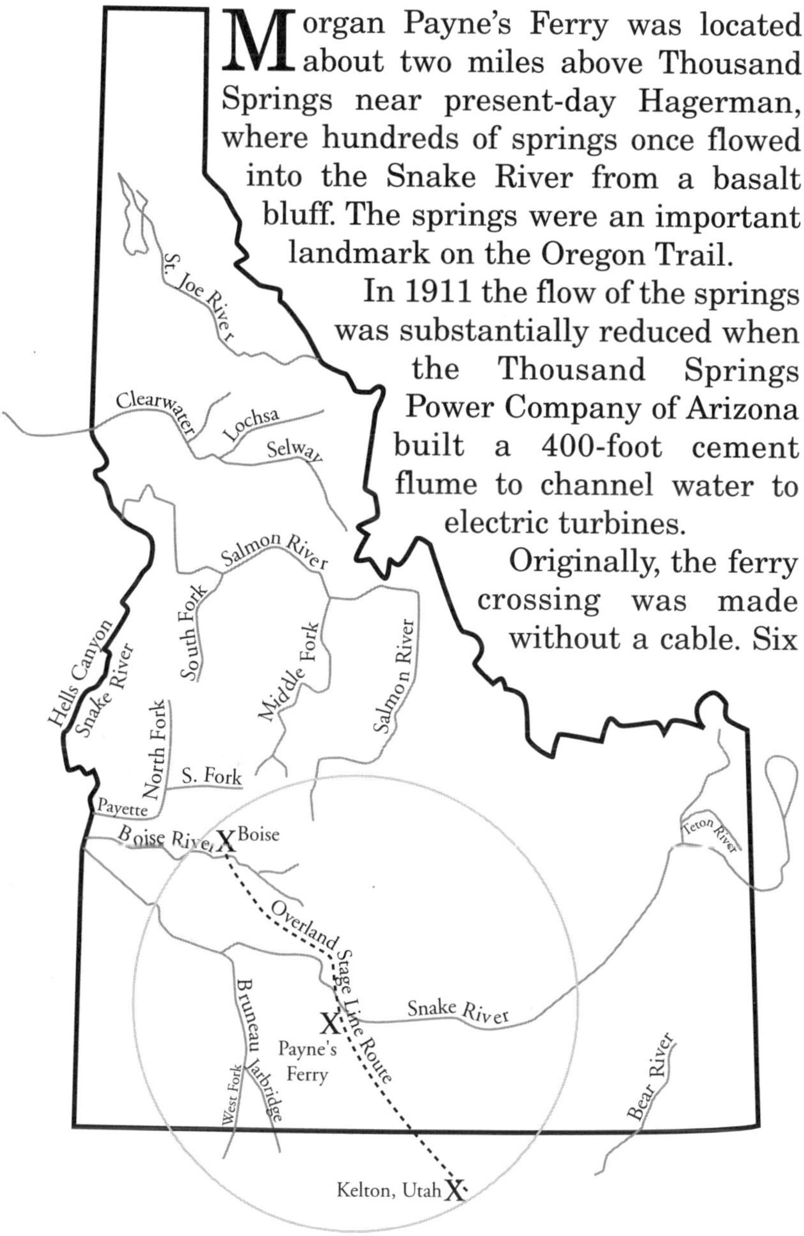

Morgan Payne's Ferry was located about two miles above Thousand Springs near present-day Hagerman, where hundreds of springs once flowed into the Snake River from a basalt bluff. The springs were an important landmark on the Oregon Trail.

In 1911 the flow of the springs was substantially reduced when the Thousand Springs Power Company of Arizona built a 400-foot cement flume to channel water to electric turbines.

Originally, the ferry crossing was made without a cable. Six to eight men rowed the craft across the river with long sweep oars. Most of Payne's customers were horses and riders, livestock and an occasional wagon.

In 1871 Payne established a cable ferry. The new heavy-duty boat could accommodate stagecoaches, freight and emigrant wagons. The Overland Stage Line paid $1,000 a year to use the ferry.

The Overland Stage crossed the river twice each day — at about midnight when heading for Utah and at sun-up when bound for Boise, 110 miles to the north.

In 1876, an Overland Stage went overboard.

The stage driver, a man named Mason, was traveling without passengers but carrying the all-important mail bags. After giving the customary morning greeting to the ferry operator, Mason lined his team up to the ferry and drove onto the platform.

After the ferry left the bank, the driver remembered he had a letter for the ferry operator. When he reached down to retrieve the letter from the boot, the horses took his sudden movement as a signal to move ahead. The two lead horses stepped forward onto the apron at the end of the ferry, which gave way under their weight. Team, stage and driver, plunged into about 10 feet of water.

The driver thrashed free from the sinking stage, nearly drowning in the process. After reaching the surface, Mason gulped air and dove into the cold swirling river to try to free the panicked team. Although the driver was struck several times by flailing hooves, he freed the two lead horses and swam them to shore. The two other hoses drowned under the weight of the harness and stage.

Though shaking with exhaustion and cold, Mason made one more dive to rescue the soggy mail.

TWENTY-ONE

Snake River — 1877

"The Snake River is Very High" — Chief Joseph

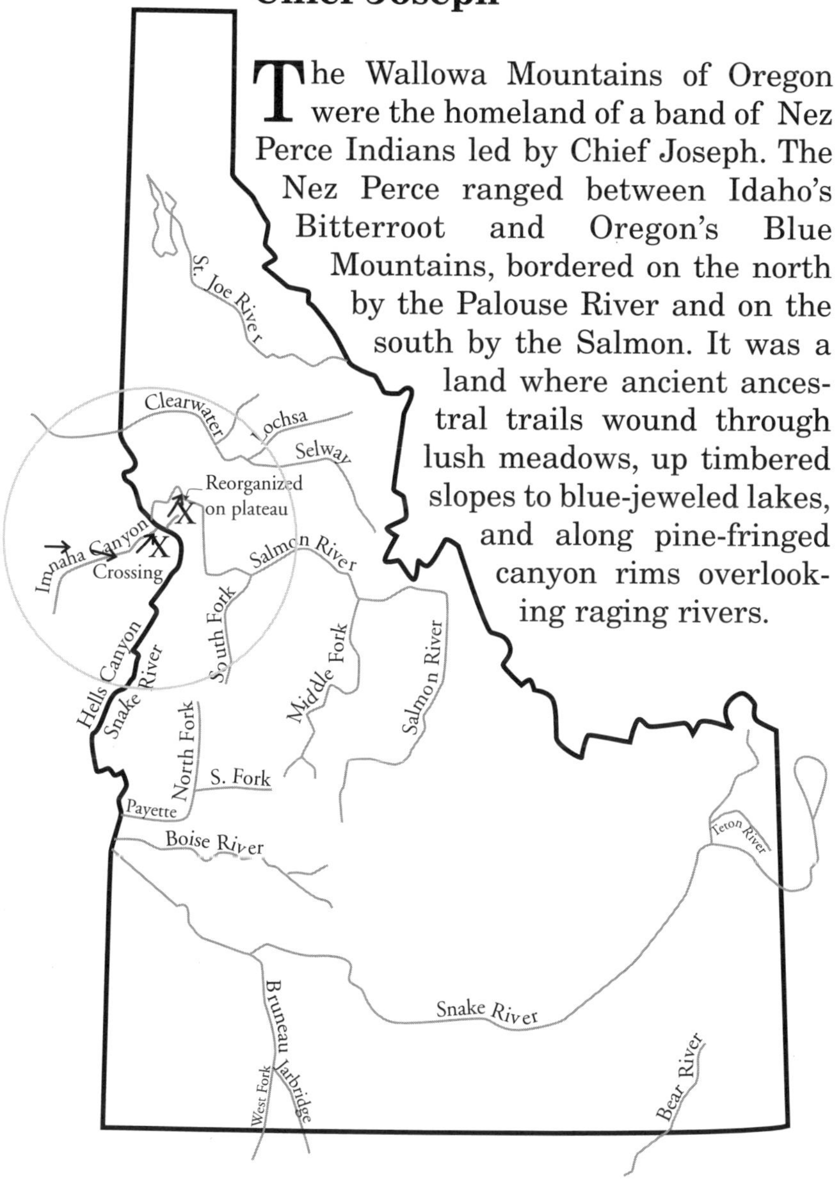

The Wallowa Mountains of Oregon were the homeland of a band of Nez Perce Indians led by Chief Joseph. The Nez Perce ranged between Idaho's Bitterroot and Oregon's Blue Mountains, bordered on the north by the Palouse River and on the south by the Salmon. It was a land where ancient ancestral trails wound through lush meadows, up timbered slopes to blue-jeweled lakes, and along pine-fringed canyon rims overlooking raging rivers.

The Treaty of 1855, accepted by most Nez Perce, gave the Indians most of their tribal lands. However, the treaty was revised in 1863, shrinking the 6.5 million-acre area to 768,000 acres — a more "manageable" piece of land worthless to the miners and settlers moving into the region. Most of the Nez Perce bands signed the new treaty, but Joseph and several other leaders refused. However, within fifteen years, they faced a proclamation by President Grant, ordering all non-treaty bands to be on the reservation by April 1, 1877. The Nez Perce were told if they didn't obey the order, troops would be sent to force them to comply.

Four bands, led by chiefs Joseph, Toohoolhoolzote, Looking Glass and White Bird, held out. The Army made no move to force the free Nez Perce to the reservation. Instead, a conference was held May 4, 1877. Toohoolhoolzote spoke for the Nez Perce. After his eloquent oration, soldiers seized him and threw him in the guardhouse. Because Toohoolhoolzote was under threat of transfer to a reservation in Oklahoma, the other non-treaty chiefs agreed to the demands of the white officials. They returned to their villages with the heart-breaking news that they would have to move. The bands were given thirty days to gather their livestock and possessions and move to the reservation at Lapwai.

Chief Joseph's people were far away at Wallowa. More that 100 men, women and children and hundreds of cattle and horses had to be moved through a steep gorge and the across the Snake River, which was running at flood level. Joseph made a plea to

General Oliver Otis Howard, the commander of the Department of Columbia, for more time.

> "War can and ought to be avoided," Joseph said. "I want no war. My people have always been friends of the white man. Why are you in such a hurry? I can not get ready to move in 30 days. Our stock is scattered and the Snake River is very high. Let us wait till fall, when the river will be low. We want to hunt up stock and gather supplies for the winter."

Howard refused to bend.

> "If you let the time run over one day," Howard wrote, "the soldiers will be there to drive you on the reservation and cattle outside the reservation at that time will fall into the hands of the white men."

Two and a half weeks later, Joseph's people gathered in the depths of Hells Canyon, on the banks of the Snake River. They had worked their way down the hot, rocky Imnaha Canyon, over the dividing ridge at its mouth, then down steep draws to the rolling, swollen brown torrent of the Snake — a quarter mile wide at that point.

The milling cattle and horses scattered along the narrow riverbank, seeking relief from the oppressive heat and searching for grass in the cervices along steep canyon walls. Small bands of white opportunists nipped at the rear of the column, stealing straggling cattle.

The Nez Perce surveyed the river. The crossing would be dangerous, but so would bullets from cavalry rifles. It was better to pit themselves against the forces of nature than those of man.

The Indians took hides normally used to cover lodges or for bedding and rolled them into tight cylinders. The hide floats were lashed together to form crude rafts. The rafts were heaped with possessions.

Four horses, known to be strong swimmers, were paired with four young men who could swim and were tough enough to endure the icy waters. The men stripped naked and mounted the horses bareback. They entered the cold swirling river with a rider at each corner of a raft. They moved slowly away from the bank and into the powerful current. Each group of raft and riders was swept several hundred feet downstream before they found firm footing near the far shore.

The crossing was repeated many times, but not always with success. Several hide rafts were swept away.

Meanwhile, marauders sneaked up on the flanks and drove several hundred horses and cattle back up the canyon to be branded as white stock.

Once the gear was across the raging river, the people began to ford. Again, the tribe's best horses played key roles. Usually, a strong man sat astride with a woman of child riding in front or clinging behind. Eyes white with fear and nostrils blowing icy spray, the horses battled across. Some were caught in the current, then flushed into eddies to spin helplessly before being sucked under. They fought back to the surface to struggle on, driven by the survival instinct.

Miraculously, all horses and people reached the far shore safely.

The remaining livestock were driven into the river. The heat of the canyon already had weakened many. Some were swept away by the current, drowning in the rapids below. The survivors climbed up the Idaho bank near the mouth of Divide Creek, trembling with exhaustion. The Indians worked their stock up the steep slopes of the canyon walls to a plateau between the Snake and Salmon rivers.

Joseph and his followers made a difficult crossing during a season when the river was exceptionally perilous. Believing they had twelve more days of freedom before beginning reservation life, they reorganized their possessions and rested their stock.

But one day prior to the deadline, circumstances forever changed the course of Nez Perce history.

TWENTY-TWO

Salmon River — 1877

"A Perfect Torrent" — General Oliver Otis Howard

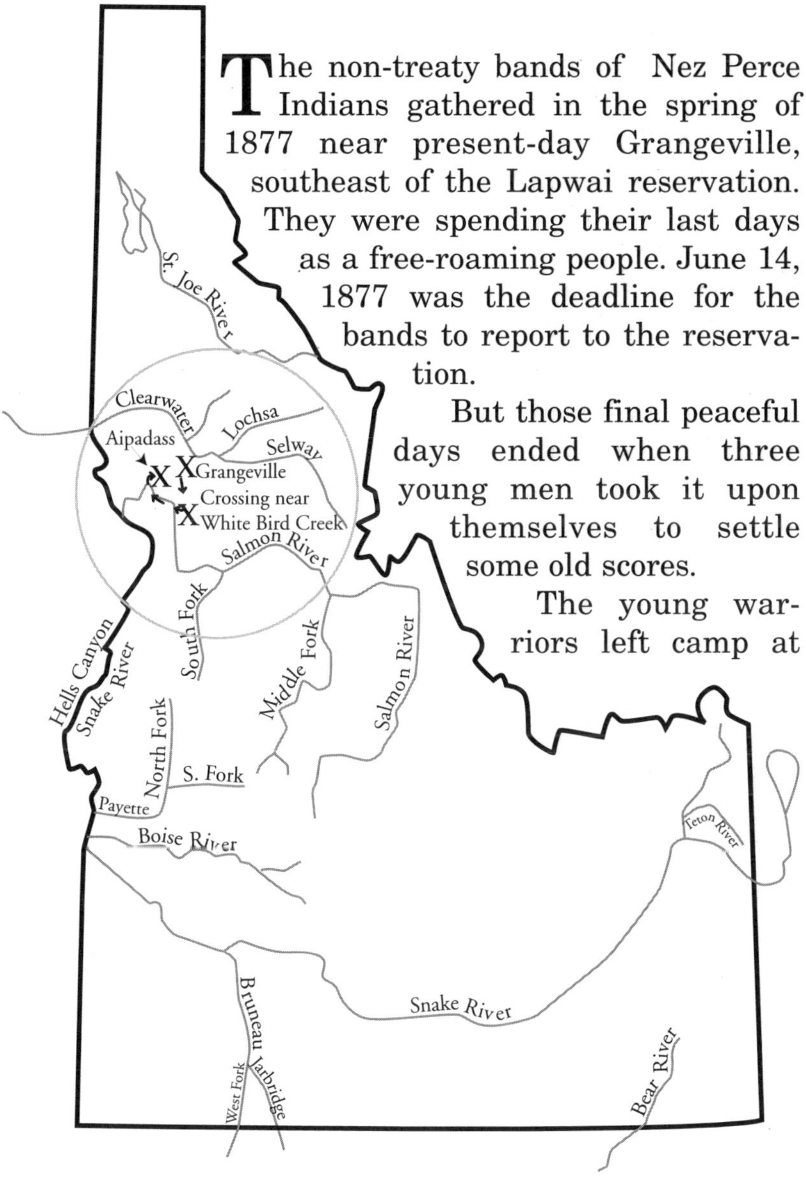

The non-treaty bands of Nez Perce Indians gathered in the spring of 1877 near present-day Grangeville, southeast of the Lapwai reservation. They were spending their last days as a free-roaming people. June 14, 1877 was the deadline for the bands to report to the reservation.

But those final peaceful days ended when three young men took it upon themselves to settle some old scores.

The young warriors left camp at

Tolo Lake and rode to the Slate Creek area on the Salmon River, looking for Larry Ott, a white man who had killed the father of one member of the trio. They didn't find Ott, but Richard Devine was home. Devine had a habit of setting his vicious dogs on any Nez Perce who passed his ranch. He died with a bullet in the head.

The three braves next killed Henry Elfers near John Day Creek. Elfers had often been hostile toward the Indians. So had Henry Beckroge and Robert Bland who died next. Samuel Benedict, a whisky merchant who had once killed a Nez Perce, also was shot. Though wounded, Benedict managed to escape into some thick underbrush.

When the avenging braves returned to the Tolo Lake encampment with stories of their bloody deeds, the news brought mixed reactions. Some men shouted war cries. Others chastised the rebels for disgracing their people. But they all realized war was inevitable.

Between June 14 and the arrival of General Howard on June 21, there were several skirmishes between the Nez Perce, settlers and troops. The Battle of White Bird Canyon claimed the lives of thirty-three soldiers.

The Nez Perce desperately needed time to reorganize before reinforcements reached General Howard. A council was held and a plan devised. Two warriors, Five Wounds and Rainbow, came up with a way to delay Howard.

The Snake and Salmon rivers were still at flood stage. The unusually-heavy snowpack from the previous winter continued to release large amounts of icy water downstream. The Indians decided they could gain time if they could force Howard to cross one of the rivers.

The Nez Perce column forded the Salmon River near the mouth of White Bird Creek. The river was swift and deep but could be crossed by the experienced natives. They made camp on the west bank and waited.

On the afternoon of June 28, Howard's troops approached the bank across the Salmon from the Nez Perce camp. Warriors rushed down from the ridges and taunted the troops. When the soldiers opened fire, the Indians scrambled back to the trees along the canyon rim.

An abandon cabin in a ravine was set on fire to draw the soldiers' attention. A sergeant and several volunteers managed to swim their horses across the river. Tethering their mounts along the bank, they crawled up the ravine to the smoldering cabin. The Nez Perce had disappeared. The men returned to General Howard with the news.

The general surmised that the Nez Perce had fled across the plateau, heading for the Snake River, where they would ford and return to their homeland at Wallowa. He knew speed was important. If he hurried, he might be able to cut off the Indians before they reached the Snake.

Howard had to figure out how to get 227 soldiers, 175 packers and guides, twenty volunteers, livestock, light artillery and all the rations and equipment necessary to maintain such a force across the Salmon.

The general summoned his engineer, Lieutenant H. G. Otis, of the Fourth Artillery. Otis surveyed the situation. Using a stick, he scribbled in the sand. He concluded that the Salmon River current was moving at about seven miles per hour. He calculated that a rope made from cavalry lariats tied together would be strong enough to hold a raft, up to 40 feet long, against the current.

A team of soldiers built a log raft and loaded it with equipment. Then several volunteers tried to paddle the craft across the Salmon — about 250 feet wide at that point. As a precaution, a rope was tied to the raft and to a large pine tree on the shore. As soon as the raft was launched, the current caught it and swept it downstream. When it reach the end of the safety tether, the rope snapped like a piece of string. The craft, with cargo and men, disappeared around a bend in the river.

When the exhausted rafters returned unharmed that evening, they had hair-raising tales to tell. They had survived nearly four miles of whitewater, as the raft hit submerged boulders; launched itself over huge breakers and dove like a gull through waves. The runaway craft swirled about in a mad frenzy before bucking free of an eddy. It seemed like an eternity to the men aboard before they found a place to abandon the fickle vessel.

Howard reported that "The river here is a perfect torrent, lost us our raft, which tumbled down the rapids at a swift rate with all on board, for three or four miles."

The general noted the amusement of one of the Indian scouts who watched the calamity. So he challenged the man to come up with a more workable solution. The scout ordered construction of a smaller raft. Then he demonstrated how four riders — one on each corner of the craft — could ferry it across to the opposite bank. But attempts were only partially successful. After several capsizings and the loss of some equipment, another method were sought.

Finally, a horseman swam the river towing a cable. The ends of the cable were tied to trees on opposite banks. A canoe was rigged so it could be guided along the cable like a crude ferry. The process was slow, but eventually the men and equipment were moved across the river.

After the troops were across, the livestock was forced into the river. Lieutenant H. L. Baily noted in his diary that some of the animals were turned over by the current and some swept downstream, but all eventually made it safely to the other bank.

Howard's force was across the Salmon River by July 1. It wasn't until July 5 that he discovered how badly he had been tricked.

After crossing the Salmon, Joseph led his band across twenty-five miles of rough country. But the Nez Perce weren't heading for the Snake River. Instead, they doubled back, re-crossed the Salmon at Craig's Ford, then headed for the Camas Prairie.

When Howard reached the second Nez Perce ford he decided crossing the Salmon there would be too dangerous. He took his force back upstream to cross near White Bird Creek, further delaying pursuit of the Indians. As the general and his men stumbled back to their starting point, Howard may have wished he had gone along with Joseph's request at the June 14 meeting — "Let us wait until fall, then the river will be low."

The Salmon River ruse gave the Nez Perce a solid head start on their pursuers. During the next four months Joseph's band traveled 1,500 miles and fought eighteen engagements involving 2,000 soldiers. It wasn't until Oct. 5, that the exhausted survivors surrendered in Montana, only a few miles short of the Canadian border.

TWENTY-THREE

Snake River — 1878

Bannock Attacks on the Snake

Early each summer, hundreds of Bannock Indians gathered on Big Camas Prairie in south central Idaho. The Indians stayed on the prairie several weeks, digging camas bulbs which they roasted in pits. Then they ground up the bulbs into meal to be used during the rest of the year.

Because camas bulbs were one of the main sources of food for the Bannock, they had a very possessive attitude toward Big Camas Prairie.

In 1868, the Bannock were assigned to the Fort

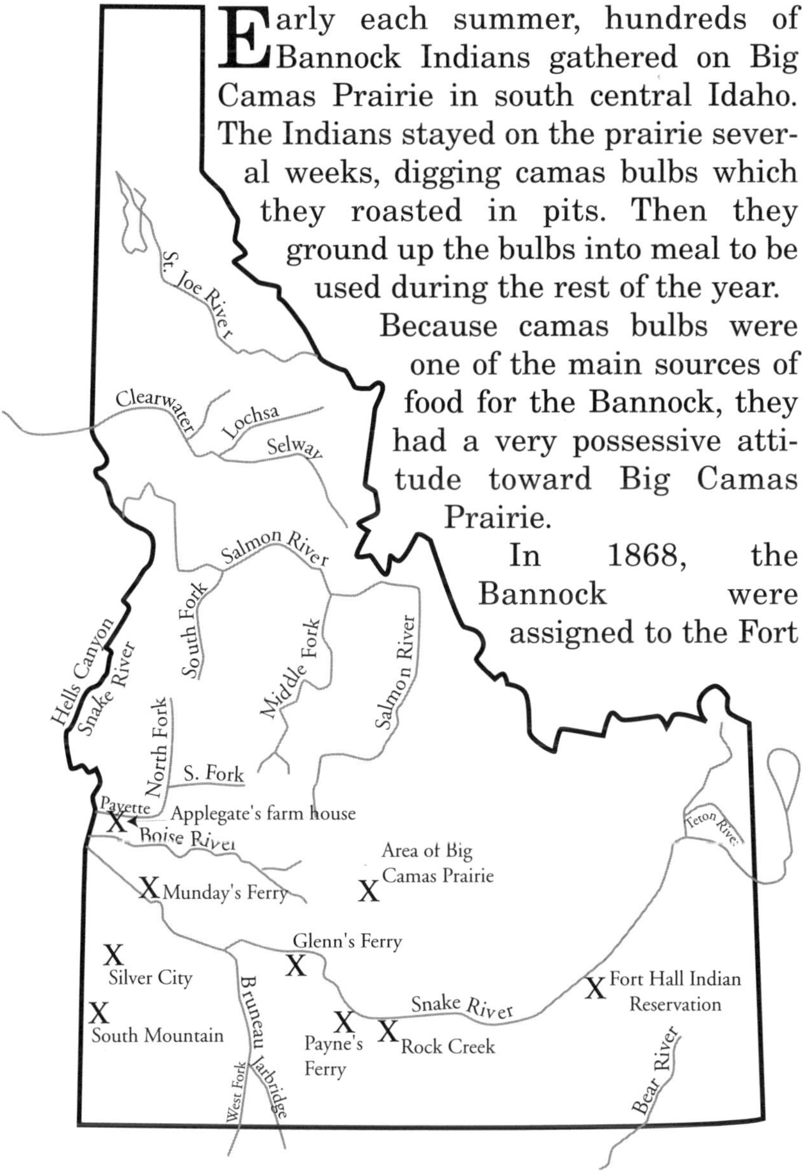

Hall Indian Reservation. Under the Treaty of 1868, the Big Camas Prairie was supposed to belong to the Fort Hall Indians. However, in transcribing the treaty, ratified by the Senate Feb. 16, a clerk in the Interior Department replaced the word Camas with "Kansas." Government officials used the error as an excuse to void Indian claims to the Big Camas Prairie and open it up for white settlement.

Settlers thought the camas bulbs were excellent hog feed. Pigs were turned loose on the prairie to root up the bulbs.

Meanwhile, the Bannock and Shoshoni Indians on the Fort Hall Reservation weren't getting enough to eat. Individual passes to leave the reservation to hunt were issued by the Indian agent at his discretion. But with so many settlers moving into the area, game was hard to find. Hunters often returned empty-handed.

General George Crook reported the situation on the reservation was getting desperate.

> "It cannot be expected that they (the Indians) will stay on the reservation where there is no possible way to get food," Crook wrote, "and see their wives and children starve and die around them … Our Indian policy has resolved itself into a question of warpath or starvation; and, being merely human, many of them will choose the former alternative where death shall at least be glorious."

When war became the only option for one group of Bannock, they chose Buffalo Horn as their war chief. The warrior was a scout for General Howard during the Nez Perce War the previous year. Buffalo Horn helped Chief Joseph's pursuers at the Canyon Creek battle in Montana. He also served with Generals Miles and Custer in their Montana wars. His military experience made him a formidable leader.

The Bannock War began in May 1878, when a small party of Indians killed a settler at Big Camas Prairie. When word reached the military, Colonel Bernard and his cavalry were dispatched to the scene.

Knowing the power of the troops, the majority of the Fort Hall Indians stayed on the reservation. Buffalo Horn and about 175 warriors choose war. Accompanied by their wives and children, the band moved west along the Snake River.

News of the uprising quickly spread among the settlers. Families gathered at Payne's Ferry. The group included forty armed men. The ferry house was fortified and windows filled with bricks and mortar, leaving just enough space for rifle barrels. A trench was dug around the building and bales of straw were stacked as breastworks. Guards were posted on nearby hilltops and around the building that sheltered the women and children.

The Bannock were spotted moving slowly along the opposite bank of the river. The settlers prepared for the worst. But the Indians continued on, the warriors riding ahead of the column of women and children.

Buffalo Horn led the band to Glenn's Ferry, thirty miles beyond Payne's. The ferryman and his wife saw the renegades coming and fled to the nearby hills. A bullwhacker camped upriver wasn't as fortunate. He was shot and killed by the warriors. His two freight wagons were ransacked, then burned. The ferry was cut loose and the ferry house burned. The smoke from the blaze could be seen upriver at Payne's Ferry. The people in the temporary fort feared the worst. Frightened that the raiders might double back, they piled into wagons and retreated to Rock Creek to join a group of ranchers and farmers fortified there.

Buffalo Horn had no plans to double back. He and his followers pressed on toward Oregon, hoping to form an alliance with the Paiute, Umatilla and Yakima tribes.

Meanwhile, a group of thirty-five volunteers formed in Silver City, headed by J. B. Harper. They rode down the east slope of South Mountain and came face-to-face with the startled Bannocks. A battle ensued. Greatly outnumbered, the volunteers pulled back, losing four men and one scout.

But the Bannock paid a price for their victory. When the skirmish ended, Buffalo Horn was dead.

The confused warriors pushed into Oregon only to be met days later by General Howard. After a series of brief battles, the Bannocks split into small groups. Some headed for the Salmon River region, some worked their way toward Montana and others tried to slip back to the reservation.

One small band came to the Snake River below the mouth of the Payette River. They tore down the unoccupied house of James Applegate, made rafts from the building materials, floated across the river and disappeared into the mountains.

Another group of braves weren't finished with the bloodshed. On July 31, at 10 A.M., the stage from

Boise to Silver City crossed the Snake River at Munday's Ferry. The driver, William Hemmingway, was carrying mail but no passengers. He talked briefly to the ferry owner, Perry Munday, and his hostler, J. W. Brown. Five bored cavalrymen assigned to guard the ferry, lounged in the background.

After Hemmingway harnessed a fresh team, he crossed on the ferry and proceeded along the river bottom road. About two miles from the ferry he spotted a group of thirty or forty Indians, some dressed in civilian clothing.

Hemmingway stopped the stage, thinking the approaching Indians were a friendly Shoshoni hunting party. But the warriors raised their weapons and charged. The driver turned his team and raced toward Munday's Ferry with the Indians close behind. A bullet stuck Hemmingway in the back.

The shots were heard at the ferry. The soldiers got the ferry to the south shore just in time for Hemmingway to board with the stage. As the ferry crossed the river, the soldiers traded shots with Bannocks lined up along the shore. Using the stage for cover, the troopers escaped injury.

When the stage and ferry were out of range, the Bannocks wheeled their horses toward Rabbit Creek and galloped away.

William Hemmingway died of his wounds four hours later.

The drainage area of the Salmon River, which lies entirely within Idaho's borders, is about 13,550 square miles.

TWENTY-FOUR

Salmon River — 1886

The First Boat Down "The River of No Return"

President Thomas Jefferson approved the nation's first overland expedition to the Pacific Ocean. In 1804 Lewis and Clark set out to write history. The explorers were forced to turn back only once during an adventure that spanned more than two years — when they faced the steep walls and white waters of the Salmon River Canyon.

The Salmon remained unconquered by white men until October

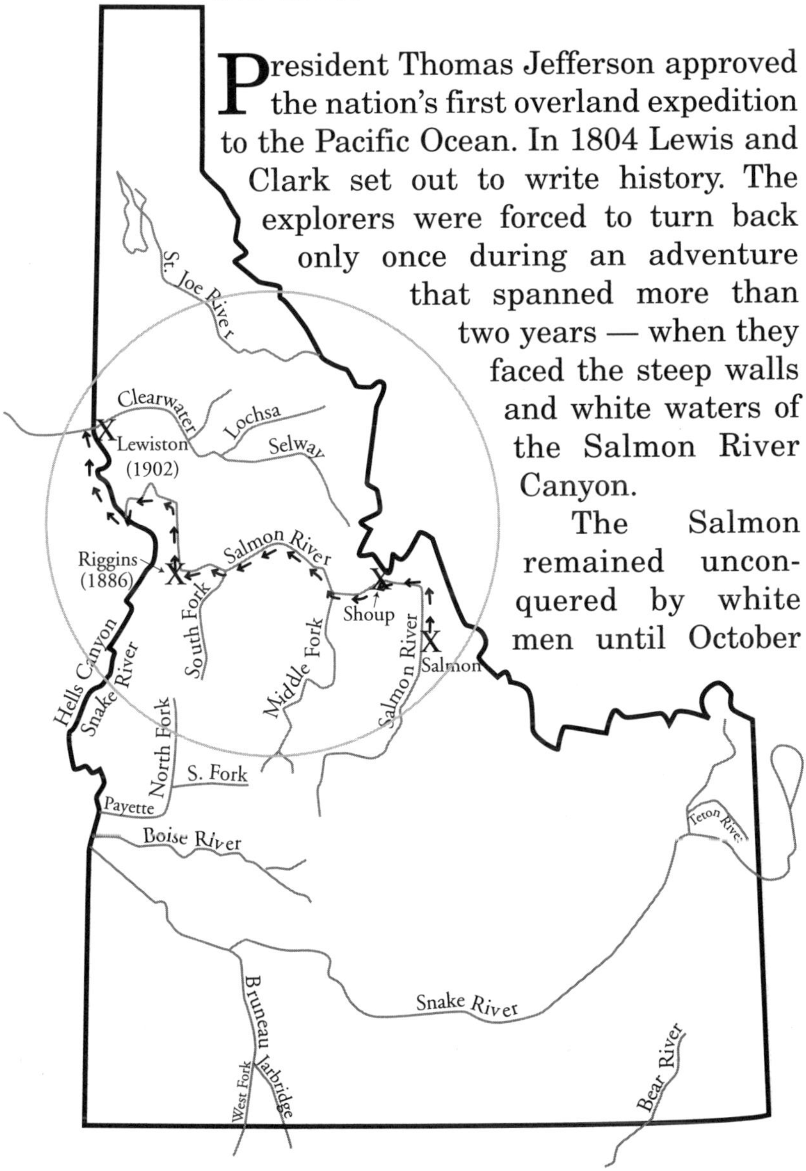

1886, when Captain Harry Guleke piloted a flat-bottomed scow through its treacherous rapids from Salmon to Riggins.

Harry Guleke was born in New York in 1862. He came to Idaho as a government trapper. Fascinated by Idaho's rivers, he gave up his job to become a bailer and swamper for a company hauling machinery and supplies downriver from Salmon to the mining town of Shoup. When Guleke's boss quit floating to work in the Shoup mines, Harry became captain of his own river fleet.

The boat Guleke and his first mate, Dave Sandiland, built for their first trip down the Salmon was thirty-two feet long, with twenty-eight-foot sweeps and six-foot blades. It was said to resemble "an antediluvian ark sired by some prehistoric mail order packing case."

The elevated platform in the center of the craft gave the boatmen a sturdy foothold and a clearer view for navigating. The bottom of the scow was double lined with green lumber to give it the buoyancy, lifting capacity and durability needed to withstand the shock of hitting submerged rocks — a frequent occurrence on the river given the time of year. Because the river was fed by snow melt and side streams, the high water rapids, relished by modern-day rafters in June, become treacherous obstacle courses by autumn. Rapids such as Devil's Teeth boldly stand in full view. But their snaggle-toothed offspring lie waiting just below the water's surface.

A raised floor was built to keep seepage water from soaking equipment and double walls were added on each side for storage. When fully loaded, Guleke's boat weighed more than four tons.

The men were ready for adventure as they embarked on their mission to conquer the Salmon. They probably paused near the mouth of Panther Creek to inspect the Sheepeater Indian paintings on a granite outcropping. Because low light made it difficult to see hidden rocks in the river, they made camp among the piles of mussel shells left at the old Indian campsite.

The scow lunged through the section now called Long Tom Rapids, just above the mouth of the Middle Fork. With tightened jaws they swept through the white-flecked crest, maneuvering around the exposed boulders.

A few miles beyond the Middle Fork, they found themselves between walls of solid rock rising straight into the vividly blue October sky. Far above, mountain goats maintained silent vigil, their light coats creating a contrast with the dark rock.

Present day Gunbarrel Rapid posed no trouble for the two boatmen, but seeing it would be necessary to be on the right-hand side of the river during high water, Guleke recorded the information in a journal. He logged the various unnamed rapids they challenged. There is no record of any serious mishaps during the celebrated journey. The explorers did have to endure some foul weather. Several times their craft became stuck on rocks and the men had to push and pull it free. At least twice, the boat had to be completely unloaded before it would budge. The gear then had to be carried over slippery boulders and along rattlesnake infested game trails to a reloading point below the rapids.

The boat, which had been built in four days, was disassembled at the end of the journey and the timber used for other purposes. One-way traffic had become a reality on the River of No Return. But boats often were smashed on hidden rocks and some lives were lost.

Sixteen years after his first trip down the Salmon, Guleke made history again. The *Lewiston Tribune* reported on Dec. 20, 1903 that "An odd-shaped scow landed at the wharf yesterday with three men — Captain Harry Guleke, R. E. Dwyer, and J. V. Dwyer. They made the trip from Salmon City to Lewiston via the wild Salmon — a voyage heretofore just dreamed of."

After his successful runs from Salmon to Riggins, Harry Guleke established his own boat yard in Salmon. Each boat was twenty feet wide and forty feet long and was equipped with a cook stove, camp outfit and tent.

The Salmon River and Guleke were constant companions for the next forty years. He floated heavy equipment and supplies to the mines and homesteads along the river. Throughout his years of challenging the River of No Return, Guleke never lost a passenger, although he did lose a few boats.

Harry died in Salmon in March 1944 at age eighty-two.

TWENTY-FIVE

Snake River — 1887

Massacre at Deep Creek

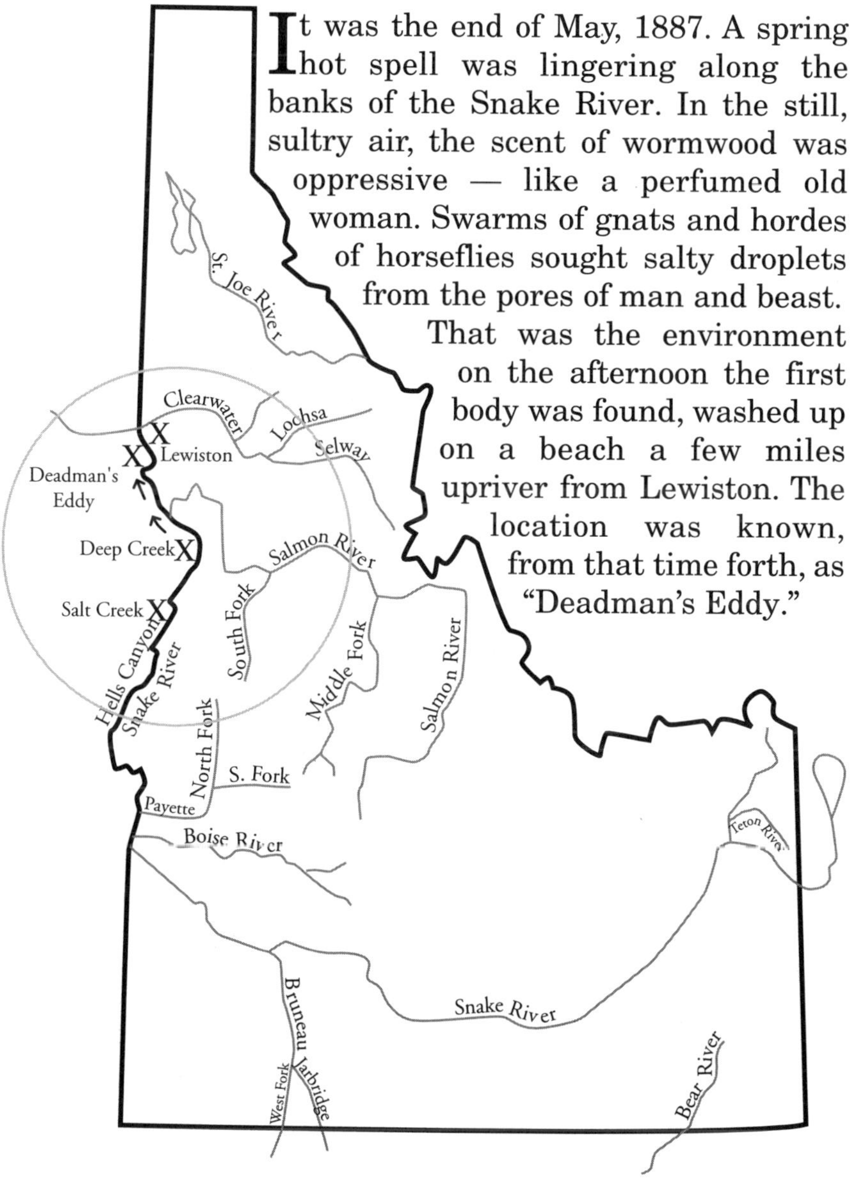

It was the end of May, 1887. A spring hot spell was lingering along the banks of the Snake River. In the still, sultry air, the scent of wormwood was oppressive — like a perfumed old woman. Swarms of gnats and hordes of horseflies sought salty droplets from the pores of man and beast. That was the environment on the afternoon the first body was found, washed up on a beach a few miles upriver from Lewiston. The location was known, from that time forth, as "Deadman's Eddy."

The corpse of a Chinese man, with a bullet hole in his head, caused little concern. Most residents of the area had little empathy for the Chinese. Many businesses in Lewiston displayed signs stating, "No Chinese employed here." The resentment toward the Chinese in the Western states during that period was so great that in 1882 Congress passed the Chinese Exclusion Act, halting immigration from that country.

Several groups of Chinese passed through Lewiston in 1886-1887, pulling supply boats upriver to remote riverside skim bars — small areas of rock and sand along the leading edge of alluvial deposits. On the skim bars, the gold content averaged less than .0015 ounces per cubic yard of earth. The tiny cup-shaped flakes of gold seldom weighed more than one ten-millionth of a ounce each, often escaping over the edge of a gold pan rather than settling to the bottom. Few white miners were willing to work the skim bars where they had less than "a Chinaman's chance" of making a profit. But the patient Chinese were willing to take the gamble.

The residents of Lewiston began to look at the situation differently when a boatman moving mining supplies upstream fished the bullet-riddled body of a second Chinese man out of the river, the same day the first corpse was found. That evening two more bodies floated past the town.

The next day, more Chinese bodies beached at Dead Man's Eddy and others were spotted in the river. The carnage was so great that even the most prejudiced whites decided it was time to find out who committed such a macabre act and why?

Authorities organized an expedition to go up the Snake and investigate the murders. The hot weather became more oppressive as the party moved deeper into Hell's Canyon.

Near the junction of the Snake and Imnaha rivers, the investigators met a group of highly agitated Chinese who told a grisly story.

During October 1886, more than fifty Chinese pulled a supply boat upriver. Part of the group set up camp at Deep Creek, on the Oregon side of the Snake. The remainder went on to Salt Creek, also on the Oregon side.

After spending the winter working a skim bar, the Salt Creek miners decided to visit their countrymen at Deep Creek. When they arrived they found the mutilated and decomposing bodies of two of their friends, each with a bullet in the head. The camp had been burned and looted. There were bloody patches of ground and drag marks leading to the river. There was no sign of the other twenty-nine members of the Deep Creek party.

Leaving the Chinese to continue on to Lewiston to make their report, the investigators pushed on the remaining six miles to Deep Creek. They found the two bodies in camp and a third snagged on a rock near the opposite bank. It appeared the man found in the river had attempted to escape by swimming but was shot as he neared the far shore. There were tidy little mounds of empty cartridges marking the spots where the murderers stood while firing at the fleeing miners.

The *Mountain Sentinel*, a LaGrande, Oregon. newspaper, called the Deep Creek murders the "crime of the century."

Learning of the crime from newspaper reports, the Chinese Consul General in San Francisco requested that the Sam Yup Company, one of six California companies controlling indentured Chinese emigrants, conduct an investigation. The company sent a representative, Lee Loi, to Lewiston. Lee Loi hired U.S. Commissioner J. K. Vincent to investigate the murders of the thirty-one Deep Creek miners and offered a $1,000 reward for the arrest of the murderers.

Nine months later, Commissioner Vincent was certain he had identified some of the guilty individuals. But it wasn't until a year after the murders that he was finally able to persuade two men, Hezikiah Huges and Frank Vaughn, to turn state's evidence. As a result of Vaughn's testimony before a Grand Jury, an indictment was issued against Hiram Maynard, Carl Huges, Robert McMilliam, J. T. Canfield, Bruce Evans and C. O. LaRue. McMillian, Carl Huges and Maynard were caught and jailed, but the other three were never caught.

A trial was held Aug. 29, 1887 in the Wallowa County Circuit Court in Oregon. Hezikiah Huges and Frank Vaughn described the murders. They said the eight men had heard rumors that the Deep Creek miners had amassed a lot of gold during the winter. The rumor was that there were seventeen flasks of gold dust — each worth more than $700 — hidden in the camp.

Huges and Vaughn said the robbers arrived at the Chinese camp in early afternoon. The miners were in the dugouts to escape the heat and didn't see the strangers coming down the trail. The murderers opened fire at close range, gunning down all but two of the Chinese. The survivors were questioned and tortured. But since the terrified men neither spoke or understood English, they were of no help to the outlaws and were put to death. The camp was ransacked but no gold was found.

The prosecution witnesses said the bodies of most of the miners were stacked in a boat. A hole was punched in the side of the craft before it was set adrift. The boat sank in a nearby rapid. But within days the bodies began to surface and float downstream.

McMillian, Carl Huges and Hiram Maynard pleaded not guilty. Despite the testimony of Hezikiah Huges and Frank Vaughn, the three defendants were found not guilty on September 1, 1888. No one was ever convicted or punished for the Deep Creek massacre.

Fifteen years later, in 1902, when a new gold boom brought renewed interest in mining in Hells Canyon, two young men found an oriental flask partially filled with gold dust while panning at Deep Creek.

In 1810, several Hawaiian members of a fur trapping party, disappeared in the rugged high desert in what is now southwest Idaho. The area was named for the lost explorers. But the word Hawaii was corrupted to Owyhee. A river and a mountain range now bear that name.

TWENTY-SIX

St. Joe River — 1888

Ladies Day on the St. Joe.

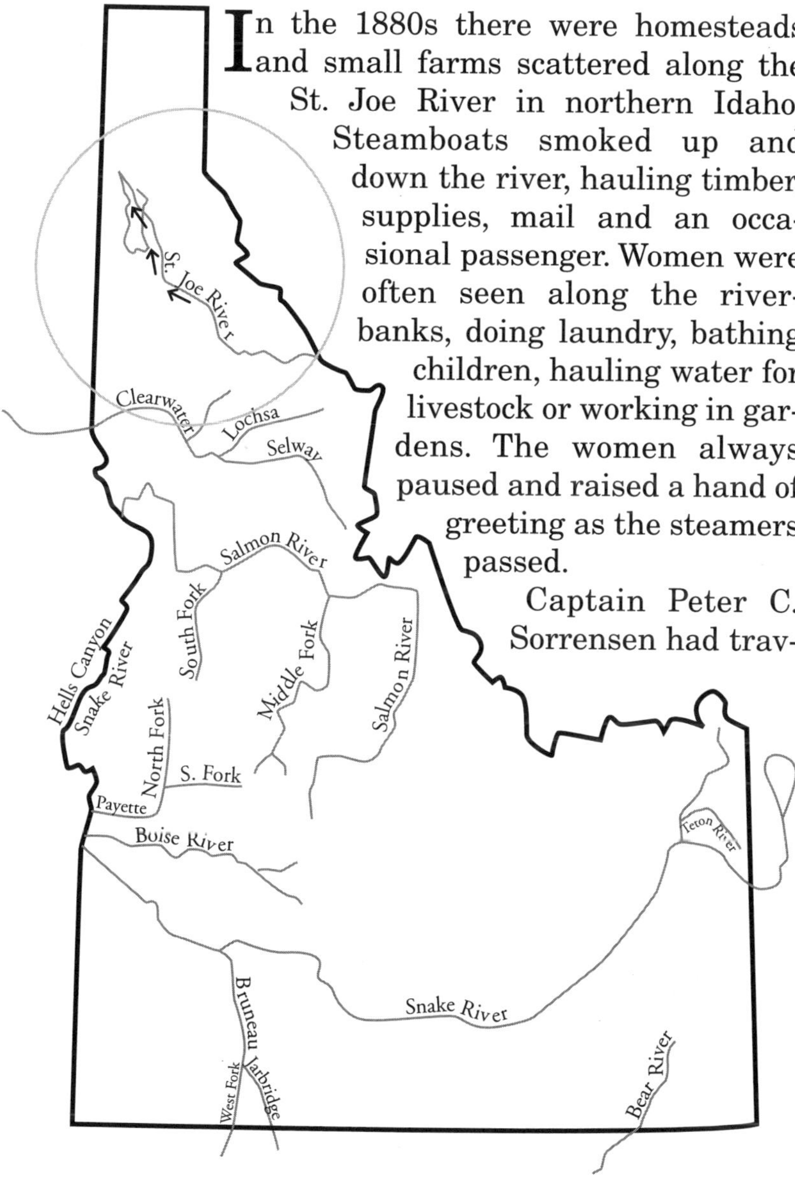

In the 1880s there were homesteads and small farms scattered along the St. Joe River in northern Idaho. Steamboats smoked up and down the river, hauling timber, supplies, mail and an occasional passenger. Women were often seen along the riverbanks, doing laundry, bathing children, hauling water for livestock or working in gardens. The women always paused and raised a hand of greeting as the steamers passed.

Captain Peter C. Sorrensen had traveled the St. Joe many times since his arrival in Idaho about 1879. During the spring of 1887, he was hired by Colonel Henry Clay Merrian of Fort Coeur d'Alene to supervise the construction of the *Amelia Wheaton*, the first steamboat on Lake Coeur d'Alene.

Captain Sorrensen was a native of Kragero, Norway. Kragero is a small fishing town on the shores of the Skagerrak, the channel separating Denmark and Norway. Although Sorrensen was an apprentice stonecutter, he also learned a lot about shipbuilding. Many of his friends were shipbuilders. Over suppers of lutefish and boiled potatoes, washed down with aquavit, he absorbed his friends' shipyard shoptalk.

The successful construction of the *Amelia Wheaton* proved Captain Sorrensen's competency as a supervisor. He received contracts to build the lake steamers *Spokane* and *Colfax*. But his favorite project was the steamer *Lottie*, which he designed and built himself. The *Lottie* was a petite, trim craft, well suited to the St. Joe.

Perhaps the women toiling along the riverbank brought back memories of Sorrensen's homeland. The ladies along the St. Joe did much of the farm work and day-to-day chores while their husbands labored in the logging camps — much as men in Norway were bound to the sea for their income.

The cheerful waves from the women as the Lottie passed lightened Captain Sorrensen's heart. He wondered how many of the women had ever had a steamboat ride?

One day in 1888, Sorrensen had an idea. He decided to sponsor a Ladies Day on the Lottie, featuring a free steamer ride on the St. Joe. A week before the

Jim Paxton

scheduled event he steamed upriver, blowing his whistle at each landing. When the women came to the river's edge to see what the hullabaloo was about, the captain passed out flyers detailing the upcoming excursion.

In the week after the announcement, dusty trunks were opened and the stored finery was mended or updated and laundered. Hat boxes were retrieved from storage under beds and in attics. High-button shoes were polished and petticoats bleached, starched and pressed. Perfumes, powder, rouge and lipstick materialized from corners of dressers and chests. Ribbons, lace, hair pins and hat pins were pressed into service. Each woman was determined to wear her finest and look her very best.

Ladies Day arrived. It was a day to sashay across the deck of the Lottie as guest of Captain Sorrensen. It was a day to forget about hoeing weeds, squatting with a scrub board, chopping wood or cleaning the hen house.

When Sorrensen steamed down the St. Joe, women were waiting at the farmside docks wearing their best attire, groomed to perfection, carrying picnic baskets brimming with gastronomical delights.

It was a gorgeous summer day. Women lined the decks of the Lottie and watched the shoreline, a landscape in motion. Men tipped their hats to the ladies while excited children ran along the banks. The passengers relished the experience, savoring each moment as one would savor each sip of a fine wine.

The sun filtered through the canopy of cottonwoods as the fractured light danced in the steamboat's wake. Many work-worn, but manicured, hands caressed the smooth, polished railing of the Lottie. Ladies Day on the St. Joe would be remembered and talked about in hushed voices at private times for years.

The Snake River drainage area totals 109,000 square miles.

TWENTY-SEVEN

Snake River — 1888

The Montgomery Ferry

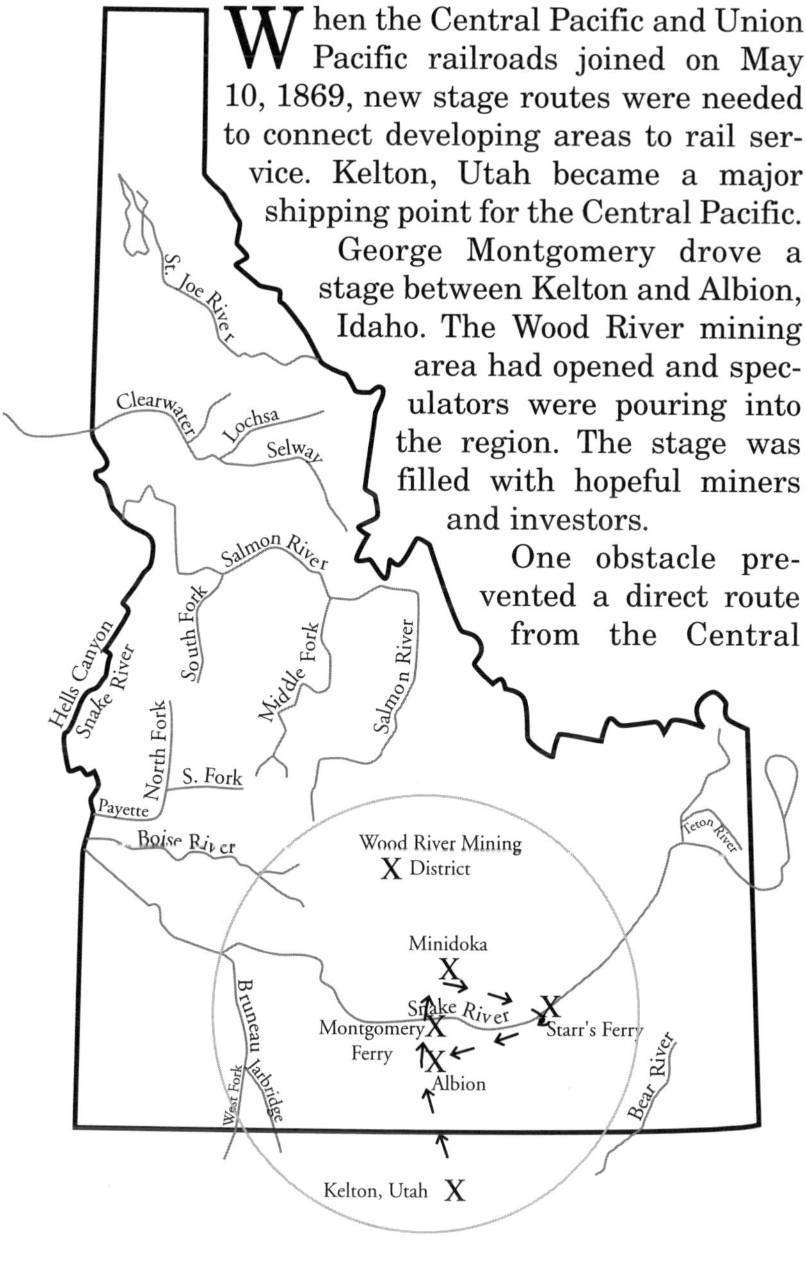

When the Central Pacific and Union Pacific railroads joined on May 10, 1869, new stage routes were needed to connect developing areas to rail service. Kelton, Utah became a major shipping point for the Central Pacific. George Montgomery drove a stage between Kelton and Albion, Idaho. The Wood River mining area had opened and speculators were pouring into the region. The stage was filled with hopeful miners and investors.

One obstacle prevented a direct route from the Central

Pacific tracks at Kelton to the Union Pacific line at Minidoka, Idaho that led to the Wood River district. The Snake River was a natural barrier. The stage had to detour nearly 100 miles to cross the river at Starr's Ferry. The problem plagued shippers and travelers for eight years.

In 1884, George Montgomery moved his family from Corrine, Utah to Albion where he started a furniture business and boarding house. Frustrated by the roundabout route necessary to freight his goods to Minidoka, George searched along the steep banks of the Snake for a location for a new ferry. He found it sixteen miles north of Albion, where he established the Montgomery Ferry.

A hired man operated the ferry while George's wife, Alice, managed their businesses in Albion. George operated the new stage route created by the ferry.

During the winter months when the river froze, George spread straw on the ice and strapped cleats to the hooves of the stage team. The stage crossed the river on the ice and rarely was late reaching its destination.

In 1895, a house and office were built at the Montgomery Ferry. It became the summer home of George, Alice and their children. They wintered in Albion.

By 1902, the Montgomerys had sold their holdings in Albion and moved permanently to the tranquil oasis at the ferry.

Herds of migrating deer passed the Montgomery home in late autumn and early spring. Pronghorn antelope bounded through the bunch grass and sage, as eagles and hawks glided overhead.

Life on the unpredictable Snake was always a challenge. Gales whipped the river, blowing the ferry under the cable and creating the danger of capsizing. Whitecaps sometimes made the river too choppy to cross. Thick sleet and snow restricted visibility.

When the weather got bad, the ferry closed down, leaving long lines of wagons, freighters and stages waiting at the landings.

Alice Montgomery enjoyed the pauses caused by nature. They gave her a chance to socialize with travelers, sometimes sharing vegetables and flowers from her garden during the summer. Her warm hospitality and bright flower beds were a welcome change for travelers who had seen little but sagebrush and jackrabbits. In the winter, the hot coffee and spiced cider created lasting memories for wayfarers.

The construction of the Minidoka Dam so slowed the Snake that the cable ferry wouldn't work properly. In 1915, George fitted the boat with a three-horsepower motor to propel the ferry through the slack water.

In 1919, a bridge was built across the Snake, making the ferry obsolete. The Montgomery home was destroyed by fire the same year.

George and Alice only outlived their ferry by three years. Alice died in January 1922. George died on Christmas Day the same year.

The Lochsa River parallels Idaho State Highway 12. It follows the route of the Lolo Trail, used by the Lewis and Clark Expedition to cross the Rockies.

TWENTY-EIGHT

Lochsa River — 1893

The Abandonment of George Colgate

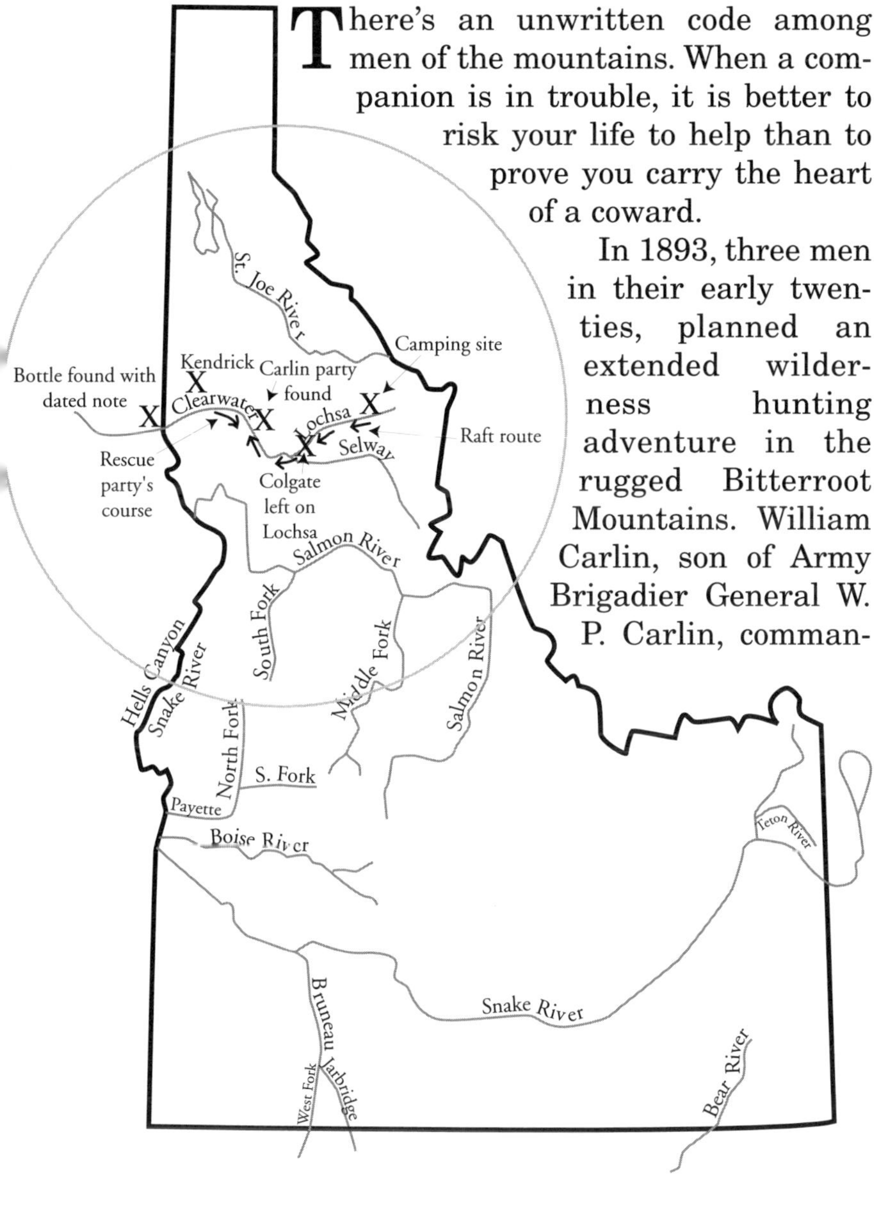

There's an unwritten code among men of the mountains. When a companion is in trouble, it is better to risk your life to help than to prove you carry the heart of a coward.

In 1893, three men in their early twenties, planned an extended wilderness hunting adventure in the rugged Bitterroot Mountains. William Carlin, son of Army Brigadier General W. P. Carlin, commander at Fort Sherman, Idaho, led the expedition. William's brother-in-law, John Pierce, and Abe Himmelwright, a friend from Connecticut, joined him. They hired a guide, Martin Spencer, and a camp cook, George Colgate. Colgate had accompanied Carlin on a previous hunting trip and proved to be an accomplished woodsman and trapper, as well as cook.

Horses, tents, camping equipment and provisions for three months were purchased in Spokane, Wash., then shipped by train to Kendrick, Idaho. The party assembled there, in high spirits. On September 18, 1893, the five men headed for the Bitterroots. After traveling for nearly a week through magnificent foothills, they climbed through rugged wilderness to reach a campsite about thirty miles from the crest of the mountain range.

The members of the Carlin party were surprised to find two men already at the campsite. Jerry Johnson and Ben Keeley had built a small cabin. Keeley planned to spend the winter trapping in the area. The newcomers set up an elaborate camp nearby, at the present-day Jerry Johnson Hot Springs.

The area was covered with dense growths of lodgepole pine, cedar, spruce and fir trees. There were small meadows nearby where the livestock grazed. Hot springs flowed from fissures along the banks of a brook now known as Warm Springs Creek. The men built bathing pools out of rocks and mud along the edge of the creek.

About a mile from the camp, the creek joined a river. The Nez Perce Indians called the stream Lochsa — "rough waters."

During their first month in camp, the hunters killed several bear, deer and elk. George Colgate prepared many wild game feasts, using only the choice meat. The five men spent their evenings feasting, smoking imported cigars and drinking whiskey. They played poker and whist while verbally reliving the details of their hunts. The autumn mornings wore thick cloaks of frost and the soft fall colors of midday were cast against stark blue skies. Time seemed to stand still for everyone except the guide and the cook.

Martin Spencer sensed an early winter. The squirrels had finished a frantic pine cone harvest. The cones were clustered four and five to a branch, rather than in twos and trees — indicating a long, cold winter. George Colgate felt the coming winter in his limbs. Being a married man with seven children, Colgate also felt it in his heart. It was time to return to his family and the comforts of home.

William Carlin and his companions were not about to abandon their Shangri la so readily. They decided to stay an additional week.

But the weather wasn't the only problem the campers faced. George Colgate was ill. Uremic poisoning caused his legs to swell to double normal size.

The reluctant hunters began breaking camp on October 10. Dark clouds rolled over the mountains. As the men hastened their preparations to leave, the wind began to blow from the north, bringing with it a blinding blizzard. Soon the ground was covered with thick, wet snow. Tree branches, weighted down by heavy capes of slush, bent and snapped. During the frenzy of the storm, the horses stampeded, leaving the men afoot.

A hasty retreat was needed. Leaving most of the camping equipment behind, the men headed for the Lolo Trail, carrying only the bare essentials for survival.

But it was too late. They couldn't find the trail, already covered by several feet of crusted snow. Struggling through knee-deep drifts, the hikers worked their way back to the Lochsa River, nearly two weeks after leaving camp.

During the trek, George Colgate's condition got worse. He could no longer walk. The river seemed to be their best hope of reaching civilization.

The group sought Ben Keeley's help, purchasing his food and assistance for $250. Keeley's previous logging experience in Minnesota and Wisconsin proved invaluable. Six large, dead cedars were cut down and rolled into the river. They were used to build two rafts fastened together with key-wedged crosspieces. The craft were steered with long sweeps. The vessels were christened *Clearwater* and *Carlin*.

A few miles downriver the *Carlin*, on which Colgate was riding, hit some boulders. Colgate was tossed into the river by the impact and washed beneath the craft. He was eventually rescued from the icy water.

Several times during the days that followed, the rafts had to beach so a fire could be built to warm numb hands and feet. The first few days were tolerable. But things got worse. When the rafts hung up on rocks, the men had to slip into the freezing water to push them clear. Most of the equipment was lost.

The group had traveled about thirty miles when it reached Holly Creek, above a stretch of river containing rapids known today as Omno's Hole and Castle Creek — the most difficult on the Lochsa.

It was November 10. More than a month had passed since leaving camp. The men pulled the rafts ashore for the night and scouted the rapids downstream the next morning. William Carlin recorded their findings in his diary.

> "Saturday, November 11th — It is cold and clear. We went down the river a long way this morning, and were horrified to find that we were absolutely stuck. Half a mile below camp is a ledge of rocks, and a rapid through which we cannot take a raft. Below this are two places still worse."

Nearly all the equipment and supplies had been stolen by the raging Lochsa. There was only enough food for a few days. They would have to continue their escape on foot, through waist-deep snow. On the bleak November day five men met and decided the fate of the sixth — George Colgate. Leaving Colgate asleep in his bedroll, his companions crept away.

The deep snow and rugged terrain made progress slow. They could only move one or two miles a day, staying close to the Lochsa to keep their bearings. They were plagued by frostbite and exhaustion and a new enemy — starvation.

Back in civilization, General Carlin became alarmed at his son's failure to return from his hunt. He dispatched a search party, that outfitted at Kendrick. At Lowell, deep snow forced the rescuers to leave their horses behind and continue up the Clearwater River in skiffs.

After two days of fighting their way up the river, the searchers spotted the walking skeletons of the Carlin party survivors. Ten days had passed since they abandoned George Colgate on the banks of the Lochsa.

The tired rescuers accepted the story that George Colgate was dead. No attempt was made to go upstream and check the site where the camp cook was left.

Central Idaho newspapers quickly got wind of the story. There was a storm of protest over the desertion of Colgate. William Carlin was so upset by the public criticism that he got the following statement from Colgate's doctor:

> "Mr. Colgate came to me from Post Falls last summer and I placed him in the Sacred Heart Hospital, where he remained about three weeks, and then returned to Idaho. Early last fall he again came to me to be examined and said, if he was well enough, he would start on a hunting trip as a cook. Mr. Colgate was troubled with an enlarged prostate and chronic inflammation of the bladder, and had been for 20 years compelled to use catheters to relieve the bladder. I told him he could make the trip, but to continue the use of the catheters; and from the history of this case and the symptoms described by the Carlin Party, I am satisfied Colgate's illness would have resulted fatally under any circumstances, and

when he was left behind in the condition described, he could not have survived twenty-four hours."

W. Q. Webb
Spokane, Wash., December 4th, 1893

Doctor Webb's statement took some of the steam out of the controversy and the story died. But almost immediately a Montana newspaper told a different story that fanned the flames again:

GEORGE COLGATE FOUND
He bitterly Denounces the Carlin Party for Deserting Him

MISSOULA, Mon., Dec. 15. — It was reported here to-day that George Colgate, who was the cook for the Carlin Party which narrowly escaped death in the hills, has been found. John Mack, a railroad brakeman on the Northern Pacific road, is responsible for the story.

Mack says that Colgate was found by two trappers wandering through the mountains in a heavy snowstorm and almost dead. They took him to a cabin they had erected, and later to Lewiston, where he is now being cared for.

Mack says that Colgate was bitter in his denunciations of the other members of the Carlin party, who, he said, left him to starve and freeze to death.

He says they deserted him because he was unable to walk any longer. After he had rested, he started to follow his party, got lost and wandered about the mountains for three weeks with scarcely anything to eat and no shelter. Then he was found by the two trappers.

The other members of the Carlin party are not inclined to believe the story, and insist that when they left Colgate he was barely alive and could live but a few hours.

Trapper Keely denounces the action of the Carlin party as most inhuman. He says that he wished to leave Colgate some food, but they would not permit it, saying that they had purchased the eatables and had not enough for themselves.

Trapper Keely is suing Gen. Carlin for the reward for finding the party."

George Colgate wasn't at the Lewiston hospital. Nor was there any record he ever was there.

In June 1894, William Carlin and Himmelwright again hired Martin Spencer to guide them into the Bitterroot Mountains. Their goal was to recover the remains of George Colgate and to salvage the camping gear left at the hot springs. The gear was recovered, but the only item found on the banks of the Lochsa was the missing man's bedroll.

During August, an Army expedition explored the St. Joseph and Clearwater river basins. A member of that group chanced upon the remains of George Colgate eight miles from where he was abandoned. Papers found on the corpse confirmed the identity. The body was buried where it was found.

The local press again picked up the story, citing that Colgate had managed to work his way four miles beyond the point where his companions were rescued. There was new public outrage.

Some believed high water in the spring washed George Colgate's body eight miles downstream. That theory gave an acceptable ending to the story — at least for the men who left Colgate to his fate. In December 1894, however, about a year after Colgate was abandoned, a small medicine bottle was found floating in a Snake River eddy near Lewiston. The bottle contained a scrap of paper with Colgate's signature, dated November 27, 1893 — sixteen days after he was left for dead.

French trappers who first explored the headwaters of the Snake River, named the stream "The Accursed Mad River."

TWENTY-NINE

Snake River — 1893

The *Annie Faxon*

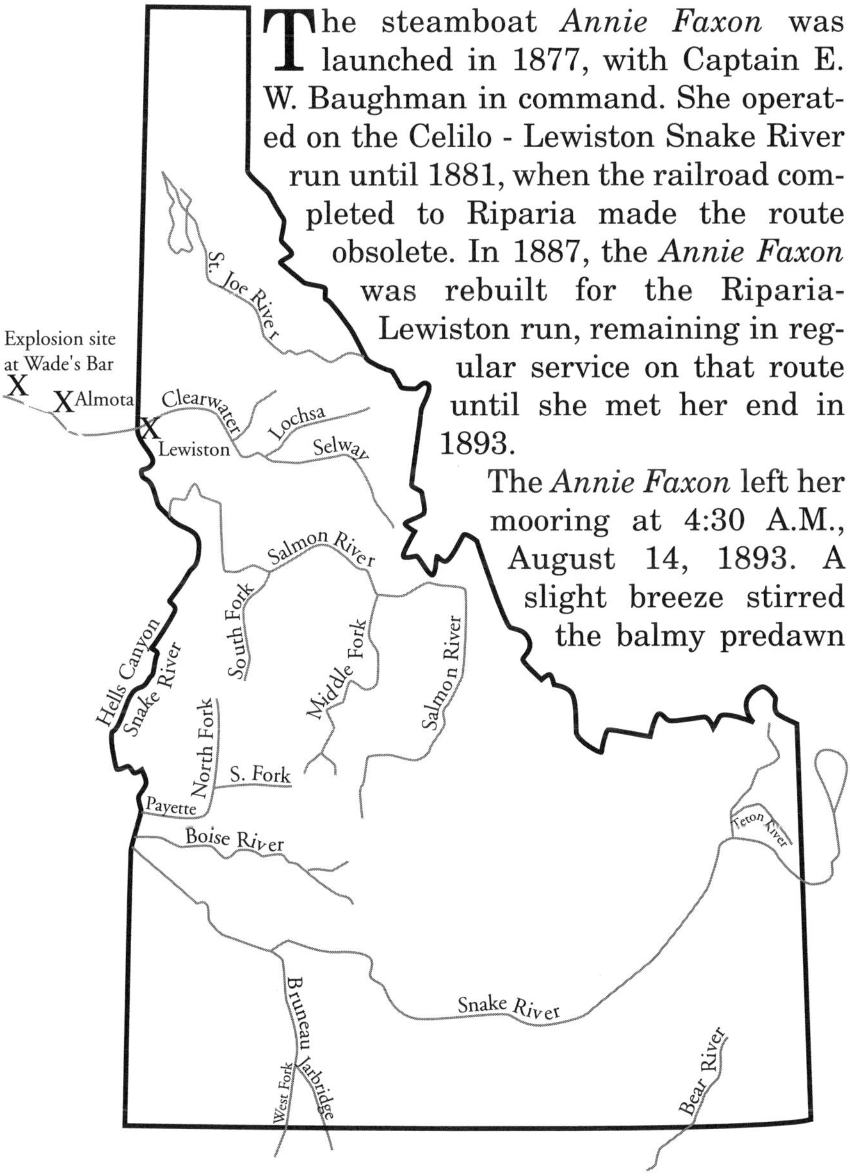

The steamboat *Annie Faxon* was launched in 1877, with Captain E. W. Baughman in command. She operated on the Celilo - Lewiston Snake River run until 1881, when the railroad completed to Riparia made the route obsolete. In 1887, the *Annie Faxon* was rebuilt for the Riparia-Lewiston run, remaining in regular service on that route until she met her end in 1893.

The *Annie Faxon* left her mooring at 4:30 A.M., August 14, 1893. A slight breeze stirred the balmy predawn air as crew members and passengers settled into their places. Captain Baughman was out of town. He left his son, Acting Mate Harry Baughman, in charge.

As the sun rose over the mountains to cast its glow upon the placid Snake, passengers left their seats to stand aft and watch the shimmering reflections dance through the wake of the steamer.

Homesteads and orchards lined the banks of the Snake as the *Annie Faxon* made her way downstream toward her scheduled stop at Riparia, a small fruit growing community in Washington state.

After three hours on the river, the steamboat was hailed from Wade's Bar, a fruit ranch forty miles from Lewiston. Boxes of late summer peaches, plums, early pears and apples lined the landing, waiting for transport.

The passengers crowded the deck of the steamer to watch her nose to shore. Just before the craft reached the bank, a giant explosion shook her. The blast toppled the smokestack into the dining room of the boat. The entire rear section of the *Annie Faxon* was destroyed. Debris from the explosion floated downriver, while larger pieces settled to the Snake's rocky bottom.

Mrs. Tappen, the purser's wife, was pinned in the sunken wreckage. Her body wasn't recovered until a week later. Five other crew members and two passengers died in the blast. Fourteen people were injured.

Two crew members were able to get a gangplank close enough to the bank to jump off and tie up the sinking steamboat before it drifted into deeper and swifter water. The dead and injured were carried off.

Jim Paxton

Acting Mate Baughman, though badly wounded, walked twelve miles through the searing heat to Almota to telegraph the news of the disaster to Lewiston.

A steamer bringing medical help reached the scene nine hours after the explosion. Most of the people who were hurt received burns and lacerations from the blast. The wounded were taken aboard the steamboat *Spokane* where they were treated by several doctors. The following morning, when it was light enough to travel, the *Spokane* transported the injured to Riparia. A train carried them to Sisters Hospital in Walla Walla, Washington.

Several weeks earlier, a marine inspector had found leaks in the *Annie Faxon's* boilers. Because the season was nearing its end, the inspector agreed to let the steamboat operate until she docked for the winter. The boilers were scheduled to be replaced before the spring season.

THIRTY

Clearwater River — 1894

The Flood of 1894

June 1894 was a balmy month. It was also the month the Clearwater River jumped its banks and a dike erected by the citizens of Lewiston. The renegade river sped into town as the warning bell sounded at half past two on what should have been a quiet Sunday afternoon.

Main Street merchants, who underestimated the height of the overflow, dashed about grabbing items of highest value. The rest of the inventory was left to sink or bob about, adding to the general confusion.

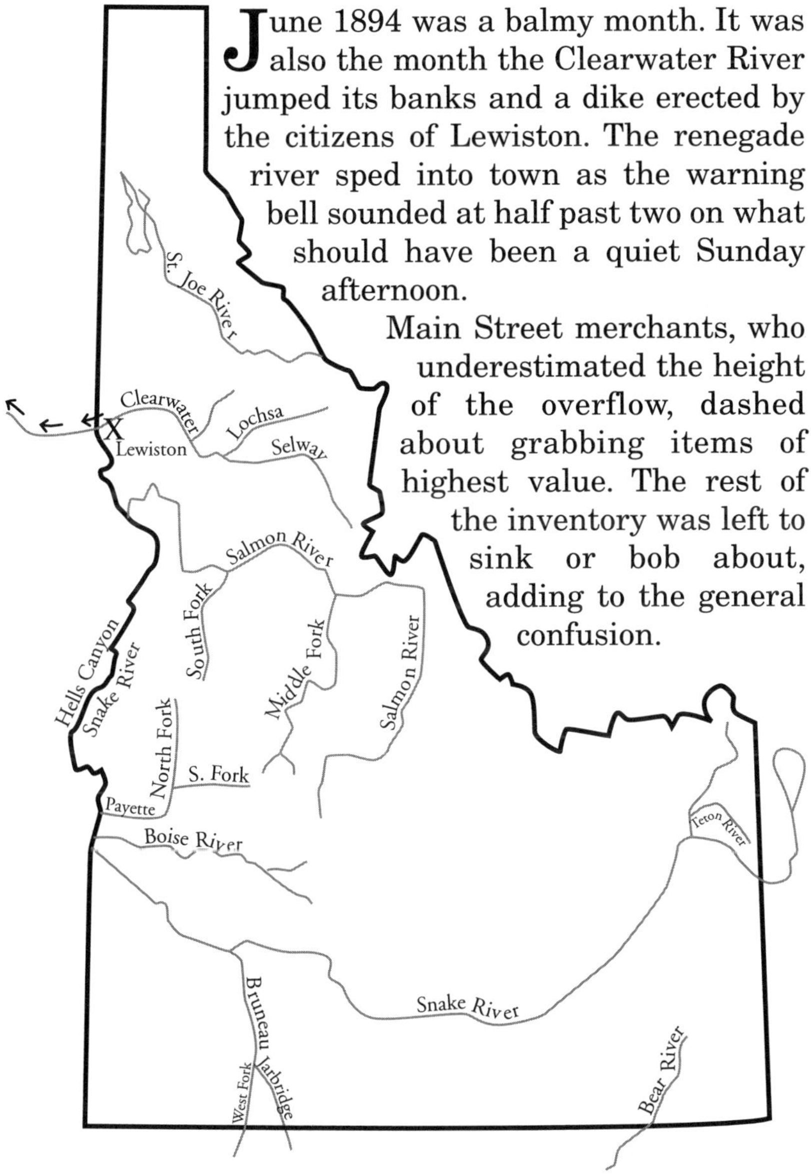

Every square inch of land from the post office to the Squires residence on the far side of town was flooded. Boardwalks floated up and down the avenues, accompanied by numerous wooden fences of various designs.

Small boys put some sections of walk to use, piloting them up and down the new waterways, ignoring mothers who splashed after them, long skirts gathered above their knees, fearful that the rafts would be caught by the main current and swept down the Snake and Columbia to the Pacific Ocean.

Dogs howled pitifully, or yapped in excitement. Some joined the youngsters on the rafts. Young girls hung from upstairs windows, some probably convinced their bedrooms would become their tombs if the water kept rising.

Down on C Street, the water was fifteen to twenty feet deep.

By Monday evening, the river tired of its sport and rapidly receded, leaving the citizens of Lewiston to clean up the mess. And the small boys were left afoot as the rafts turned back into sidewalks.

LIVERY STABLE
Jim Paxton

Farewell Bend, on the Snake River, was the point where Oregon bound pioneers left the river, after following it for nearly 400 miles.

THIRTY-ONE

Snake River — 1895

The *Norma*

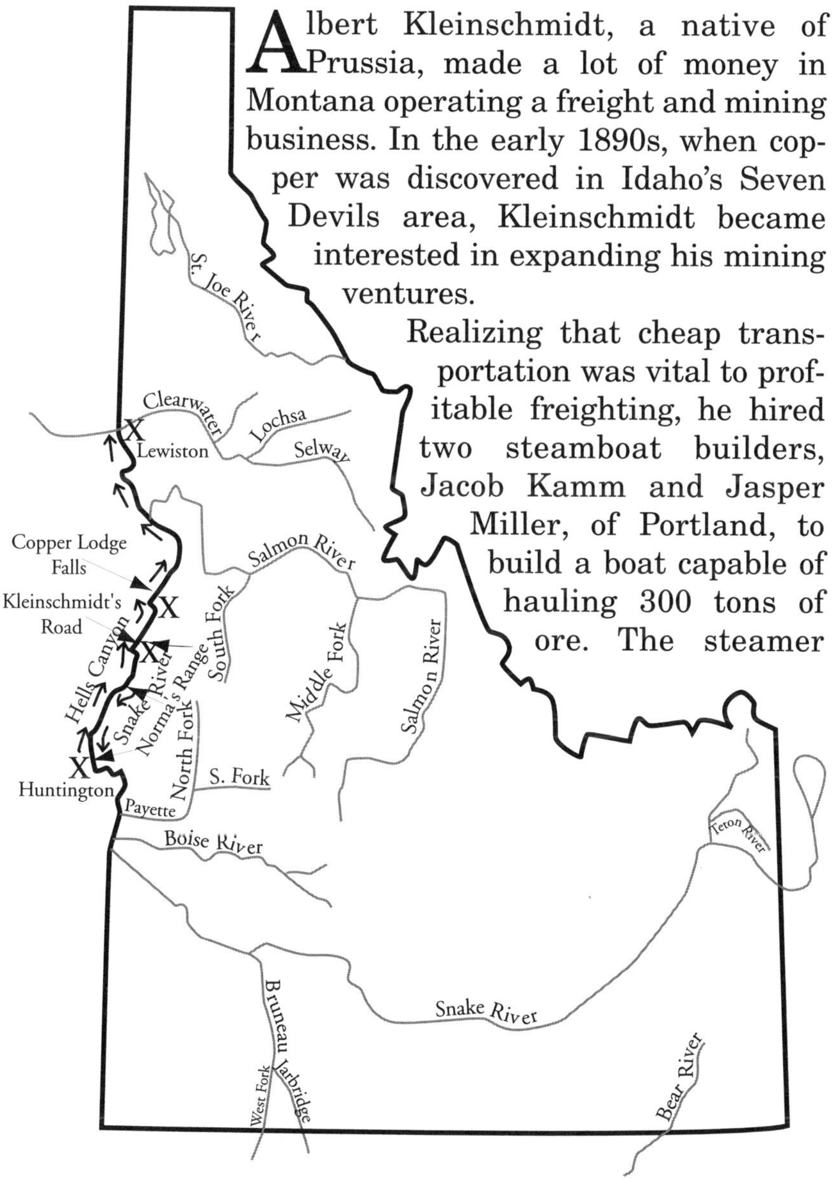

Albert Kleinschmidt, a native of Prussia, made a lot of money in Montana operating a freight and mining business. In the early 1890s, when copper was discovered in Idaho's Seven Devils area, Kleinschmidt became interested in expanding his mining ventures.

Realizing that cheap transportation was vital to profitable freighting, he hired two steamboat builders, Jacob Kamm and Jasper Miller, of Portland, to build a boat capable of hauling 300 tons of ore. The steamer had to travel less than twenty miles between a road Kleinschmidt planned to build on the Idaho side of the Snake River, and the Oregon Short Line Railroad, on the Oregon side of the stream.

The steamboat was built in 1891, in the small town of Huntington, Oregon, upstream from the mouth of Hells Canyon. It was a light, eight-foot draft sternwheeler. The vessel was 165 feet long, thirty-five feet wide, with a hull depth of six and one half feet. The deck house was 120 x 35 x10 feet.; the cabin measured 80 x 35 x 9 feet; and the pilot house was 12 x 8 x 8 feet.

The boat was christened the *Norma*, named after Albert Kleinschmidt's oldest daughter. In March 1891, Captain Sebastian E. Miller was appointed to command the steamer. But the river was too low and Miller had to wait for the spring run-off to make a trial run.

On April 21, Captain Miller piloted the *Norma* up and down the river past Devil's Gate, Bay Horse Rapids and Blacksmith Point without difficulty. Three months after the trial run, Kleinschmidt's road was finished.

But after all the planning, the *Norma* only made two ore-hauling trips. Shortly after the road was finished, the price of copper plummeted. Kleinschmidt suffered great financial losses and couldn't pay for the boat. Ownership of the *Norma* reverted to the builders, Kamm and Miller.

The steamboat was next to useless. A railroad bridge blocked the river just above Huntington. Even in low water, the boat was too big to slip under the bridge. She was trapped between the bridge and the head of Hells Canyon, thirty miles downriver.

Kamm and Miller sold the boat at a loss to C. W. Williams in 1892. Williams took the Oregon Short Line to federal court to force the railroad to put a draw in its Snake River bridge. That would allow the boat to operate in the Silver City region of the Snake in southwest Idaho. When Williams lost the case, he petitioned the Secretary of War to force the O. S. L. to open the bridge. That effort failed, too. Since he still owed money on the *Norma*, the boat passed back to the builders again.

The *Norma* stood idle at Huntington until May 1895. Kamm and Miller decided their only hope of getting their money back was to take the steamboat through Hells Canyon to Lewiston, where she would be of some value. They knew the journey would be perilous and that the chances of the boat perishing in the dark depths of the canyon were far greater than the chances of her reaching her destination.

William Polk Gray was chosen to make the Hells Canyon attempt. The soft-spoken fifty-year-old had more than thirty years experience as a pilot on the Columbia and lower Snake rivers. Gray was considered one of the best sternwheeler captains in the United States. He was thc only man to ever run the Priest Rapids on the Columbia with a full load of passengers.

Captain Gray brought most of his crew with him from Portland, Oregon. They included his brother, A. W. Gray, first mate; Ed Lyons, second mate; C. H. Jennings, engineer; E. D. Kellogg, second engineer; A. B. Gardner, fireman; J. Duffey, watchman; George

Binnard, cook and steward and Thomas Wright, carpenter. Deckhands were W. Young, M. Quigley, M. Condrey and P. Westwood. F. D. Farwell, a newspaper reporter, went along to document the adventure. The captain and crew arrived in Huntington on May 14, 1895.

On May 16, Gray and his crew took the *Norma* on a trial run. She performed well.

At 3:00 P.M. on May 17, Gray cast off and headed downriver.

There was trouble almost immediately. The Army Corps of Engineers was improving the river channel. The captain, who was unfamiliar with the stretch of river, depended on charts the engineers had prepared for him to guide him as far as Oxbow Bend.

Three miles below Huntington, the *Norma* was churning through Bay Horse Rapids when she was impaled on the broken end of a two-inch steel drill the engineers had left sticking up in the middle of the channel. The drill tore several holes in the hull before snagging the boat. The *Norma* swung sideways and slammed into a large boulder. It took hours of work with lines and spars to wrench her off the drill, and two more days to repair the damage,

The journey resumed. A short distance downriver Captain Gray spotted riffles in the water ahead. He asked the first mate to check the charts. A. W. Gray studied the chart and proclaimed the area clear.

The all clear statement was barely out of the first mate's mouth when the *Norma* rammed a partially-submerged rock, ripping a forty-foot gash in her starboard side. The enraged captain threw the Corps of Engineers charts into the river.

The boat began taking on water but the captain hesitated to put to shore. He was afraid the nervous crew might jump ship. Gray took a calculated risk and ran on downriver past Sturgill Rapids. Once beyond that point, it was impossible for the vessel to return to Huntington. They were committed to reaching Lewiston. Anyone trying to abandon the boat would have a long climb out of Hells Canyon.

The crew stayed with the boat. They spent three days below Sturgill Rapids patching the *Norma*.

Back on the river, the *Norma* immediately faced another obstacle. As she rounded a bend, she almost hit a heavy steel cable at Brownlee Ferry, hanging less than eight feet above the river. Captain Gray stopped the steamer in time and backed the boat upstream into an eddy. The crew lashed her to nearby boulders while the captain blew the whistle to alert the ferryman.

The first mate and two crew members were sent ashore to find out why the ferryman wouldn't lower the cable. He said he was doing it to prolong their lives. He expressed the opinion that the boat had a bull-headed fool for a captain and not a soul would live through the canyon.

Under the threat of bodily harm, the Good Samaritan reluctantly lowered the cable and the *Norma* continued on her way. Captain Gray nosed the boat ashore above Copper Ledge Falls. The eighteen-foot drop had delayed the steamboat *Shoshone* for a year in 1869, then nearly wrecked her when she went through the following season.

Perpendicular rock walls rose nearly 500 feet on both sides of the river. Captain Gray and the crew scouted the rapids from a ledge, studying the currents, eddies and backlashes. They decided the Norma would suffer the least damage on the right side of the river by dropping into a hole where the backlash of water would cushion the sternwheeler and keep it away from the cliff.

The captain decided the starboard side was most likely to be damaged. Carpenter Thomas Wright was instructed to run guard timbers from the point of likely impact, all the way to the midship keelson. The first mate was ordered to have cord wood stacked against the interior of the hull, the length of the guards, in case water tore away the bulkhead.

The next morning, Captain Gray dropped the *Norma* over the right side of the falls. She shuddered down the cataract. As she hit the hole, the captain slammed her into reverse with the helm hard to starboard. The *Norma* rammed the point of the cliff with just enough force to break three of the guard timbers, leaving the hull undamaged.

A triumphant cry rose from the crew. The *Norma* has successfully run the most difficult section of Hells Canyon.

On May 24, the *Norma* arrived in Lewiston. She was the second and last steamboat to travel the entire narrow, rapid-filled length of Hells Canyon.

From 1895 to 1907, the *Norma* hauled grain from Lewiston to Rapaira. During the building of the Deschutes railroad bridge above Celilo Falls, she served as a ferry across the Columbia River. Upon completion of the bridge in 1915, the *Norma* was taken to Portland and dismantled.

THIRTY-TWO

Snake River — 1896

The Idaho Canal Company Fraud

The original home of the Northern Shoshoni Indians was the upper Snake River Valley. The Shoshoni called the place Shawnt-Shawnip — land of plenty. Before the establishment of Fort Hall and the Oregon Trail, the land was also home to herds of buffalo and other large game animals.

The Bannock, a division of the Shoshoni family, were a more migratory tribe. Their territory covered much of southern Idaho and western Wyoming.

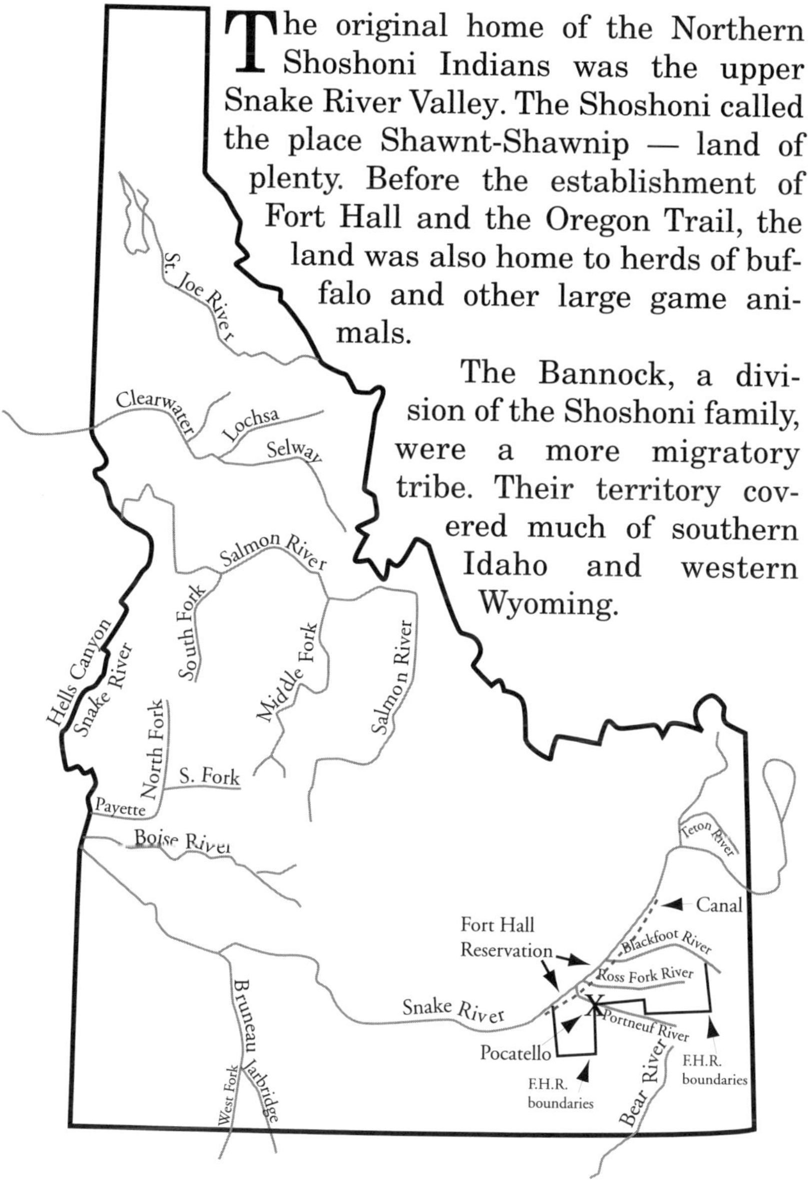

A reservation was created for the Northern Shoshoni on a portion of their homeland, on June 14, 1867 by presidential executive order. It was named the Fort Hall Reservation. A year later, on July 30, 1869, President Ulysses S. Grant signed an executive order placing the Bannock on the Fort Hall Reservation.

With the coming of the white man in the mid 1800s, most of the game disappeared from the Upper Snake River Valley. That didn't seem to concern reservation officials. They were confident they could transform a race of hunters into peaceful farmers. A grand plan was devised for nearly 600 Bannock and 500 Shoshoni on the reservation. Each head of family would get 320 acres of land and each individual over eighteen years of age, and not the head of family would get eighty acres. The assigned farms would no longer be held in common, but belong to those who cultivated and tended them. Each farmer would receive $100 worth of seed and agricultural implements (shovels and hoes) the first year, and twenty-five dollars for each of the succeeding three years. As a further incentive, the ten most productive farmers would receive awards of $500 each for three years.

When the Indians refused to rush forward to embrace the new scheme, Commissioner Charles Powell decided to demonstrate farming techniques. The reservation residents would be shown how to farm and have a chance to see what results were possible from their manual labors.

A white farmer was hired to plow thirty-five acres, build a small irrigation ditch and plant grain, potatoes and other vegetables. The demonstration was of little interest to the Shoshoni and Bannock men who considered digging and harvesting work for women. They were hunters. The Indians did notice, however, that only seven acres of the demonstration farm produced some potatoes and turnips. The rest of the crops were destroyed by drought and grasshoppers.

Delays caused by government red tape postponed the distribution of land to the Indians throughout the 1880s. Even when the concept was approve, Fort Hall agents realized the farming effort would fail without irrigation. The Indians now were more interested in farming because there wasn't enough game to feed their families. They faced near starvation.

The need for an irrigation canal was emphasized by agent S. G. Fisher.

> "Until some provisions are made for an increased supply of water, it is absurd to ask the Indians to take their land seriously, from the fact that not one in ten of those willing to farm could get their 160 or even 80 acres covered by water. In most cases their 'farms' comprise from two to ten acres; scattered along in the bends of the creeks coming out of the mountains. In many instances, 160 acres would take in a dozen or more of their little cultivated patches called farms, including their log cabins and fences."

In 1889 the Indians were told a canal would be built through the reservation, bringing water from the Snake River. The ditch was to leave the river a few miles below Idaho Falls, cross the Blackfoot and

Portneuf rivers and terminate at American Falls. The canal was to be thirty-eight feet wide at the bottom, sixty-two feet at the top, and eight feet deep. The canal would irrigate an estimated 300,000 acres, two-thirds of it on the reservation. The estimated project cost was $238,000.

On March 3, 1891, Congress authorized the Secretary of the Interior to contract with responsible companies for the construction of an irrigation canal on the Fort Hall reservation. The project cost was to be paid out of money belonging to the Bannock and Shoshoni people, held by the United States Treasury.

The act also granted a right-of-way across the reservation for the canal company to carry water to the nearby town of Pocatello. Only surplus water from the ditch was to be used by the Indians.

The only party to submit a proposal was the Idaho Canal Company, a new business that had not yet incorporated. Government representatives agreed to grant the company a contract as soon as a map of definite location was filed.

Apparently, the contract was never completed. By 1895, the Indian Bureau had decided to hire a superintendent to establish an irrigation system on the Fort Hall reservation. The plan failed because of Pocatello's prior water rights. Indian Agent Teter wrote about the mess.

> "I can not too strongly condemn the short-sighted policy, the gross neglect, or worse, which allowed the settler to file upon the water in the streams on or adjacent to the reservation, thereby preventing the Indians from

> obtaining water, save for personal uses, and putting them at an expense of thousands of dollars to obtain water on the reservation for irrigation."

The Bannock and Shoshoni drafted their own statement on the situation:

> "Our agent (Teter) says Washington wants us to pay the white man to make a ditch on our land and pay him for taking care of it, and then buy the water out of a ditch our money has built on our land, and which rightfully should belong to us. We think he is mistaken."

But the complaints from the agent and the Indians were ignored.

The government advertised for bids on the canal project. On January 25, 1896, the Idaho Canal Company, now incorporated, was awarded the bid and signed a contract to build the canal. A new plan called for it to begin at the Snake River, run through a flume across the Blackfoot River and end at Ross Fork Creek. The company also agreed to extend the canal from Ross Fork Creek as far as necessary toward the Portneuf River to supply water to future white farmers who might settle in that area.

Water was to be conveyed to reservation land for five dollars an acre, plus an annual charge of seventy-five cents an acre for maintenance. For the construction north of Ross Fork Creek and the delivery of 300 cubic feet of water, through the canal, the Idaho Canal Company was to receive $90,000, with an annual maintenance charge of fifteen dollars per cubic foot ($4,500).

An engineer employed by the government, suggested some changes in the canal route. His ideas resulted in a new contract with the canal company requiring two dams to be built across the Blackfoot River to divert water into the reservation canal. Part of the canal already was completed, at a cost of $30,000, but little water flowed into it.

In July, 1897, more unexpected expenses had to be paid by the Indians. A section of the finished canal, was washed out that spring and the canal company refused to repair it. Using mostly Indian labor, repairs were made at a cost of $16,929.

The two diversion dams on the Snake River were not yet completed. Work had not started on the main canal across the reservation from the Blackfoot River to Ross Fork Creek. The Indians, angry about the wanton spending of their money, submitted a petition to the Secretary of the Interior protesting the continuation of the project.

In December 1897, the two diversion dams were finally completed. One year later the entire project was finished.

Inspector W. H. Graves examined the canal project and reported it did not meet the terms of the agreement. The channel was not sufficiently excavated. It was a "built-up" canal made cheaply by scraping up loose dirt along the outside of the channel. Two attempts were made to bring water through the canal and both resulted in major washouts which covered fertile land with a deep layer of sand. Inspector Graves also documented the reaction of the Indians.

He said the Bannock and Shoshoni were so upset and convinced they had been deceived that, "they will not talk about it nor listen with any patience to any explanations concerning the matter."

Problems with the canal continued. It became so frustrating to the Indians that when water finally became available in 1903, most refused to begin farming. They were afraid the canal would fail again.

In 1908 the federal government purchased the canal system. But the irrigation program continued to be run in a slipshod manner. Even today, the Fort Hall reservation irrigation system is incomplete and water rights are uncertain due to the mix-motives behind the original project.

There are about 50 major irrigation reservoirs on the Snake River and its tributaries.

THIRTY-THREE

Snake River — 1900

Swan Falls Ferry

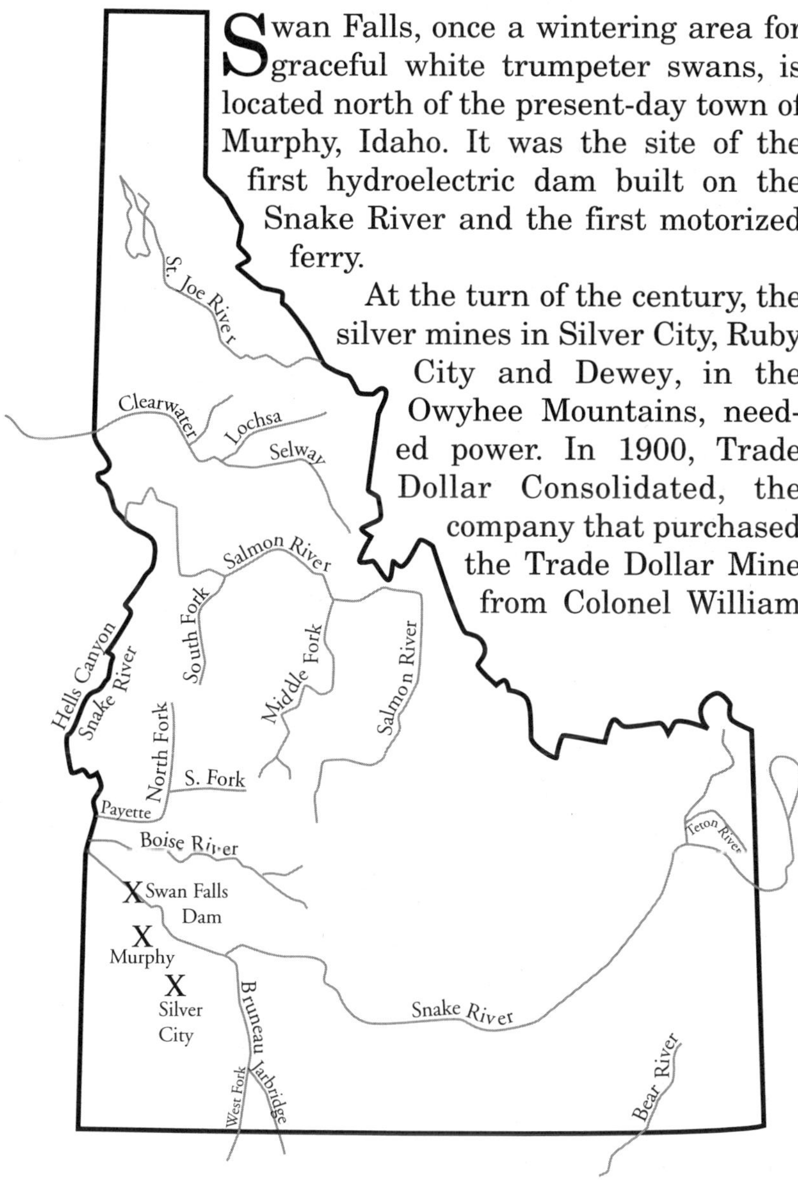

Swan Falls, once a wintering area for graceful white trumpeter swans, is located north of the present-day town of Murphy, Idaho. It was the site of the first hydroelectric dam built on the Snake River and the first motorized ferry.

At the turn of the century, the silver mines in Silver City, Ruby City and Dewey, in the Owyhee Mountains, needed power. In 1900, Trade Dollar Consolidated, the company that purchased the Trade Dollar Mine from Colonel William

Dewey, decided to build a dam to generate the needed electricity.

A. J. Wiley, a young Boise engineer, was hired to design the dam. Wiley took advantage of a rock shelf across the river, and the five-foot drop of the falls. He designed a concrete structure twelve feet high and forty-five feet long on the east end of the shelf. The remaining 424-foot gap across the river was closed with a stone and wooden crib dam. The power plant, located on the concrete section, was equipped with four vertical turbines that turned a shaft belted to three generators. The dam was completed in 1901. Surplus electricity was routed through a 4,400-volt line to Nampa and Caldwell to power an interurban railway line.

A reservoir formed behind the dam, widening the river and making it more difficult for residents of the neighboring towns of Melba, Guffey and Murphy to cross the Snake. To appease local citizens, Trade Dollar Consolidated installed a ferry, one-half mile above the dam. Because there wasn't any current in the reservoir to push a cable ferry, a motorized vessel was installed.

The boat was fitted with a pair of side wheels powered by electric motors. Electricity was carried to the motors by an overhead line. The ferry resembled a cross between a miniature steamboat and a flattened cable car. Since ferry operators had to be paid, the craft was designed so anyone could operate it by stepping aboard and throwing a stitch.

Intrigued by the only motorized ferry on the river, area residents quickly adopted the site for Sunday get-togethers. After church, people with picnic baskets, sun umbrellas and impatient children would line the banks awaiting their turns on the ferry. When too many passengers crowded the boat, the electric motors whined in complaint.

Before long, the ferry owners found someone to operate it on weekends and holidays and eliminated the carnival atmosphere and overloads. The electric Swan Falls Ferry remained in operation until the 1930s.

A larger powerhouse was built within a couple of years after the completion of the dam. In 1910 Trade Dollar Consolidated formed the Swan Falls Power Company and added two new generators. In 1914 two more turbines and generators were added, along with a spillway. In 1916 Swan Falls Dam was purchased by the Idaho Power Company. At the time, the dam had the greatest generating capacity in the state.

Idaho Power replaced the stone and wooden crib in 1920 with a concrete dam. In 1936 another spillway and ten new gates were added on the east end of the dam.

The construction of the Swan Falls hydroelectric dam ended Chinook salmon and steelhead fish runs to points upstream from the site.

In 1860, the Colonel Wright *became the first steamboat to operate on Idaho rivers. The boat had to stop near the junction of the Snake and Clearwater, while passengers cut trees for fuel on a rattlesnake infested island.*

THIRTY-FOUR

St. Joe River — 1902

The St. Joe Boom Company

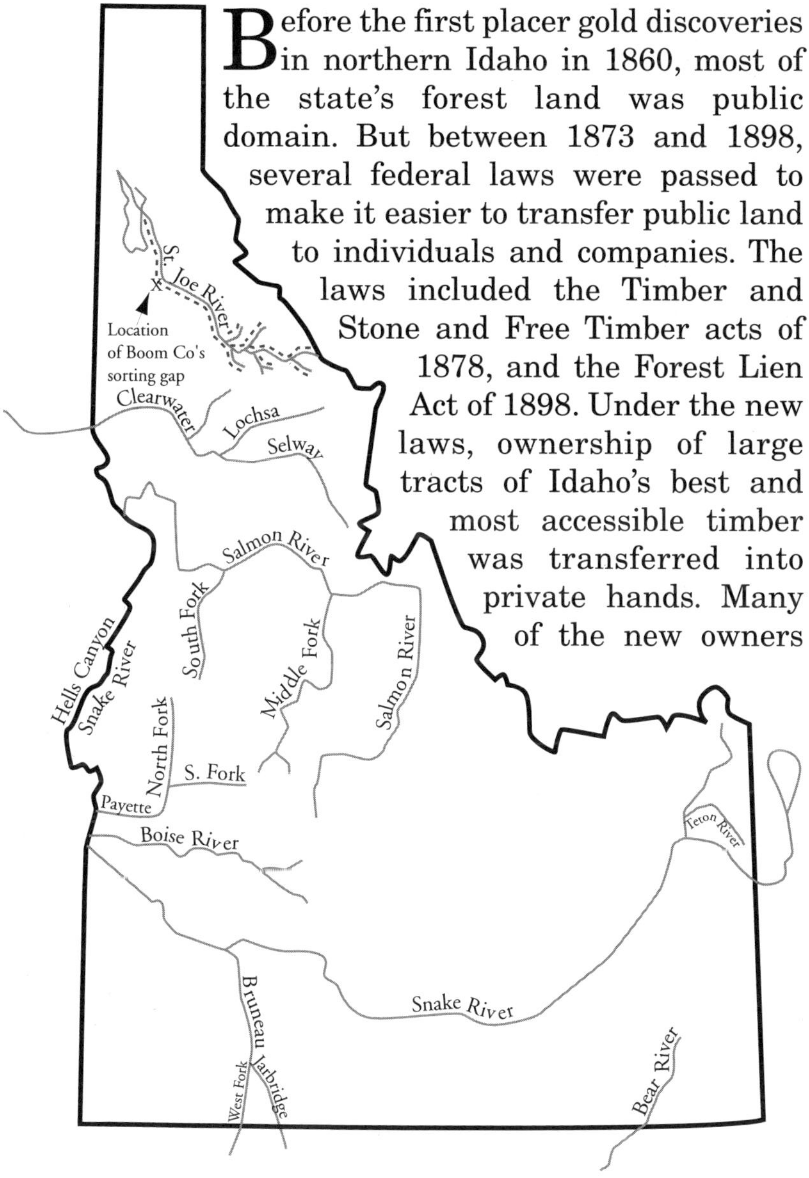

Before the first placer gold discoveries in northern Idaho in 1860, most of the state's forest land was public domain. But between 1873 and 1898, several federal laws were passed to make it easier to transfer public land to individuals and companies. The laws included the Timber and Stone and Free Timber acts of 1878, and the Forest Lien Act of 1898. Under the new laws, ownership of large tracts of Idaho's best and most accessible timber was transferred into private hands. Many of the new owners were seasoned timber barons who had left the rapidly-disappearing forests of the eastern United States for pristine timber stands in the West.

In April 1878, a detachment of cavalry from Fort Lapwai set up camp along Lake Coeur d'Alene. The mission of the soldiers, commanded by Colonel Henry Clay Merrian, was to build a fort on the shoreline. All the equipment needed for a sawmill was hauled to the site, including a large circular saw and a steam power plant. By winter, the mill was in full operation.

From 1878 to 1898, the cavalry mill employed twenty to thirty civilian workers, producing all the lumber for the fort buildings, for the steamboat *Amelia Wheaton*, and for a school.

Glassford T. Hawley built the area's first commercial sawmill in 1883 and the lumbering town of Coeur d'Alene sprang to life. Within five years, the town had more than 1,000 people.

The three Fisher brothers built the first sawmill at St. Maries, on the St. Joe River, in 1887. Privately-owned lumber companies were soon popping up around the region like morel mushrooms after a spring rain.

There were more than forty million board feet of timber standing in the Coeur d'Alene, St. Joe area alone. White pine (Idaho's state tree) was most abundant. It was considered the king of the softwoods. Stands of larch (tamarack), Engleman spruce, western red cedar, Douglas fir, and western yellow pine kept company with the noble white pine.

Most of the timber was harvested in the St. Joe drainage, where the northern section of the Bitterroot Mountains form the northernmost boundary and the

Clearwater Mountains are the southern barrier. Logs were cut along the river tributaries and slid down greased chutes into water-fed flumes. The flumes carried the logs to holding ponds called splash dams. When the ponds were filled with logs, the dams were opened, flushing the timber downriver to mills in St. Maries and along Lake Coeur d'Alene.

Men followed the logs to keep them from jamming. But they couldn't keep their logs from mixing with those from competing companies. Log ownership sometimes resulted in arguments and fist fights.

There also was strife between the loggers and steamboat operators. Unattended or unclaimed logs sometimes drifted into the lake creating a hazard for the boats.

In 1902, F. J. Davis of Rutledge Timber Company, suggested that all the competing timber companies form a co-op to move logs to the mills. The St. Joe Boom Company was formed.

Under the agreement, logs were stamped several times on each end with a hammer brand before being released from the splash dams. Each company registered its brand with the state, eliminating timber ownership disputes.

A permanent crew was housed downriver at a sorting gap just above a wide stretch of water. Each company had a designated "corral." The corrals were made of long slender logs called boomsticks, chained end-to-end, forming a circle. As logs arrived from upstream they were sorted by brand into the corrals.

Once a booomstick corral was full, cables were stretched across it to pull the logs into a tight, narrow mass called a braile. A tug then pulled the braile the final thirty miles downriver to Lake Coeur d'Alene.

Each tugboat carried two pilots, a cook, fireman and lineman. Because a tug's steam engine could consume up to fifty-five cords of wood during the trip, it also pulled a wood barge loaded with fuel.

The average tow for a tug was a braile one and one half miles long. The vessel pulled the braile on a 1,200-foot towline. That kept the propwash from the tug from hitting the braile.

Once the logs reached the lake, they were held in larger booms until needed by the sawmills. River transportation of logs peaked in the 1920s. Like the eastern forests, those in Idaho began to shrink. Most of the sawmills are gone, their skeletons casting ghostlike reflections on the shadowy waters of the St. Joe and Lake Coeur d'Alene.

THIRTY-FIVE

Salmon River — 1903

Winter Journey Down the Salmon

R. E. and J. V. Dwyer, two brothers from Omaha, Nebraska, came to Idaho to do some hunting and to float the Salmon River during November 1903. Captain Harry Guleke, a seasoned river-runner, was to join them on the adventure.

The brothers left Salmon City on November 18, riding horseback along a trail bordering the river. After following the Salmon for thirty-five miles, they saw the smoke stacks of the Kitty Burton Gold Mining Company in

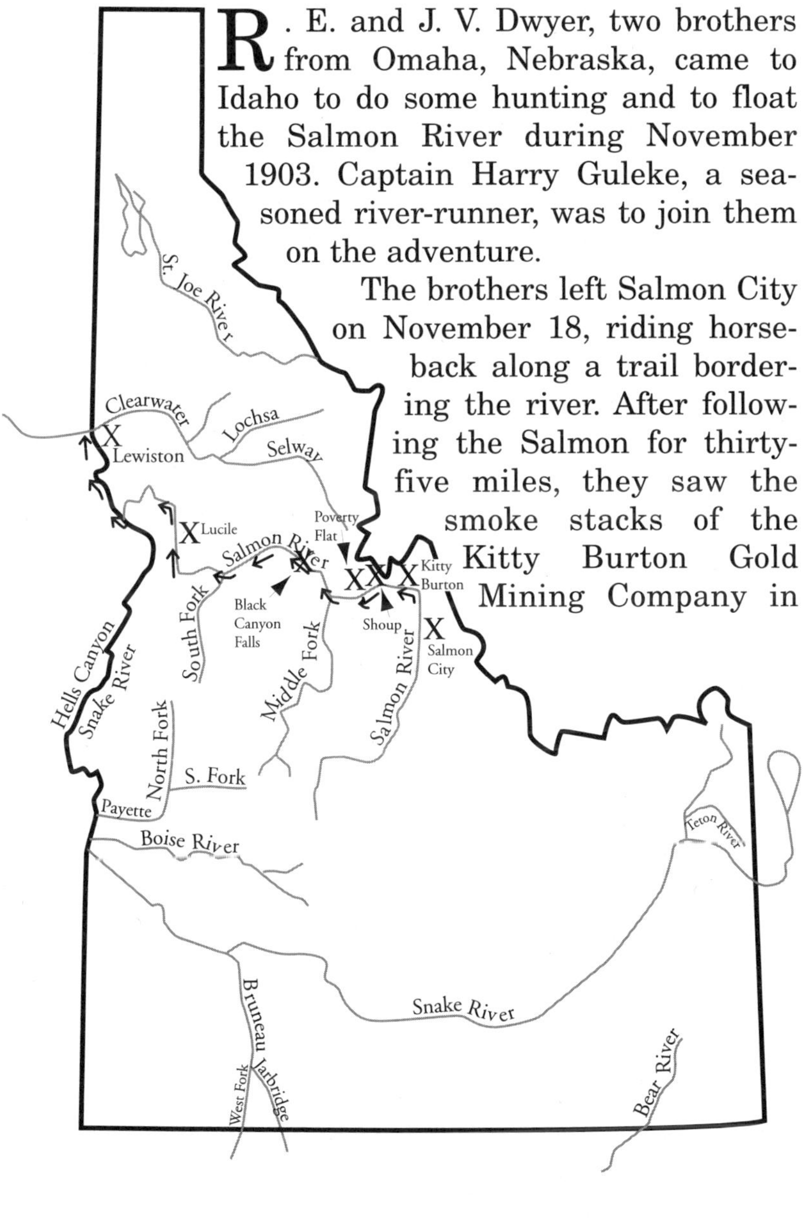

the distance. They rented a room for the night at the mine.

A crude road had been forced up the steep embankment of the Indian Creek drainage from the river. Rafts, barges and sweep boats unloaded cargo and mining equipment from Salmon City. The landing served the two mines five miles up the draw, the Kitty Burton and the Ulysses. Because there was no way to return the craft upstream, they were docked and sold to those who ventured farther down "The River of No Return."

The Dwyer brothers outfitted for their journey at a mine supply store. They also purchased a flat-bottom sweep boat, thirty-six feet long and ten feet wide. The manager of the Kitty Burton couldn't believe his luck at selling the boat during November. Most craft wouldn't find buyers until late spring.

After loading their supplies, the Dwyers headed downriver. They floated eight miles before coming to the settlement of Shoup, a town located at the Grunter Mine. The mine's mill had once been powered by a large wooden waterwheel. The massive wheel stood silent and still, shrouded in late-morning mist. A narrow suspension bridge emerged from the foggy background. It led to Eli Suydam's mine, the Clipper Bullion, located on the left bank of the river. A ten-inch water pipe, held up by a labyrinth of cables and wooden supports, sagged across the Salmon.

Two miles beyond Shoup, the men came to Pine Creek. Another mine stood on the hillside. An idle aerial tramway could be seen through the ponderosa pines. The brothers were so engrossed in the sights they nearly lost their balance as their sweep boat

Jim Paxton

plunged into the first rapids. Fortunately, the waves were biggest at the beginning and the wave train smoothed out below.

George Sandiland, a seasoned river man, had lost his life in the same rapid during high water. Six years earlier, he was hauling freight with Guleke when he caught a rock with the rear sweep. He was catapulted into the river and lodged beneath the boat.

Sixteen miles downriver the Dwyers reached their predetermined campsite, on a gravel bar just above Big Creek (now known as Panther Creek). That was where Guleke was to join them. From that point on, the river was no place for novices.

The brothers set up an elaborate camp and spent several days hunting in the surrounding hills for deer and mountain sheep. The weather turned wintry. Wind whistled up the river channel as snow swirled and drifted. Nearly a foot of snow soon accumulated on the ground. Temperatures dropped and ice formed on the river's edge.

Captain Guleke didn't show up in camp at the expected time. The two men finally decided they needed to start their journey before they became locked in the ice. Five miles downriver, at Poverty Flat, their fears were realized. The river was choked with ice and slush three to four feet thick. Using long poles to push the ice out of the way, they worked to clear the channel. Ice and slush drifting down the river, backed up behind their craft. But the brothers made progress. By nightfall they had cleared all but about 300 feet of the blockage. Exhausted and numb from the cold, the Dwyers crawled into their bedrolls. In the morning they were disappointed to find there was more ice in the river than there had been the previous day. Some of the ice was seven to ten feet thick..

The brothers fought the ice jam as snow continued to accumulate on the hillsides. On the third day, as they took a break from their work, Captain Guleke appeared on the scene.

The men hoped that with a third person working they could conquer the barrier. But on day four it was clear to Guleke that their efforts were in vain. He suggested they remodel the sweep boat, making it small enough to be carried around the ice jam. Using a hatchet and old hand saw, they built a new boat. A toboggan was constructed from planks salvaged from an abandoned boat. Leaving most of their supplies behind, the trio portaged the remodeled craft past the block on the toboggan.

At the junction of the Middle and Main forks of the Salmon the adventurers had to carry their craft around another ice dam. The following day they entered Black Canyon. It took three days to negotiate the ten-mile canyon. They had to portage seven ices dams, some fifteen feet deep. Solid ice reached out from shore on both sides of the river, leaving a narrow channel filled with slush and snow.

There also was a major rapid in the canyon. The rapid, today called Salmon Falls, usually disappears during high water. During low water, large boulders poke above the water, waiting to trap careless river runners. Two of the three openings in the rocks were clogged with ice. The boat managed to slip through the open channel on the left side of the river.

Beyond Black Canyon, the journey became more pleasant. The lower elevation meant warmer temperatures. But a bone-chilling wind sometimes howled up the canyon in the afternoon.

Guleke captained the boat, with the Dwyers taking turns at the sweep in calm water. Guleke skillfully jockeyed the boat down the right-hand side of Split Rock Rapid. At Big Mallard he pulled the boat to shore and scouted the rapid from the path above. He ran the boat close to the left bank, squeezing through a slot on the left of a big boulder, while avoiding a yawning hole on the right. After Elkhorn and Vinegar rapids, the boat drifted through long, flat stretches. Mostly drop-pool rapids remained. The heart-stopping sections were left behind on the upper river.

The men beached their craft at Lucile and replenished their supplies. The wilderness was behind them — now homesteads dotted the riverbank.

The men reached Lewiston December 19, glad the adventure was over.

THIRTY-SIX

Snake River — 1903

The Steamboat *Imnaha*

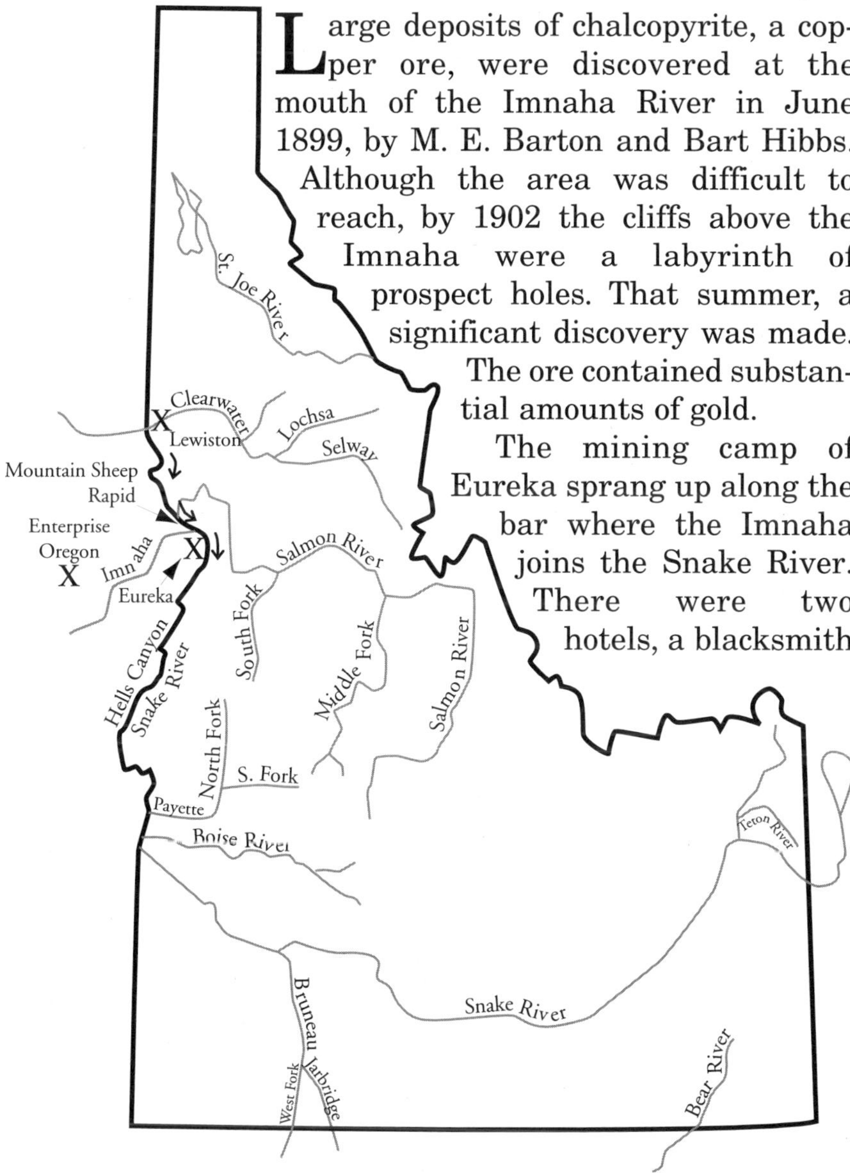

Large deposits of chalcopyrite, a copper ore, were discovered at the mouth of the Imnaha River in June 1899, by M. E. Barton and Bart Hibbs. Although the area was difficult to reach, by 1902 the cliffs above the Imnaha were a labyrinth of prospect holes. That summer, a significant discovery was made. The ore contained substantial amounts of gold.

The mining camp of Eureka sprang up along the bar where the Imnaha joins the Snake River. There were two hotels, a blacksmith shop and store. Mail arrived once a week from Enterprise, Oregon, sixty miles away. The town quickly grew to 200 people.

The Eureka Mining Company owned controlling interest in the copper mines. In early spring 1903, a subsidiary — the Lewiston Southern Company — was formed to operate a steamboat between Lewiston and Eureka.

The boat was built cheap and quick. Named the *Imnaha*, it cost $35,000. There were only five bulkheads in her 125-foot length. Instead of four-inch timbers the *Imnaha* had two-inch sheathing. She floated on June 30, 1903, making her maiden voyage under Captain Harry Baughman,

The first half of her fifty-six-mile run to Eureka was without difficulty. As the *Imnaha* passed the mouth of the Salmon River, however, she couldn't climb the rapid under her own power and had to be hauled up with lines.

Farther upstream, it took two days for the crew to line the *Imnaha* through Mountain Sheep Rapids, only two miles below Eureka. To the untrained eye the rapid didn't seem threatening. It was a smooth-surfaced stretch of fast-moving water. The difficulty stemmed from the narrow nature of the passage — only sixty-two feet from cliff-to-cliff.

After the steamboat's initial problems ascending the Snake, the boat owners asked the Army Corps of Engineers to improve the channel. The Corps dynamited several obstructions. At the three most difficult rapids, where lining was necessary, sturdy iron rings and eyebolts were set in solid rock and sulfur hardened. Heavy wire cables were attached to the rings.

An empty steel barrel was attached to the free end of each cable to mark it and keep it afloat.

The *Imnaha* was fitted with a powerful steam capstan (winch). On arrival at a rapid, crew members located the floating barrel and hauled the steel cable aboard using a hooked pole. The cable was wrapped around the capstan and the boat pulled itself into calmer water. The cable was then reattached to the barrel and thrown back into the river so it could float back to the base of the rapid.

The cables allowed the *Imnaha* to make regular runs to Eureka carrying passengers, supplies, mining equipment and timber. The lumber delivered by the boat was used to support an ore stamping mill.

The machinery for the stamp mill, which cost Eureka Mining Company $65,000 arrived at Lewiston November 7, 1903. The equipment was loaded on the *Imnaha*. The load also included a thirty-horsepower steam engine, needed to power the mill. On a Sunday morning, the steamboat departed Lewiston for Eureka on her fourteenth and final voyage.

The trip went smoothly until the boat reached Mountain Sheep Rapids late in the evening. Following routine, a crew member fished the steel barrel from the river and fastened the cable to the capstan. The cable strained under the extra weight of the mill equipment as the boat pulled itself through the rapid.

When the *Imnaha* reached calm water, the captain engaged the engine and ordered the cable and attached barrel to be thrown back. Unfortunately, the barrel floated under the paddlewheel and tangled the eccentric rods. Grating sounds echoed above the roar of the rapids as the rods shattered, disabling the paddlewheel and killing the engine.

Spinning helplessly in the current, the *Imnaha* drifted back into the Mountain Sheep Rapid where it lodged crosswise in the narrow channel, damning the river. The passengers, crew and captain scrambled up the slick, boulder-strewn bank on the Oregon side of the Snake. In silence they watched as the river backed up behind the wedged boat. In the dim light cast by a quarter moon they saw the hull crack like fragile eggshell. The stamp mill and steam engine dropped into the dark depths of the river, grinding metal against stone as it fell. The survivors stood in disbelief, long after the spine-tingling echoes of the accident had faded.

The Lewiston Southern Company planned another sternwheeler, the *Mountain Gem*. But the company couldn't make a profit without it's own stamp mill. Soon there were layoffs. Within two years, Eureka was a ghost town. The ruins of the mill's sprawling foundation are still visible behind Eureka Bar.

THIRTY-SEVEN

St. Joe River — 1905

Steamboat Feud

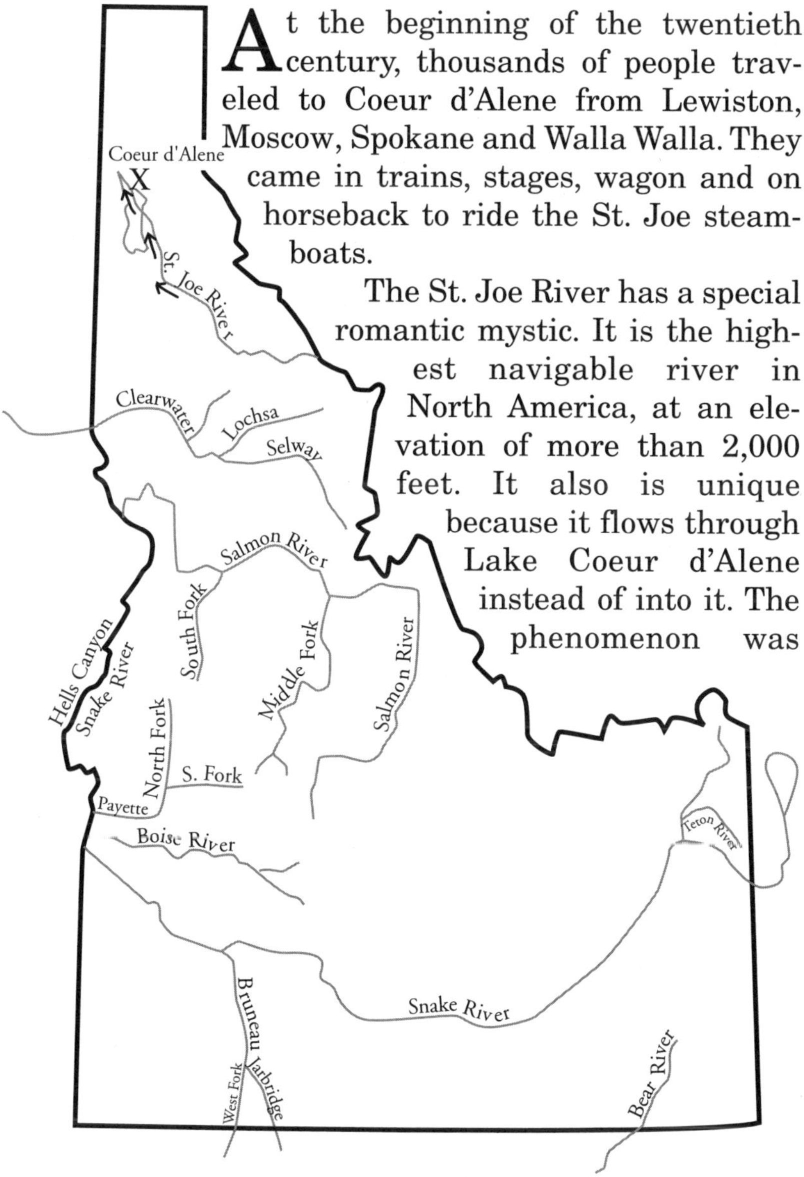

At the beginning of the twentieth century, thousands of people traveled to Coeur d'Alene from Lewiston, Moscow, Spokane and Walla Walla. They came in trains, stages, wagon and on horseback to ride the St. Joe steamboats.

The St. Joe River has a special romantic mystic. It is the highest navigable river in North America, at an elevation of more than 2,000 feet. It also is unique because it flows through Lake Coeur d'Alene instead of into it. The phenomenon was created by a delta formed in the lake by sediment from the river. The delta pushed farther into the lake over the years, until it reached the other side. Cottonwoods, willows and other moisture-loving plants took root in the silt, making it appear that there was a broad, tree-lined boulevard running the length of the lake.

Steamboating on the St. Joe was a fashionable holiday excursion. It was a way to escape the summer heat and the weariness of everyday toil. Stylish boats were built to carry the increasing tourist traffic. The 100-foot *Spokane* had staterooms, special upper deck cabins and a smoking room. A sister ship, the *Colfax,* was slightly larger than the *Spokane*.

Gourmet meals were offered aboard the vessels, as was dancing to music provided by shipboard bands. The steamboats docked at various locations so passengers could sight-see, picnic or swim in the river. The steamboat business boomed.

A local businessman, Joseph C. White, decided to get in on the action. White formed a partnership with H. Spaulding and Spaulding's son. The three launched the steamboat *Idaho*, to compete for the tourist trade. The 190-foot sidewheeler could carry 1,000 passengers. The owners painted red bands around the *Idaho's* smokestack and called the company the Red Collar Line.

The *Idaho* had larger staterooms, a bigger dance floor and a finer dining room than the competing boats. It wasn't long before it was the most popular tour boat on the St. Joe River and Coeur d'Alene Lake.

The owners of the *Spokane* and *Colfax* struggled to stay in business. As customer numbers dwindled, the management cut back the services and cut prices. But passengers wanted pizzazz, not bargains. The *Spokane* and *Colfax* eventually were sold to the owners of the *Idaho*. The previous owners agreed not to compete with the Red Collar Line in the future.

But the no competition agreement proved worthless. The sellers of the two boats used the money from the sale to reorganize into the White Star Navigation Company and build a ninety-six-foot sternwheeler called the *Boneta*. The new boat started drawing customers away from the Red Collar steamships, infuriating the owners, who vowed revenge.

One summer day, as the *Boneta* gracefully glided through the quiet, dark waters of the St. Joe, she was rammed by the *Idaho*. The *Boneta* took on water and slowly sank. The White Star Navigation Company managed to raise her, but couldn't restore the boat to her former beauty. The grand dame of the St. Joe became a common freighter.

The Red Collar Line and White Star Navigation Company continued to fight for passengers. As customers lined the wharves, the competing boats jostled each other for docking positions and to be the first to leave. Races between the boats weren't in good sport. They often were vicious.

The Red Collar eventually bought out the competition a second time, creating a steamship monopoly on the St. Joe and Coeur d'Alene. But the glory was short-lived. When the automobile arrived the steamboats lost much of their appeal and slid into the shadowy depths of oblivion.

Workers building the steamboat Shoshone *in 1866, near Farewell Bend on the Snake River, sometimes had to stop work and duck for cover when Indian war parties fired shots in their direction.*

THIRTY-EIGHT

Snake River — 1905

Milner Dam

Parched, arid desert once stretched across southern Idaho — a sage-covered, barren landscape inhabited by jack rabbits and rattlesnakes. The Snake River, flowed through a deep cut in the wasteland. But the Snake's water was of little benefit to the surrounding countryside.

In 1889, federal government engineers and agricultural experts were sent to Idaho's Snake River Plain to assess its potential as farmland. They determined it would be possible to irrigate more than 300,000 acres

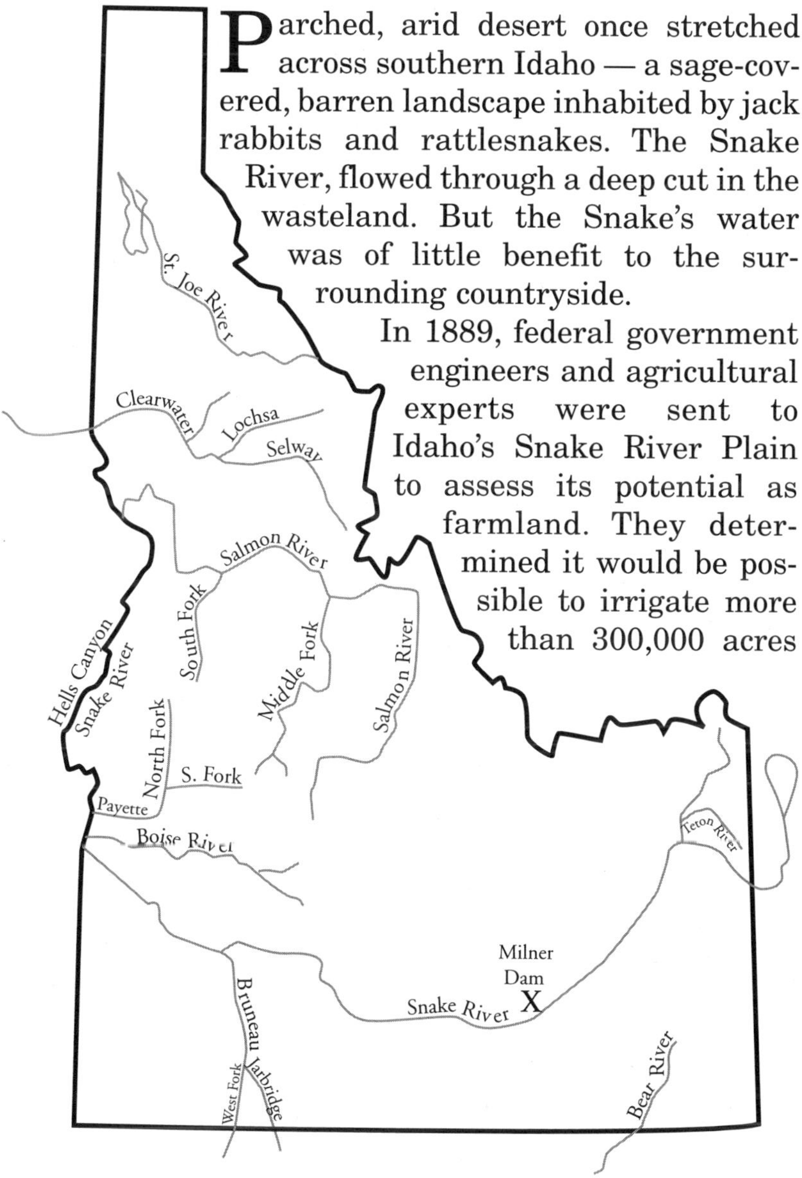

of rich volcanic soil with gravity flow irrigation. Southern Idaho became one of the first areas in the nation to test the reclamation theory.

Under the 1894 Carey Act, settlers who agreed to pay for irrigation systems were given government land. The original law had flaws and two amendments to the act were adopted — the last in 1901.

Landholders struggled under the financial burden of paying for dams to provide water for their projects. To help ease those woes, President Theodore Roosevelt signed the 1902 Reclamation Act. The act allowed the loaning of federal money to build large dams and other facilities vital to major irrigation projects.

On October 24, 1903, D. W. Ross, a district engineer for the Idaho Reclamation Service, presented a report covering preliminary investigations for building a rock and earth dam on the Snake River. The proposed site was 157 miles below present day Idaho Falls; seven miles upriver from Caldron Linn.

The Secretary of the Interior authorized the Idaho project on April 23, 1904 and allocated $2,600,000 to build the dam. The plan called for the construction of the North Side Canal and its distribution system in Minidoka County. The South Side canal system would be located in Cassia County and include three lift pumping stations to deliver water to the area's higher elevations. The project was designed to irrigate 120,000 acres on both sides of the river. The area extended east and west for twenty-one miles and north and south for eighteen miles.

Settlers, most with little money, were elated. Their arid land could finally be cultivated. They believed the irrigation water would make it possible to make a living off the land.

But plans sometimes change. The government took some of the funds earmarked for Milner Dam and transferred them farther west to the Boise-Payette irrigation project. There was enough federal money left to finish the pumps and three lift stations. But there weren't any funds to complete the dam or build necessary canals.

The pioneers of Minidoka and Cassia counties realized that when a fly lands in the ointment, you don't throw away the jar — you get rid of the fly. They formed the South Side Minidoka Water Users, Ltd. and found private funding to complete the project.

Stanley Milner, a Salt Lake City businessman, invested $30,000 in the project. Frank H. Bunn, a Pennsylvania steel tycoon, also invested. The Kuhn family, of Pittsburgh, financed much of the North Side distribution system.

Because of the shortage of funds, men digging the canals were often paid in "script" — a written promise to pay when money became available.

A completion date was set for the project. President Roosevelt assigned Secretary of the Interior James R. Garfield to make an on-site inspection. Preparing for Garfield's visit was a race against time with men and women working around the clock. The diggers carried their bedrolls with them and slept along the canal banks. Women traveled up and down the canals delivering hot food and coffee. The dam, canals and temporary wooden headgates were finished in time for Garfield's inspection.

Water stored behind Milner Dam totals 5.7 million acre-feet during an average year.

When the headgates were opened, cries of "Water's in! Water's in!" were heard up and down the system. The canals channeled the water from the reservoir, and the arterial ditches carried it to the land.

Settlers had individual headgates that, when opened, directed the water into their ditches. Only the watermaster could open the gates. He knew the amount of water allotted each farm and set the hours for the water to be used. If it was a dry year and water was scarce, it was the job of the watermaster to see that is was divided fairly among the users.

The water behind Milner Dam became the lifeblood of the settlers and their land. When the watermaster opened a headgate, the farmer was there with his shovel to open and close furrows and to watch for breaks in his ditches. During his turn with the water he worked around the clock to make the most of it. The term, "he has the water," excused a man from all other obligations, including funerals.

Turning desert into productive farmland had a price. The Snake River is America's classic example of a major stream nearly dried up by diversions. Fish, waterfowl habitat and recreation opportunities have been lost. Above Milner Dam, more than 300 canals and pumps divert Snake River water. During an average summer, the river flows at 8,000 cubic feet per second above the dam. Only about six cfs slip through cracks in the structure.

The rapids below Milner Dam once were the longest in Idaho, several times the length and challenge of the famed Lava Falls of the Colorado River.

Rafters and kayakers still run the section in early spring during high water years, before irrigation begins. But by the end of June, the riverbed below the dam virtually dries up.

Farther downstream, a "new" river forms. Streams and creeks feed into the Snake channel, partially filling it again.

Only two steamboats successfully navigated Hells Canyon — the Shoshone *in 1869, and the* Norma, *in 1895. Both made one-way trips downstream.*

THIRTY-NINE

Snake River — 1907

Peril Above the Falls

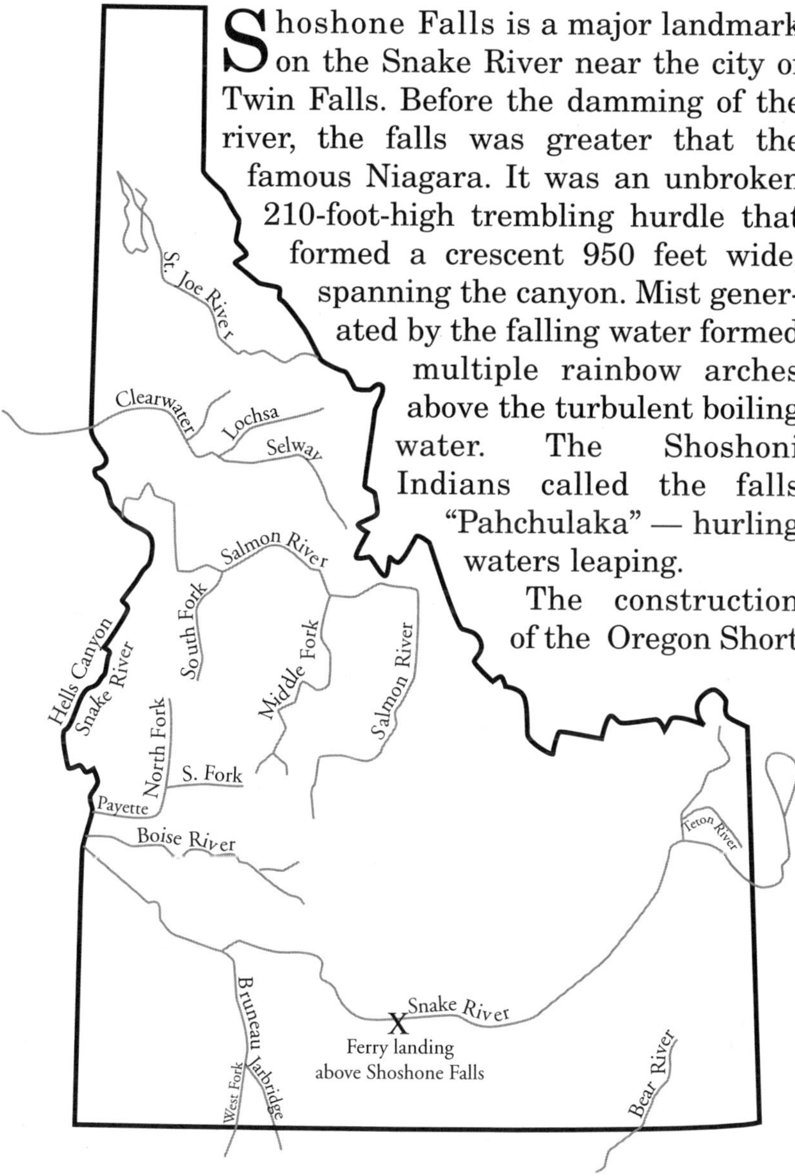

Shoshone Falls is a major landmark on the Snake River near the city of Twin Falls. Before the damming of the river, the falls was greater that the famous Niagara. It was an unbroken 210-foot-high trembling hurdle that formed a crescent 950 feet wide, spanning the canyon. Mist generated by the falling water formed multiple rainbow arches above the turbulent boiling water. The Shoshoni Indians called the falls "Pahchulaka" — hurling waters leaping.

The construction of the Oregon Short

Line Railroad, in 1889, created the need for a ferry. One was built about 200 yards above the falls. The flat-bottomed boat, guided by wire cables wound by a windlass — was called Shoshone Ferry. A rough wagon trail wound down the north canyon wall to river level, where the water was deep, wide and smooth. The surrounding cliffs reflected on the tranquil water as if the emerald-green Snake was a mirror.

Despite all the beauty, the sound of the water booming on the rocks below the nearby falls caused many travelers to worry that the ferry cable might break, catapulting them to certain death.

One May afternoon in 1907, two wooing men and their coy lady friends took a ride on the Shoshone Ferry, even though the river was swollen from the spring runoff. The party included Miss Belle Chambelain, State Superintendent of Public Instruction, Miss Louise Johnson, State Librarian; and their escorts, I. B. Todd of Chicago and H. M. Hebben of Boston.

The warm spring air was filled with the pungent scent of the surrounding sagebrush steppes. Calls of the canyon wren echoed among cliffs dressed in hues of gray. It seemed the perfect time to embark on a romantic journey across the river.

The ferry carrying the two couples slid smoothly across the river, as the ferryman onshore worked the windlass. But midway across the river, an ominous snap was heard. Four people felt their stomachs churn as the ferry swung to race toward the falls.

Fortunately, the two men were able to grab the broken cable before it slithered off the raft and into the river. They tied the cable to their craft. Held by the tether, the ferry snaked back and forth in the current like a hooked sturgeon. The horrified women stood with their backs to the beckoning falls and their eyes focused hopefully toward the shore.

The thunderous sound of the Snake falling over the lava cliff and billowing mists provided an appropriate backdrop for the drama. The men on the ferry and the worker on shore battled the river for more than a half an hour, feet braced and muscles straining.

The crippled ferry inched toward the bank where a skiff waited to take them back to the landing. After the women were safely ashore, the city gentlemen proved their mettle by staying on the ferry until it was secured.

Business was never very good for the Shoshone Ferry owner. He barely made a living. In 1921 he was ordered to give up his license because of numerous reports that he was operating the ferry while intoxicated. That's when officials discovered the ferryman couldn't give up his license because he didn't have one in the first place.

Lewiston, located 470 river miles inland, is Idaho's only seaport.

FORTY

Salmon River — 1908

Taylor's Ferry Tale

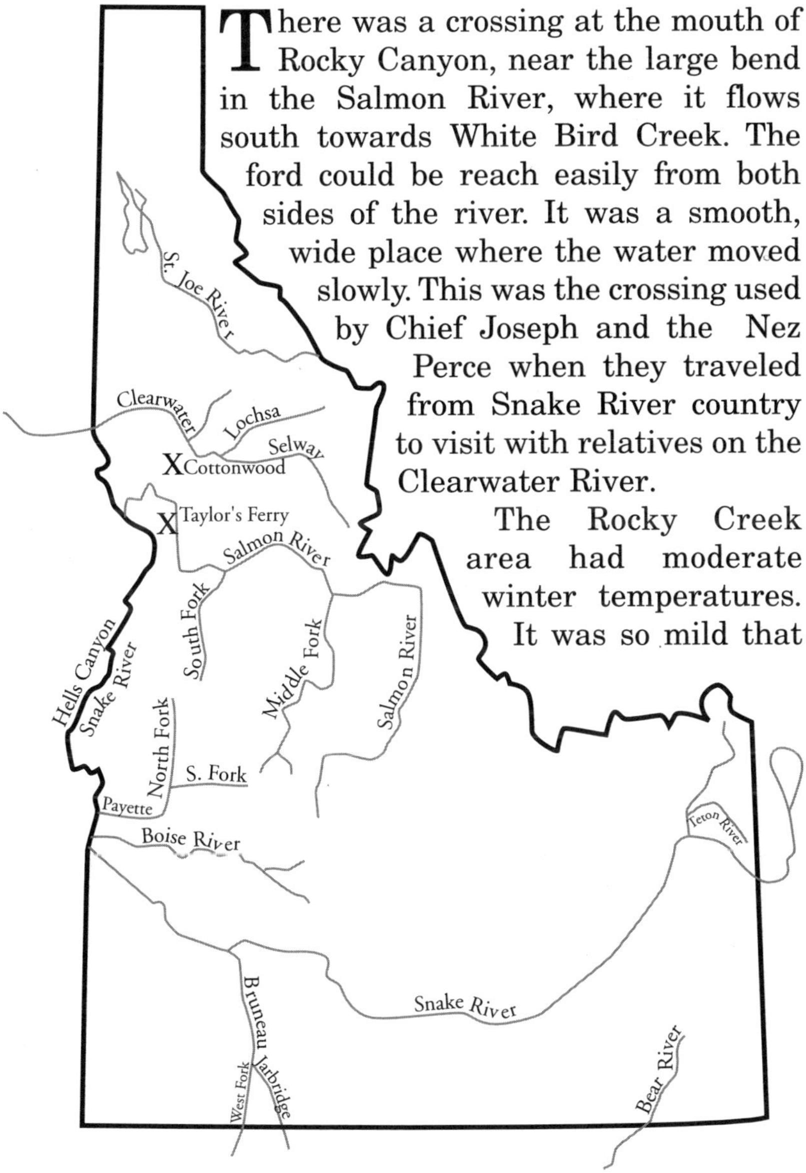

There was a crossing at the mouth of Rocky Canyon, near the large bend in the Salmon River, where it flows south towards White Bird Creek. The ford could be reach easily from both sides of the river. It was a smooth, wide place where the water moved slowly. This was the crossing used by Chief Joseph and the Nez Perce when they traveled from Snake River country to visit with relatives on the Clearwater River.

The Rocky Creek area had moderate winter temperatures. It was so mild that during the 1860s, prospectors from nearby mining town of Florence came down the mountain to winter near the crossing. They placer mined along the Salmon River and White Bird Creek during the winter, then returned to the mountains in the spring.

In the late 1800s, a man named Ed Taylor homesteaded near the mouth of Rocky Canyon. Ed was a farmer. He planted a large vegetable garden on the bar above the river, where the soil was rich and fertile.

Ed sold his produce at the settlement of Cottonwood, about a day's ride from the crossing. The route to Cottonwood was rough. So with the aid of a neighbor, George Burgund, he improved the road using pick and shovel. The road became the first wagon route down Graves Creek and Rocky Canyon to the Salmon River.

Because the road was rough, the two men built a heavy-duty wagon with solid wood wheels. During their journey's to Cottonwood, one man drove the wagon slowly while his partner walked behind with a crowbar. When the axle hit a high stump or rock, the crowbar was used to free it.

Traffic increased on the improved road. More settlers forded the river at the Rocky Canyon crossing to reach the road. That inspired Ed Taylor to build a ferry to supplement seasonal income from his vegetables. The cable ferry featured a boat fitted with pontoons. The pontoons reduced the force of the swift spring current on the cable and the ferry.

The ferry was a success but Ed's first love was his garden. He spent as much time as possible among his vegetables. His tomatoes were his most outstanding

Jim Paxton

achievement. The vines grew stout and strong to support the large red orbs of ambrosia. When the citizens of Cottonwood praised Ed's tomatoes, he swelled with pride.

One spring day Ed was summoned from his garden to ferry two men and some cattle across the river. Normally, Bill Eller and Rich Nash swam their stock across the river. But an unusually high spring runoff made that method dangerous.

Because of the weight of the cattle the ferry should have made two trips. But Ed was eager to get back to his garden, so he crammed the entire herd on the ferry at once.

The ferry creaked and groaned, and the extra weight nearly submerged the pontoons. The cable sagged. Suddenly, one of the anchors gave way, freeing the ferry.

Taylor's Ferry plunged into the first big wave at the top of a long rapid, drenching men and cattle. Normally, the stretch would have been filled with boulders. But with the river running high, it became a series of standing waves. The weight of the cattle kept the craft from capsizing. Instead of going over the waves, the ferry plowed straight through them. The three men clung to the rails, trying to keep their balance while avoiding the wild-eyed cattle.

It was a wild ride unlike anything previously experienced by the men or the cattle.

Above the roar of the river, Bill Eller heard his name being called. He looked at Ed Taylor, whose eyes remained fixed on his homestead back upriver. "Bill," Ed yelled above the clamor of the wave breaking over the disabled ferry. "You can raise more tomatoes on that high bar than any place on the Salmon River."

Suddenly, the ferry ground to a halt — stuck fast on the gravel bar of a small island. Men and cattle made it safely to shore.

Ed gave up his ferry business after the cattle episode. People soon forgot the ferry, but Ed Taylor's tomatoes were long remembered.

The first electric lights in Boise, Idaho were powered by two small water turbines. The electricity flowed for the first time on July 4, 1887.

FORTY-ONE

Snake River — 1908-1939

McKeeth's Ferry: Idaho's Last

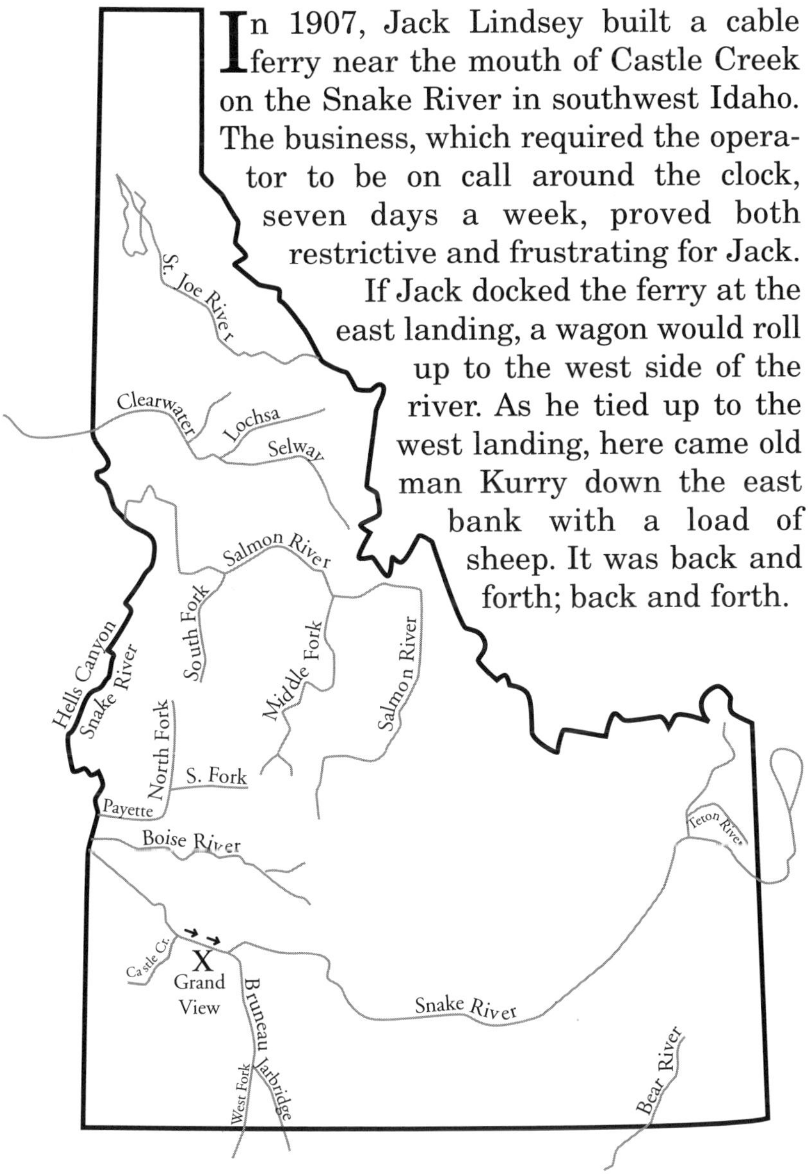

In 1907, Jack Lindsey built a cable ferry near the mouth of Castle Creek on the Snake River in southwest Idaho. The business, which required the operator to be on call around the clock, seven days a week, proved both restrictive and frustrating for Jack. If Jack docked the ferry at the east landing, a wagon would roll up to the west side of the river. As he tied up to the west landing, here came old man Kurry down the east bank with a load of sheep. It was back and forth; back and forth.

Sometimes lines formed at the landings as Jack scrambled in the summer heat or winter cold to get everyone across. But he spent some days swatting flies or skipping stones waiting for fares that never came. After a year of operating the ferry, Jack was tired of the whole business.

During a sweltering summer day in 1908, as Jack sat fanning flies, two of the McKeeth brothers, Vaughn and Lynn, rode up to the landing. By the time they reached the far shore of the river, Jack had talked them into buying the ferry for $500.

The young men were excited about their acquisition. They faced a major problem, however. The boat had to be moved eighteen miles upriver to their family's homestead. The silver-tongued duo talked two of their brothers, Roy and Ross, into handling the task while they built the landing for their new operation.

A team of horses was hitched to the ferry by a series of ropes and pulleys. One of the brothers handled the team while the other rode the ferry. As the sweat-soaked horses strained along the bank, the man on the ferry used a long pole to keep the craft from running aground or striking a boulder. At night, the muscle-weary men camped on sandbars along the river. It took four days to complete the trip.

Lynn and Vaughn alternated on ferry duty, rotating every week. Business boomed, since the ferry was located near the growing town of Grand View.

By 1921 all the ferries operating along the Owyhee County stretch of the Snake River had been discontinued or replaced by bridges — except McKeeth's Ferry. The brothers sold their operation to Dave Hood, who lived in a small cottage on the west bank with two goats. Dave operated the business for seven years without a break.

In 1928, Dave made a deal with a neighbor's twelve-year-old son, James Hallford. James agreed to operate the ferry for a year while Dave took a vacation. The young man was expected to keep the ferry, bullwheel, cable and landing in good order. In return, Hallford got all the ferry receipts collected during the year.

Dave Hood returned the following summer to a smooth-running business and resumed his ferry career. But the next summer season, as Dave was sweeping the deck of his boat, he suffered a heart attack and died.

Several people operated the ferry during the next nine years. Idaho's last operating ferry sank in 1939 while hauling sheep. Twenty years later, a portion of the deck was salvaged and used as a private fishing pier.

About 100 miles of the Snake River — from Hells Canyon Dam, to Lewiston — is much the same as it was when the first white explorers came to the region.

FORTY-TWO

Boise River — 1911

Arrowrock Dam

In 1894 Congress passed the Carey Act, named for Wyoming Senator Joseph M. Carey, the bill's author. The act was designed to help farmers claim arid lands in seventeen western states. The land gave each of the states in the dry region one million acres, providing they build the necessary dams, reservoirs and canals to irrigate the land. Two-thirds of all Carey Act claims — nineteen — were filed in Idaho.

Persons who wished to secure

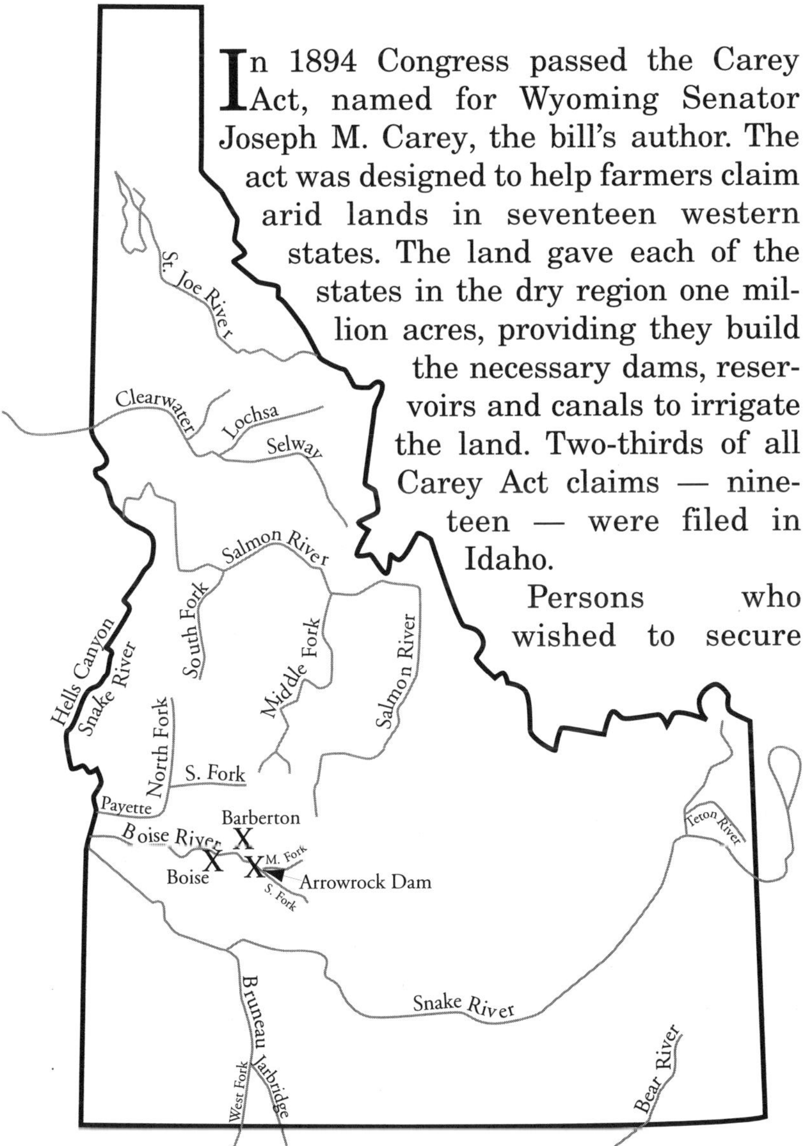

farmland under the act first applied to the state Board of Land Commissioners. If the board approved, the application was submitted to the Secretary of the Interior. Once approved by that federal agency, it was passed back to the state level. Individuals making claims were given liens to the land in lieu of payment for the irrigation systems they were expected to build and maintain.

By 1900, there were nearly 1,600 farms scattered across the Boise Valley in southwest Idaho. The settlers eked out meager livings on land covered with sagebrush and infested with jackrabbits. Although some canals were built to bring water to the desert, there wasn't enough to meet the growing demand.

Idaho, just ten years into statehood, faced the threat of losing population unless a method could be found to turn the arid desert into irrigated farmland.

Congress passed the Reclamation Act of 1902 to solve problems faced by Idaho and neighboring states. The act spawned the Bureau of Reclamation. It allowed the federal government to advance funds to build large dams and other facilities vital to major irrigation projects. The no-interest federal loans were to be repaid by the water users over a period of years.

In 1905, the Secretary of the Interior approved an irrigation project on the Boise River. By the summer of 1910, enough money was available to begin construction of the dam, to be located twenty-two miles upstream from the city of Boise. A large stone outcropping, known as Arrow Rock, jutted into the river near the dam site. The project became known as Arrowrock Dam.

Frank T. Crowe, considered one of the world's greatest dam builders, was hired as construction supervisor. James Munn was project superintendent. Engineers were told to include a special log chute at the dam that could send one million board feet of logs a day from the reservoir to the lumber mills downstream. The design also included provisions for future hydroelectric generators.

The first step was to build a diversion dam to channel water around the construction site. It was completed in 1912. A temporary hydroelectric generator was installed at the diversion dam to supply electricity for construction equipment and worker living quarters.

A small town, Arrowrock City, rose on a flat below the dam site. It could accommodate 1,500 men. It had a fully-functioning YMCA, hospital, movie theater and large clubhouse with billiard tables. There also was a gymnasium, commissary, mess hall and bath house. The town had running water, electric lights and a sewer system. The common laborer made $2.40 to $2.50 an hour, plus room and board.

A telephone system with fifty-four miles of line connected the Boise Reclamation Service office to the various work sites. A sawmill, seventeen miles away, provided lumber for building forms for the massive concrete structure.

A seventeen-mile standard-gauge railroad was built connecting Arrowrock with Barberton, located on the edge of Boise, the nearest link to the Oregon Short Line Railroad. The rail line was used to haul building material, food, supplies and mail.

Excavation for the foundation of the dam and spillway began in 1913. More than 250,000 cubic yards of rock, sand and clay had to be removed from the riverbed. A plant was built thirteen miles away to supply gravel for 600,000 cubic yards of cement for the dam. A sixteen-car train left the plant for the dam site every two hours. At the dam, aggregate was combined with cement and delivered through three-inch pipes by compressed air to mixers that prepared two tons of concrete per minute. The concrete was hauled through a tunnel in small electric cars to the distribution tower. A cable-tram carried buckets from the tower to hoppers above the forms.

By January 1914, the grouting of the foundation and abutments and the drilling of drainage holes was completed.

The men worked in two shifts. The day shift began at 8 A.M. and ended at 5 P.M. The night shift ran from 5:30 P.M. to 1:30 A.M., with the crew working by spotlight.

By April 1914, as the dam neared completion, work went on around the clock. The dam was finished before the end of 1914 — two years ahead of schedule, at a cost of $12 million. At that time, Arrowrock was the highest dam in the world at 328 feet. The reservoir was eighteen miles long and could hold 276,500 acre-feet of water.

The benefits of the dam were immediate. The summer of 1915 was one of the driest on record. The reservoir provided badly-needed water for 1,600 settlers.

The completion of Arrowrock also brought more newcomers to the Boise Valley. Thousands of acres were offered for sale to the new arrivals. Blistering stretches of wasteland bloomed into fruitful orchards and gardens. Within twenty years, the amount of farmland in the area tripled, with 374,218 acres under irrigated cultivation.

In 1937, the Bureau of Reclamation added five feet to the crest of Arrowrock Dam, providing additional 30,000 acre-feet of water storage.

The Snake River white sturgeon, a fish that has changed little since prehistoric times, can reach lengths of twelve feet and weigh as much as 1,500 pounds.

FORTY-THREE

Snake River — 1911

The River versus the Railroad

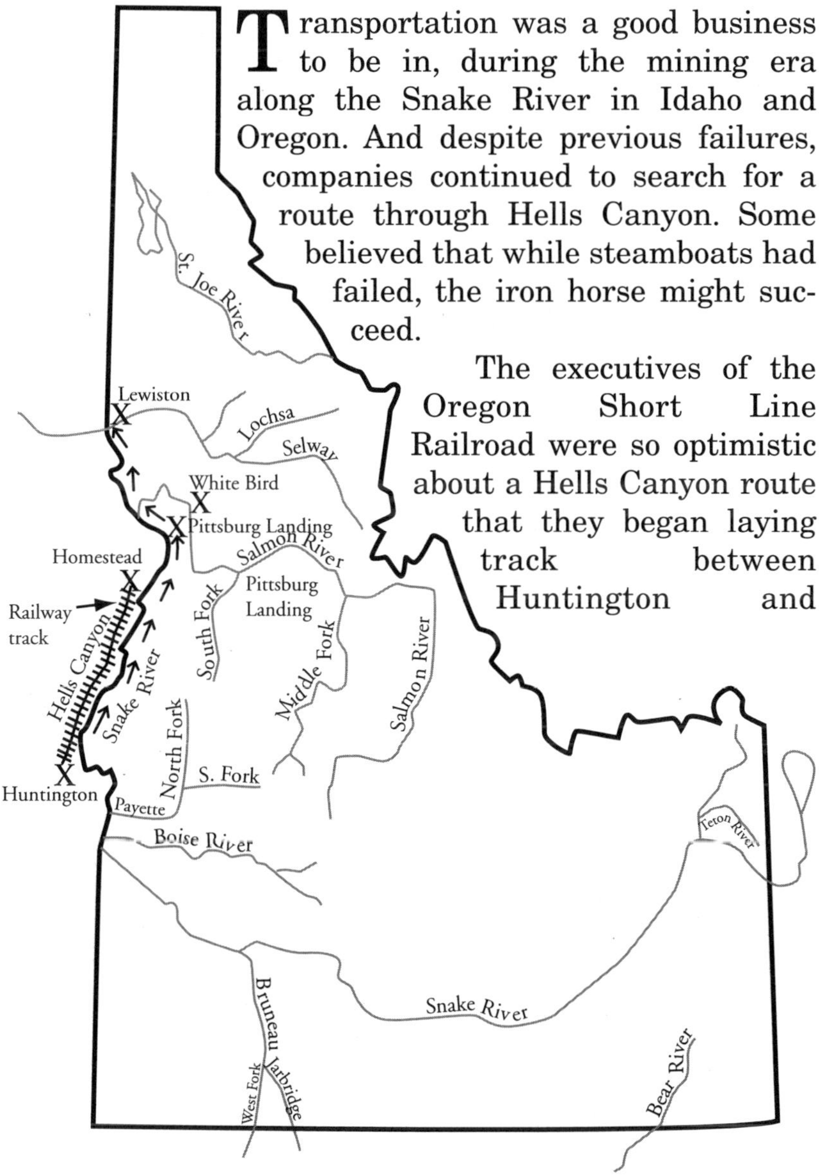

Transportation was a good business to be in, during the mining era along the Snake River in Idaho and Oregon. And despite previous failures, companies continued to search for a route through Hells Canyon. Some believed that while steamboats had failed, the iron horse might succeed.

The executives of the Oregon Short Line Railroad were so optimistic about a Hells Canyon route that they began laying track between Huntington and

Homestead, Oregon before the route survey was completed.

On October 3, 1911, sixteen men left Homestead in six rowboats loaded with survey gear and camping equipment. The men had been hired by the Northwestern Railroad Company, a subsidiary of the Oregon Short Line Railroad. The project was directed by Chief Engineer Carl Stradley and Assistant Engineer Stacy.

There were no problems for the first fifteen miles of the trip. Then the travelers encountered the fierce waters of Lynch Creek Rapid. The first boat flipped. The three passengers tumbled down the white torrent. One man seemed to have particular difficulty reaching shore. When he reached safety the reason for his problem was evident. Tightly clutched in one hand was a heavy survey transit he had grabbed as he went overboard. Several pieces of equipment were lost, along with some personal belongings. A chest containing writing paper was found floating in an eddy one and one-half miles downriver. The boat wrapped around a boulder and broke in half.

Camp was made above Lynch Creek Rapid. The next day was spent portaging around the rough water. It was hard work carrying the supplies and equipment along the rough shoreline. The empty boats were set adrift, then caught when they emerged from the lower end of the rapids.

Another mile brought the party to Squaw Creek Rapid. It took all day to line the five boats through the rough water and portage the equipment.

At noon on October 6, the survey party reached a rapid called "Big Bad Buck." One boat shot through before the crew could get it to shore. The men clung to the sides of the boat as it dove over the ledge, then pitched through the breakers below. The remaining boats were lined down, with two of them flipping. One boat was recovered but the heavy iron camp stove it carried was lost. With so many items stolen by the cantankerous Snake, the men and equipment could all fit in the four remaining boats.

The weather changed from Indian summer to rain.

On the fifth day of the trip, six hours were spent repairing damage on a boat that smashed into a boulder. At Fisher's Ranch, above Steamboat Rapid, the renegade boat that had disappeared at Buck Rapid two days earlier was found beached on a bar. A young rancher had captured it as it floated past. The surveyors bought pears, apples and bear meat from the homesteader.

Rain continued to fall during the following days — days spent lining and portaging.

By October 15, the party had only traveled forty miles in twelve days. At Wannick Ranch they sent word to the outside world that they had lost their stove, a tent and several bedrolls. Assistant Engineer Stacey rode in with a packer from Imnaha with the needed items.

A camp was set up and surveying began. Eleven days later camp was moved five miles downstream from Wannick Ranch. George Heydrick, a rodman, had been ill several days. He was moved two miles downstream to Pittsburg Landing, where he was taken by buggy to White Bird for medical attention. Within three days the entire camp moved to the landing. Surveying the area took ten days. Then camp was moved to Summer's Creek.

The day after they arrived at Summer's Creek, the men learned George Heydrick had died of typhoid pneumonia.

Winter arrived and ice formed along the banks of the Snake. Moving six miles downstream to Rowland's Bar was difficult. The survey line had to be pushed along cliffs while one member of the party brought the boats downriver.

The survey crew reached the range of the *Flyer*, a thirty-six-foot-long boat powered by a twenty-five horsepower engine, that made weekly runs upriver from Lewiston. The *Flyer* transported the camp to Cache Creek. Five men stayed behind to bring down the boats.

By Christmas, snow covered the ground and the river was clogged with ice. The survey moved slowly, the men spending much of their time looking for firewood. They didn't reach the mouth of the Grande Ronde River until January 6. Seven days later the crew broke camp for the last time.

The river was filled with large cakes of ice, making it nearly impossible to maneuver the boats. The men entrusted themselves to the current. Several rapids were run with the boat passengers clinging to their bobbing craft. At times the ice-free portion of the channel was barely wide enough for the boats to pass through.

Thirty-nine miles later, on January 6, at 2:30 P.M., an exuberant survey crew arrived at Lewiston.

The men challenged forty-three rapids and portaged twelve, during nearly four months surveying Hells Canyon and the Snake River. An analysis of their report showed the cost of laying track along the route would be about $198,000 per mile! The rails from Huntington to Homestead were pulled up.

The river had won.

The Middle Fork of the Salmon River is ranked one of the top ten whitewater rivers in the world.

FORTY-FOUR

Snake River — 1912

Silas' Sturgeon Hole

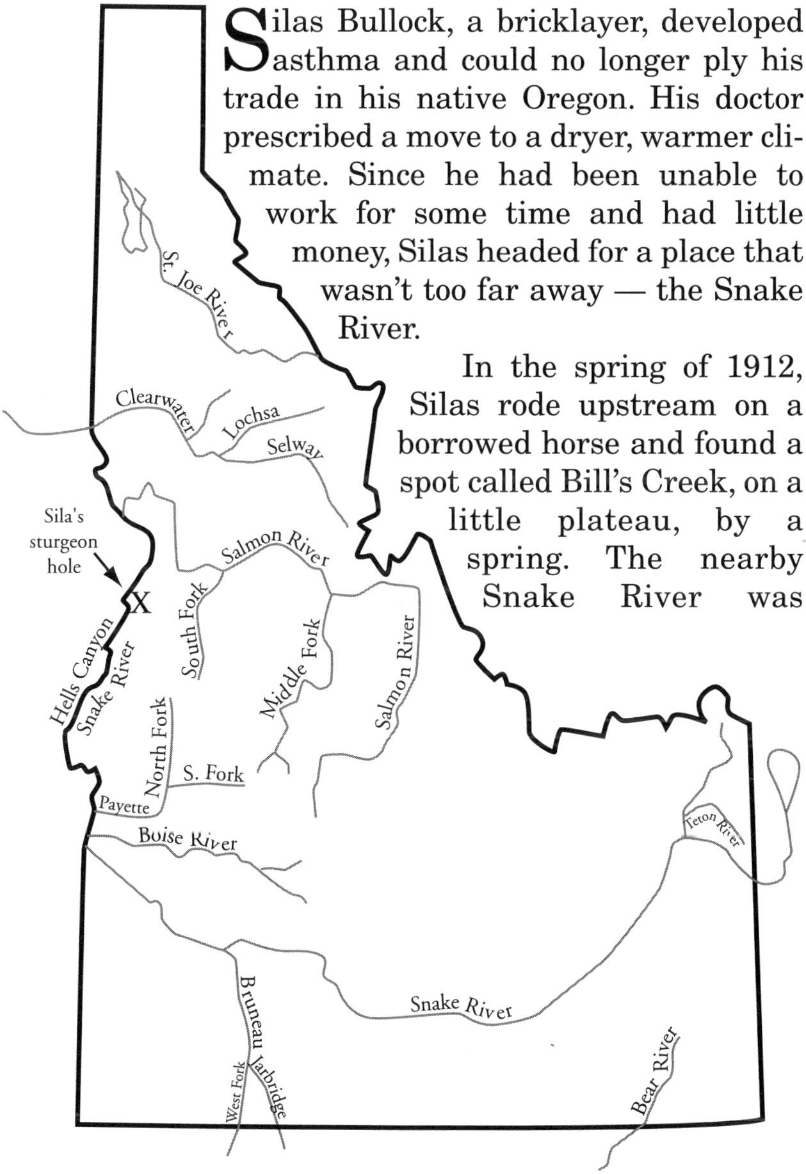

Silas Bullock, a bricklayer, developed asthma and could no longer ply his trade in his native Oregon. His doctor prescribed a move to a dryer, warmer climate. Since he had been unable to work for some time and had little money, Silas headed for a place that wasn't too far away — the Snake River.

In the spring of 1912, Silas rode upstream on a borrowed horse and found a spot called Bill's Creek, on a little plateau, by a spring. The nearby Snake River was smooth and formed a deep pool fringed by a stretch of soft, white sand.

Silas took the horse back to its owner, and returned to Bill's Creek to homestead. His first project was a garden, which thrived under his care. He built a stone lined root cellar to store the harvest.

His second project was a cabin. Wood was scarce in the area but rocks were plentiful. Using his mason skills, Silas used chunks of granite as bricks and soon had a fine, one-room cabin. The windows and doorway were framed with boards found in an upstream eddy. Timbers for the roof and floor were salvaged from a collapsed bridge.

Because he was so busy during the first year getting settled in, Silas paid little attention to the river. But one hot spring day during his second year on the homestead he decided to take a swim and relax in the sun on the sandbar.

The water was cold and invigorating. Silas dove into the river and was swimming along when he saw something that nearly made his heart stop. Directly below loomed a dark form nearly ten feet long. Silas thrashed to shore in a panic, beaching himself half out of the water as he gasped for breath. Peering over his shoulder, he saw a foot-long section of tail and dorsal fin showing above the water. He let out a startled cry and clawed his way up the sandbar.

Silas stayed away from the river for the next few weeks. Then one morning as he was working in his garden, he saw a curious sight. Two scruffy-looking men came downriver in a small boat and speared one of the shark-like creatures in the pool. He rushed down to the sandbar and helped haul the monster out of the river.

The men were commercial sturgeon fishermen, and spent most of the year along the river. Pack trains met them a various locations to collect their catch and haul it to Lewiston. Silas learned the roe from the sturgeon was valuable. It was salted down and shipped to large cities such as Portland and San Francisco, and sold as caviar.

The men were towing several logs. The sturgeon were tied to the logs to keep them alive until the fishermen met a pack train. The fish were then killed and cleaned.

The ten-foot monster from Silas' hole weighed more than 500 pounds. He examined the prehistoric-looking gray fish. It had bony plates rather than scales along its sides. He was told the skeleton was cartilage rather than bone. The sucker month, shaped like a large, short tube, was used to grub about in the sand and ooze for mussels and minnows.

The sturgeon didn't look like anything a person would want to eat. However, the fishermen gave Silas a three-foot sturgeon and encouraged him to try it.

When his guests departed, Silas fried some of the fish. After the first hesitant bite of the succulent, fine-grained white flesh, he knew that thereafter, no man would be allowed to trespass in his fishing hole. He filleted and salted the remaining meat, then packed most of it away in a ten-pound lard bucket and submerged it in the creek to keep it cool.

Silas decided to make his own fishing gear. He made a spear and fastened one end of a long rope to the handle. He tied the other end to a stout mountain mahogany bush near the bank.

After several days of watching and waiting, Silas was beginning to think he might never taste sturgeon again. Then one morning he fixed himself some lard biscuits for breakfast. There was a large ball of dough left over. He attached the dough and some bacon to a large steel fishing hook.

Sinking the bait deep in the pool, Silas crouched on the sandbar and waited. Eventually, he became discouraged and went off to tend his garden. Later than day, he saw the mahogany bush shaking violently. There was a fish on the line!

Silas wore himself out trying to get the sturgeon ashore. He tumbled into bed that night with the fish still in the water. He fought for two more days and failed to land it.

Ken Taylor, an engineer for the Union Pacific Railroad, was investigating the possibilities of a train route along the river. While traveling the rocky trail, his horse went lame. Being an engineer, not a farrier, he didn't check to see if his mount had picked up a stone in its hoof. Leading the limping animal, he spied a small rock cabin perched on a flat above the river. Smoke snaked lazily from the chimney. He was approaching the dwelling when a short, stout man rushed out carrying a shotgun in one hand and a butcher knife in the other. He had a full beard and long, curly, gray-streaked brown hair. With hazel eyes agleam, Silas proclaimed with glee, "You're just the guy I'm looking for! Get your horse and follow me!"

A shaken Taylor protested that his horse was lame. After examining the hoof, his host dislodged a small stone, then reissued his original command.

Taylor reluctantly followed the excited man to the river. Silas untied the rope from the bush and looped it around the saddle horn. Taylor was instructed to slowly lead his horse away from the river. When the rope tightened, he looked back and saw a giant fish thrashing in the shallows. His horse strained forward and inched the sturgeon up onto land. Silas shot the monster in the head with his shotgun and then went at it with the butcher knife.

The sturgeon was the first Taylor had ever seen. He was nearly as excited about the catch as Silas. He helped cut up the eight-foot fish, then stayed for lunch to feast on the bounty.

After Silas learned the proper fishing technique he caught plenty of sturgeon. Many a traveler was recruited to haul a thrashing giant from the river. Silas' hole was the best on the river and he guarded it zealously.

In 1926, Silas moved to California to be close to relatives. His years on the Snake River had cured his asthma and he resumed his career as a bricklayer. He died of heart failure two years later.

Five Mile Rapid, on the Bruneau River, drops 100 feet per mile for almost five miles.

FORTY-FIVE

Snake River — 1925

Amos Burg

In 1915, a fourteen-year-old youth, Amos Burg, traveled from his Portland, Oregon home to Lewiston, Idaho to visit a friend. At Lewiston, Amos purchased a canoe and convinced his friend to join him on a river adventure. The two journeyed down the Snake to the Columbia and paddled all the way to Portland.

During the next ten years, Amos canoed Alaska's Inland Passage to the mouth of the Fraser River, twice floated the Columbia from its Canadian source to

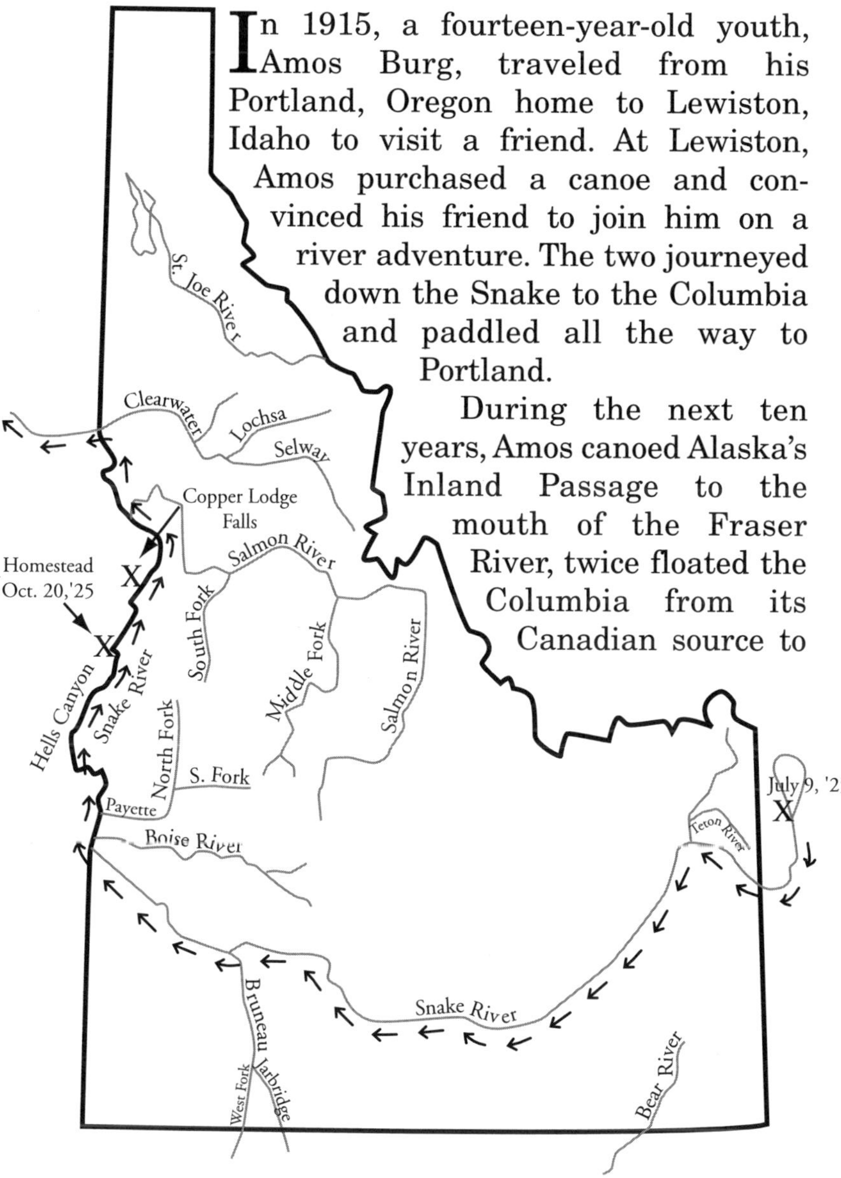

the Pacific, and canoed the Yellowstone, Missouri and Mississippi rivers.

On July 9, 1925, Amos began a canoe journey at the headwaters of the Snake River in Yellowstone National Park in Wyoming. By the time he reached Homestead, on the Oregon side of the Snake, above Hells Canyon, he had survived the loss of a canoe, numerous dangerous portages, and many challenging rapids.

At Homestead, Amos readied his craft, *Song o' the Wind*. Because he was unfamiliar with the territory, the twenty-four-year-old adventurer sought out someone who knew the gorge. A prospector named John Mullins claimed to know every rock, rapid and boulder in Hells Canyon. Mullins was willing to strap on a cork life jacket, climb into a canvas-clad canoe and try to make history with Amos Burg.

The two men left Brockman's Ranch on the morning of October. 20, 1925, with John in the stern manning the steering paddle and Amos rowing from the middle of the boat.

None of Amos Burg's previous river experiences had been as stimulating and the canyon's first big challenge — Kern Rapid. From a hillside, the rapid seemed to be a fierce-flowing stretch of water with a long stretch of standing waves. There was a straight shot down the tongue, so the men opted to run the rapid instead of lining their empty boat through it.

As though in slow motion, the canoe slid down the shimmering green tongue, rapidly descended into a dimly-lit trough, then rose to the sparkling crest of the wave. *Song o' the Wind* roller-coastered through the quarter mile stretch, its occupant's exuberant cries lost in the ferocious growl of the river.

The next challenge was Squaw Creek Rapid, an obstacle course through a series of boulders. The canoe caught the edge of a hole and nearly capsized.

Buck Rapid, clearly the most difficult and impressive rapid on the Snake in those days, was scouted. Amos chose to line the boat through the falls, rather than carry the heavy craft along the rocky shoreline. When one of the lines broke, "Big, Bad Buck" swallowed the canoe and spit her out in the eddy below. Everything was securely fastened to the craft and little was lost in the river.

At Sawpit Rapid, the two men worked to maneuver the canoe through a series of rocky obstructions. The boat rammed into one of the boulders, shattering its stern. The wounded, half-submerged canoe, made it to shore where repairs were made.

At Steamboat Rapid (named after the winter layover of the steamboat *Shoshone*), a wave shoved the craft sideways and flushed Amos and John into the water. They bobbed to shore in their cork life jackets with the boat in tow. Just ahead was the roar of Copper Ledge Falls.

Once around the falls, the most difficult part of the journey was behind them. John Mullins was ready to return to Homestead. Seeing range horses grazing on the hillside, he roped one and rode off over the horizon. Amos Burg completed his trip to the mouth of the Columbia.

Four years later, Amos returned to the Snake River. His beloved *Song o' the Wind* was swallowed by a cataract on the upper section of the river.

Within sixteen years, Amos mastered the Yukon, Athabasha, Slave, McKenzie and Colorado rivers.

Amos made his third float through Hells Canyon in 1946. An established journalist and documentary photographer, he worked with the *National Geographic* and *Encylopedia Britannica*. His Hells Canyon mission was to film the deepest gorge in North America. Members of the team included Dr. Russell G. Frazier, Charles H. Wheeler and A. W. Patterson. The crew traveled in three rubber rafts named *Charlie*, *Junior* and *Patches*. *Junior* flipped in the rapids at the base of Eagle Island, so a twelve-foot wooden boat was purchased for fifteen dollars from a nearby ferryman. The wooden craft was converted into the camp boat, carrying 500 pounds of camera equipment, food and clothing.

The rafts were lined through Squaw and Buck rapids. The wooden camp boat was heavily damaged at Thirty-two Point Rapid while being lined through the narrow passage. Socks and towels were used to bandage its cracked hull.

The camp boat and *Patches* were lined down Wild Sheep and Granite Creek rapids while *Charlie* bucked and bounced its way through with Amos at the oars.

During the eleven-day journey, 3,000 feet of color film was shot of the magnificent Snake and the Hells Canyon gorge.

"To my mind, the scenic grandeur of Hells Canyon equals that of the Grand Canyon," Amos said, "yet its majesty is pleasingly softened by abundant wildlife and vegetation not to be found on the Colorado River run."

Amos married in 1958. Carolyn, his wife, became an avid river runner. The couple owned their own twelve-foot Avon raft and journeyed many rivers together, including the Amazon, Orinoco and Magdelena. But one river Amos wanted to share with Carolyn was the Hells Canyon stretch of the Snake. In 1978, the seventy-seven-year-old Amos brought his wife to the gorge. It was, however, too late to relive his earlier adventures and the natural beauty of an untamed river.

"Dams," Amos said, "destroyed one of nature's most magnificent masterpieces."

Lake Pend Oreille, Idaho's largest, was a naval training base during world War II . Training submaries operated in the lake.

FORTY-SIX

Clearwater River — 1927

Clearwater Log Drives

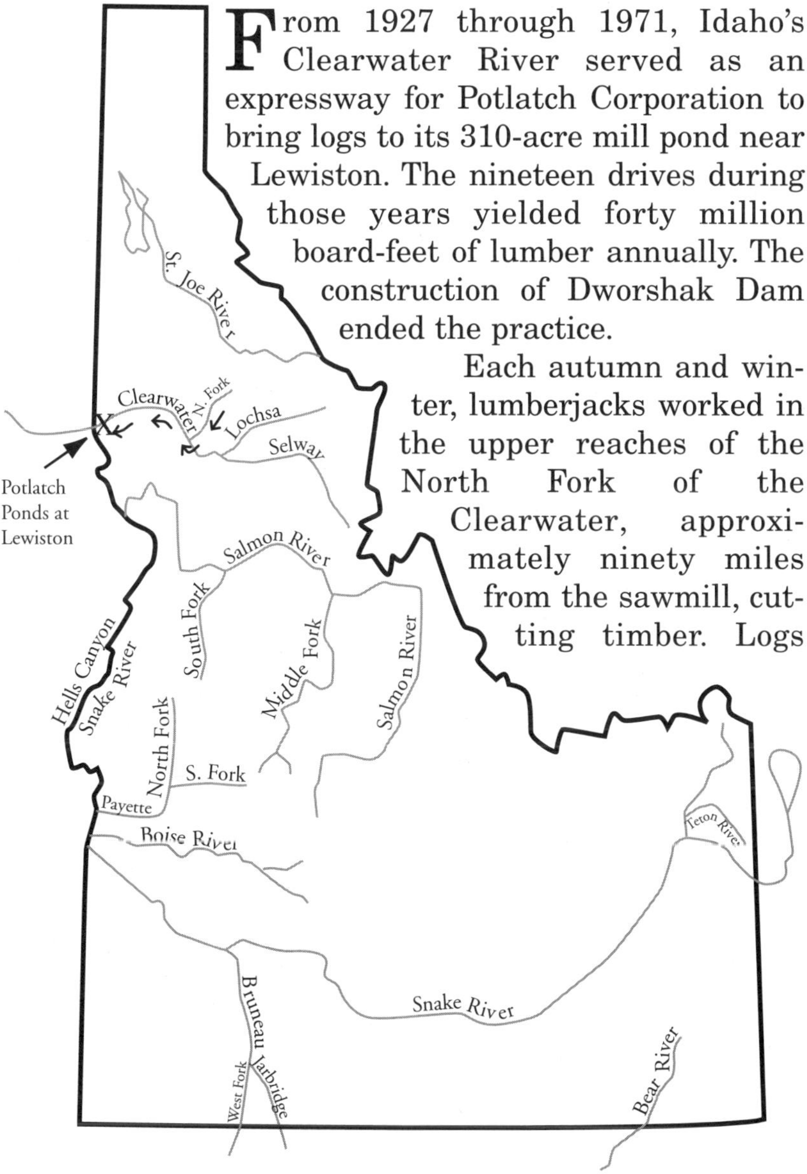

From 1927 through 1971, Idaho's Clearwater River served as an expressway for Potlatch Corporation to bring logs to its 310-acre mill pond near Lewiston. The nineteen drives during those years yielded forty million board-feet of lumber annually. The construction of Dworshak Dam ended the practice.

Each autumn and winter, lumberjacks worked in the upper reaches of the North Fork of the Clearwater, approximately ninety miles from the sawmill, cutting timber. Logs were piled in mile-long stacks until the spring run-off provided the river flow necessary to flush the timber downriver.

A high snowpack year with an early warm spell, such as occurred in 1938, washed logs to the millpond within hours. During dry years, low water caused mile-long log jams. The spring of 1933 produced such conditions, resulting in a drive lasting eighty-five days.

Preparations for the drive began in March. Three cedar rafts were built to house the portable camp. Two rafts were used as bunkhouses, holding sixteen cots each. The third served as the cookhouse. The rafts were tied together with the kitchen in the center. The floating camp was called a Wanigan.

The men cut off their pant cuffs to keep them from snagging on logs or filling with icy water. Spikes were hammered into boot soles. The spikes had to be checked nightly, throughout the drive. Missing or worn spikes were replaced and dull ones sharpened. Properly maintained spikes were essential for gripping logs and preventing tumbles into the river.

Peavey hook hinges were oiled. The indispensable Peavey was designed in 1858 by a Maine blacksmith, Joseph Peavey, after watching a river crew wrestle with a log jam. The tool consisted of a stout lever with a hinged spike used in rolling and diverting logs.

The men are awakened before daybreak on the first morning of the drive by "Cookie." The white-aproned figure bellows "roll out!" as he tolls a heavy iron triangle dangling from the side of the cookhouse. The "rearing" crew of more than thirty lumberjacks rolls from their bunks to don heavy woolens and

freshly-oiled spiked boots. They make their way to the bobbing mess hall where "flunkies" (kitchen helpers) pile their plates high with flapjacks covered with butter and molasses, and thick slices of bacon. Bowls of cereal, platters of donuts, pitchers of milk and carafes of strong tea or coffee cover the table. The men eat in silence. The mess hall is a place for fueling, not jawing.

Immediately after breakfast, the Wanigan casts off and heads down river, guided by massive sweeps fore and aft.

As the sky lightens, workers take their places in four bateaux — oar-powered boats with pointed bows. (In later years, twenty-two-horsepower engines were installed in the boats.) The men use their hooks to pry the key logs from the storage decks and logs begin spilling into the Clearwater. The drive is on!

The rearing crew trails the logs, watching for strays and jams. Thousands of logs tumble ahead, the rumble audible a mile away.

Two large logs are spotted beached on a submerged sandbar and another lodged against two boulders. A pair of bateaux tie up to shore and men jump into calf-deep water to pry the logs free. Sand and icy water flood their boots. They feet are rubbed raw as they grapple with their opponents, causing a foot condition known as "squeak heel."

The other boat follows the growling timber. The massive migration is beyond sight. There is suddenly a lull in the rumble, signaling that a jam has occurred.

The men in the boats approach the massive pile-up. Some logs are crisscrossed while others stand on end. The river backs up behind the timber dam, its pressure locking the mass into place. One bateau moves to shore. The ground crew will break the wing jam along the bank. The oarsmen in the other boat ease it to the center of the jam and try to hold it steady in the shifting current while the lumberjacks leap out.

Breaking up a jam is the most dangerous part of a drive. The logs creak and groan as the current grinds then together. With the crew boss shouting orders, men scatter across the jam searching for the key — one log locked into position that is holding back the entire drive. As men "hop the toothpicks," some logs roll beneath their feet, while others try to stand on end. Peavey hooks clatter as they probe for the key.

A lumberjack shouts above the racket of the jam — the key has been found. The crew converges on the spot to work the log loose. A cacophony of screeching drowns out the river as the jam gives way. Men scatter, some leaping into the bateau from moving timber, while others must ride the surge downstream, gripping the logs with their spiked boots.

One man looses his balance and falls in the thirty-five-degree water. He swims for his life, trying to stay clear of the racing logs. The ground crew rows into deep water to pull the swimmer to safety.

It is nearly an hour before the Wanigan appears, snubbed to shore. Most crew members are wet to their armpits, but only the violently shivering swimmer changes into dry clothes during lunch. Ham sandwiches and Paul Bunyan-sized slices of pie are washed down with tin mugs of steaming coffee. Sixty minutes pass between docking and launching back into the Clearwater.

Seven miles downstream there is another jam. It is smaller than the first, but logs are packed together tighter than sardines. Crews from all four boats work hours looking for the key. Twice it is found and twisted free, only to have the logs relock as another key wedges into place. By the time the reluctant crew boss gives the order to "blast it!" eyes can barely tell a log from a shadow.

Dynamite is set in the waning light. The explosion sends a geyser of water and splinters into the air and the stubborn mass of timber hastens on down the river.

Warm lights glowing from the Wanigan greet the crew. Men change into dry clothes before gathering for their meal. Afterwards, their boots are oiled and their spikes examined, buttons are sewn and tears in clothing mended. By nine o'clock they crawl exhausted into their cots — and dream of the clang of the "gut hammer" announcing the beginning of a new day.

FORTY-SEVEN

Salmon River — 1935

National Geographic Down the "River of No Return"

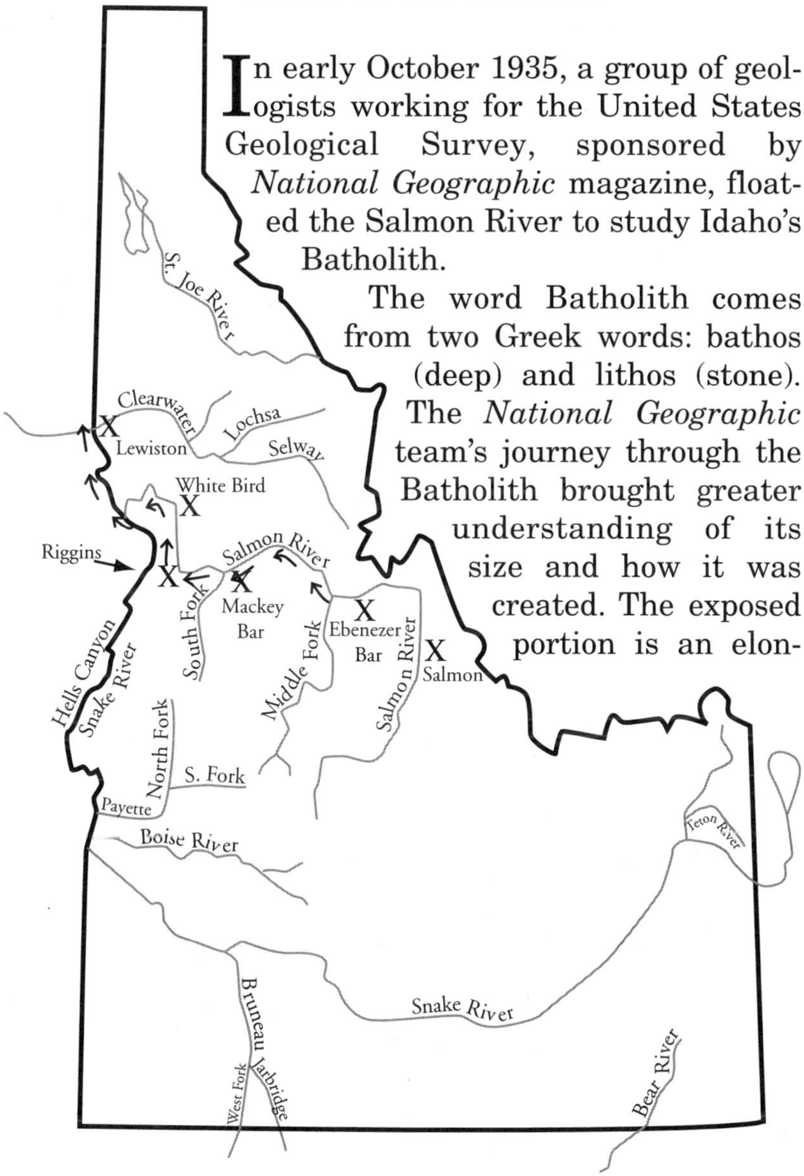

In early October 1935, a group of geologists working for the United States Geological Survey, sponsored by *National Geographic* magazine, floated the Salmon River to study Idaho's Batholith.

The word Batholith comes from two Greek words: bathos (deep) and lithos (stone). The *National Geographic* team's journey through the Batholith brought greater understanding of its size and how it was created. The exposed portion is an elongate, indented area with a north-south length of nearly 200 miles and an east-west width of approximately 100 miles. A myriad of mountains give relief to the stark angles of granite. The main Salmon River has cut a mile-deep east-west incision through the largest of Idaho's physical provinces, creating a geological feast.

Leaders of the expedition included Philip J. Shenon and John C. Reed. Dr. Maynard Owen, a writer and photographer for *National Geographic*, accompanied the group along with A.W. Fahrenwald, director of the Idaho Bureau of Mines and Geology. Howard R. Flint, regional Forest Service inspector was assigned to study the plants and animals. Idaho Representative D. Worth Clark, joined the adventurers to get a first hand view of the state's primitive area.

The party's boat was designed and built by Captain Harry Guleke. The thirty-two-foot craft had twenty-eight-foot sweeps located fore and aft. Each sweep had a six-foot blade. Sweeps are used to steer, not propel a river craft. Unlike rudders, they are held above the surface, except when needed to change course. The boat simply floats downriver with the current.

An elevated platform in the center of the scow provided footholds for the boatmen, as well as a better view of the river while steering. The boat bottom was double lined with green timber to withstand shocks from submerged boulders. A raised floor kept any water seepage from soaking the equipment. The sides of the hull were double-walled, creating storage compartments for canned goods and sleeping bags. The boat weighed nearly five tons when fully loaded.

Two boatmen were hired. The wife of Captain Monroe Hancock claimed he was "fit only for the rear sweep, since he could never make up his mind which way to go." John Cunningham manned the second sweep. Dave Chard, a colleague of Hancock, went along as cook.

Because it was autumn, the river was too low for the boat to carry a full load on the first leg of the journey — the fifty-six-mile stretch between Salmon and Ebenezer Bar. But a crowd gathered on the newly-built Salmon bridge to see the expedition off. So all the members boarded the craft and floated under the bridge to appease the spectators.

The men met the scow October 6, at Ebenezer Bar, where another crowd gathered to see them on their way. But because it was late in the day, camp was made for the night.

Dave Chard installed his galley, a full-size iron cook stove, in one corner of the boat. Work benches were added on each side of the stove. After breakfast of sourdough pancakes, the men began the 2,355-foot descent to Lewiston, 253 miles away.

The first rapid, Long Tom, was just above the mouth of the Middle Fork of the Salmon. The scow glided effortlessly through the rough water. Then camp was made, because Shenon, Reed and Williams planned a side trip up the rugged Middle Fork drainage to look for the Batholith edge.

Clyde Smith, an experienced boatman who lived nearby, joined the group at the camp for the pre-arranged excursion. Equipment was loaded into his small bateau. Members of the expedition left behind entertained themselves fishing for steelhead (Fahrenwald caught a fifteen-pounder). Meanwhile, Reed, Williams, Smith and Shenon fought their way up the Middle Fork. Three miles were covered before the muscle-sore men made camp.

No sign of the Batholith edge was found the next morning. Having no desire to tow the boat any farther up the river, the men boarded her and had a glorious whitewater ride back to the camp on the Salmon.

The scow continued down river after the men returned. The next camp was made five miles downstream at Bear Basin Creek. Hancock and Howard Flint were suffering from colds and enjoyed getting to bed early after a short day on the river.

The next day the boat shot down Killum, Gunbarrel and Horse Creek rapids. Camp was made on a sandbar. The four miles covered had been wet ones.

Beyond Horse Creek, the excited geologists entered the Batholith and for the next ninety miles passed between canyon walls carved deep into the great granite mass.

During the afternoon, the boatmen guided the heavy craft safely along the left side of a large hole near the top of Rainier Rapid. Five miles downriver they eased through the two jagged rocks of Devil's Teeth.

On the fifth day of the trip, the Salmon counted it first coup. At low flow, the river pours through three slots at Salmon Falls. Two of the slots were too narrow for the scow, so the crew had no choice but to take the third option. The boat wedged between two boulders and became stuck fast. Two placer miners who were in the area helped pry the craft free. The drenched men welcomed the hot water at Barth Hot Springs, two miles beyond the falls. Everyone felt better after a steaming soak.

It rained that night. Flint, still suffering from his cold, was in a feverish state. He rolled out of his bedroll and became soaking wet. When camp-mates discovered him in the morning, he was chilled and extremely weak. They decided to get Flint to a hospital as quickly as possible. One member of the group went downriver to find a cabin and radio for help. The nearest emergency landing strip was at MacKay Bar, twenty-five river miles and two days distant.

At Split Rock Rapid, just beyond Allison Ranch, all except the cook, oarsman, and Flint disembarked to lighten the boat. While swinging to avoid one boulder, the craft slammed into another rock, nearly capsizing. At Big Mallard, the craft was maneuvered to the left of a large boulder. Three miles downstream, skillful navigating was needed at Elkhorn Rapid. Less that a mile beyond, they approached Growler Rapid. With Flint confined in his sleeping bag, Hancock didn't want to take any chances upsetting the boat in deep water. He chose a shallow water route. The heavily loaded craft hung up on submerged rocks.

The men struggled for two hours to free the boat from the trap. Finally, a bridge of saplings was built so a ton and a half of cargo could be off loaded and carried to a sandbar downstream. Night fell before the scow was freed. After reloading, the expedition pushed on to Zaunmiller's Ranch, where the ailing Flint was given hot broth and a warm bed.

In the frosty chill of predawn, Flint was carried to the boat on an improvised stretcher. Groundhog Rapid, known as Whiplash during high flows, was of little consequence when run in the autumn. Eight miles downstream, the group briefly paused at Painter's Lodge for a meal. Then it was on to Mackay Bar, four miles downstream.

Pilot Dick Johnson was waiting at Mackay Bar to fly Flint to a hospital in Missoula, Montana. Flint was secured in an improvised bed in the front cockpit of the plane. His farewell words were, "Well, fellows, if the doc lets me, I'll join you in Riggins."

Flint died several days later.

After spending the night at Mackay Bar, the expedition continued. After passing the mouth of the South Fork of the Salmon, they encountered long stretches of smooth water. Reed and Chard tried to turn the slow-moving scow into a "windjammer" by making a sail out of a tarp. It obstructed the pilot's view of the river. But that wasn't the main problem. A wind started blowing the boat upstream. Camp was made at Sheep Creek

Sheep Creek Rapid and Carey Falls were challenged the following day, with no problems. But by midday, a strong wind again blew upriver, driving the heavy vessel backwards. Crude oars were unlimbered. For a time, the scow became a rowboat.

At French Creek, the party encountered a road after more that 100 miles of wilderness. The Civilian Conservation Corps boys were blasting a road upriver to Carey Creek. Two truckloads of C.C.C. lads followed the scow downstream, cheering as it approached the town of Riggins.

After spending two days in Riggins, the men resumed their trip October 20. From Riggins to White Bird the river paralleled the Idaho north-south highway for thirty-three miles. Riggins residents drove along the highway pacing the scow. They often raced ahead to vantage points above rapids to watch the craft plunge through.

At a rapid just beyond Freedom, the vessel caught on some submerged boulders near shore. Exuberant onlookers jumped from their parked vehicles and helped drag the boat off the rocks.

Below White Bird Creek, the group entered the little known, but thrilling lower canyon of the Salmon. The depth and rugged character of the gorge had previous made it nearly inaccessible. The characteristic feature of the area is the ancient lava flows that create a stair-step landscape. A few miles beyond is Green Canyon. The lower portions of the canyon walls are made of a dense, green rock called greenstone. The rock faces are so smooth that there are few places to tie the boat to shore. Green Canyon ends at Pine Bar Rapids, one of the worst on the river.

The boatmen scouted the rapid from the right bank and selected a course through the steep, tight, rocky stretch. Captain Hancock and John Cunningham successfully ran the gauntlet. At dusk, the boat approached Rice Creek, where a narrow gravel road from Cottonwood crosses the river at a bridge. The swift current swept the boat under the bridge where it hit submerged rocks and stopped. Philip Shenon was thrown against some cargo and badly bruised his hip. Fast water flowed around the craft. The men used poles to pry the scow off the rocks. Camp was made below Rice Creek.

It was late morning on October 25 before sunshine reached the bottom of the canyon. The explorers floated through a gorge strewn with pillars and angular blocks of lava as they approached Snow Hole Rapid.

Snow Hole, the most difficult rapid in the lower gorge during low water, was named for the white foam frothing in the eddy below. The boatmen scouted from the left bank. The course was just to the right of center, with no room for error. The cumbersome scow pressed through, then dove into the eddy, showering the cheering passengers with icy foam.

Near the mouth of Flynn Creek, the colorful greenstone replaced the lava again. This marked the beginning of Blue Canyon, home of The Slide (or Devil's Slide) rapid. It features a dreaded high water cataract formed by a landslide on the left side of the river. But low water reduced the rapid to amusement park status. It gave the passengers in the boat one last thrilling ride before the Salmon spat the scow into the lumbering Snake River.

The party's last camp was made at Asotin, Washington after floating thirty miles on the Snake. The next day, October 28, they arrived it Lewiston at 10 A.M.

Philip Shenon and John Reed's article, Down Idaho's River of No Return, appeared in the July 1936 issue of *National Geographic*. It contained photographs plus two maps.

FORTY-EIGHT

Salmon River — 1936

Middle Fork Adventures

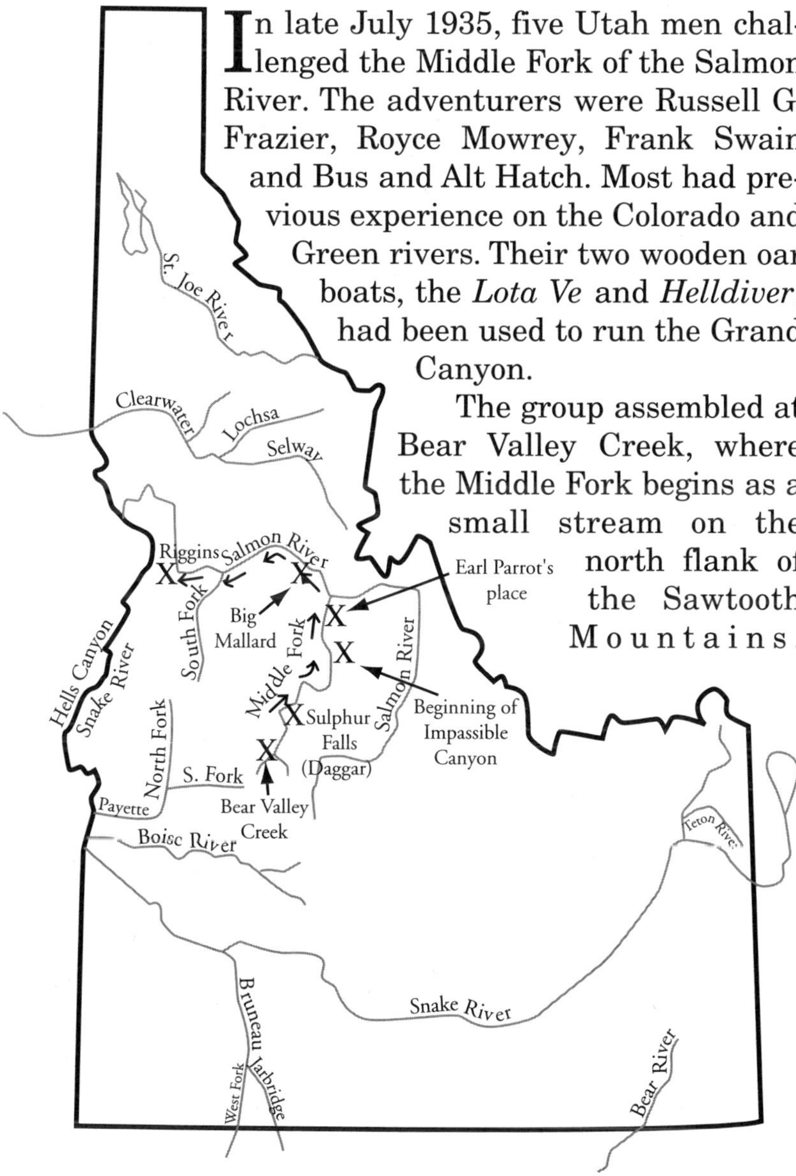

In late July 1935, five Utah men challenged the Middle Fork of the Salmon River. The adventurers were Russell G. Frazier, Royce Mowrey, Frank Swain and Bus and Alt Hatch. Most had previous experience on the Colorado and Green rivers. Their two wooden oar boats, the *Lota Ve* and *Helldiver*, had been used to run the Grand Canyon.

The group assembled at Bear Valley Creek, where the Middle Fork begins as a small stream on the north flank of the Sawtooth Mountains.

Modern rafters and kayakers avoid the stretch from Bear Valley Creek to Dagger Falls.

Nineteen thirty-five was a low water year, making passage on the upper Middle Fork extremely difficult. Some stretches were choked with fallen trees or sharp granite boulders. The bottoms of the boats frequently were torn while the craft were pushed and pulled through the maze. Twice, lodge pole pines had to be cut and split to replace battered flooring. Leaking seams constantly needed tar caulking.

Four days were spent struggling through the shallow water. When the tar ran out, the adventure had to be aborted. *Lota Ve* and *Helldiver* were cached above Sulphur Falls (now known as Dagger Falls). Frazier and his party hiked out.

The following winter featured heavy snow, so the adventurers planned to return to give the Middle Fork another try. They would have to float 108 miles down the Middle Fork to the main Salmon River, plus another 112 miles to Riggins.

For the second attempt, Frazier brought along some rubber belting from a conveyor to use to repair the hulls of the cached boats.

Bus Hatch and Royce built two additional boats. The bottoms of the shallow-draft vessels were made of three-quarter-inch plywood. The new boats were light enough to be carried by two men. They were named *What Next* and *Who Cares*.

The party, with two additional members — Wallace Calder and Bill Fahrni — arrived at Bear Valley Creek on July 6, 1936. *What Next* and *Who Cares* were loaded with enough supplies for two days. Bus Hatch and Wallace Calder took one boat, while

Frank Swain rowed the other. They pushed off at 5 A.M. July 7. They reached Sulphur Falls a day and a half later.

Russel Frazier, Alt Hatch, Bill Fahrni and Royce Mowrey took a pack train loaded with supplies to Sulphur Falls, where they refloored the cached boats with the conveyor belt. They arrived a day after the gloating boatmen. Enroute, the Frazier group encountered a "wanna be" boatman, John Marshall, and invited him to join the party.

All four boats had to be portaged (carried) around Sulphur Falls. Morley and Fahrni took *What Next*; Alt Hatch commanded *Who Cares*; Swain and Frazier piloted *Helldiver* and Bus Hatch and Marshall handled *Lota Ve*.

The first twenty-two miles below the falls passed swiftly. One rapid after another propelled the craft downriver at a pace that left little time to enjoy the scenery along the banks. The boatmen tried to avoid the holes that greeted them around almost every bend in the snaking river. They were only partially successful. With only one man in each boat free to bail, the river came in faster than it could be tossed out. At times that was a positive factor.

Velvet Falls, a short, deep drop into a large, swirling eddy, would have turned some of the boats over had they not been heavy with water. However, the sluggish vessels nearly found trouble at Pistol Creek Rapid, where a large boulder on the left side of the river had to be dodged at the beginning of the descent. The boatmen strained to get the craft into position to safely shoot the narrow passage.

Below Pistol Creek, the river mellowed out. Six miles downriver they glided past Pungo Creek where trappers Ed Bundell and Harry Jones had two log cabins and a large garden. Seven miles beyond, they stopped at Pottie's Spring, now called Sunflower Hot Springs. They had planned to stop at Sheepeater Hot Springs, twenty-two miles upstream. But the river hurried them along and they couldn't get their boats ashore in time.

Pottie's Spring did not have a large pool, but hot water bubbled up and trickled down the rocks into a bath-sized hole. The men took turns relaxing in the steaming water and soaking muscles strained at Pistol Creek.

A mile beyond Pottie's Spring was Milt Hood's commercial hunting and fishing camp. Middle Fork Lodge was the first such enterprise on the river.

Two days into their journey, the men floated past Falconberry Ranch at Loon Creek, an historical tributary on the Middle Fork. Gold was discovered there in 1869. More than 600 claims were staked along the creek. Sixteen miles beyond Loon Creek, the party stopped to visit with George Crandall and his wife. The land later became the Flying B Ranch.

Crandall had fenced his property to restrict a small herd of cattle. The rancher's home had carpeted floors, an unusual luxury on the Middle Fork. A gramophone entertained the guests. Even with few amenities, Mrs. Crandall enjoyed her primitive surroundings. She led a sheltered life, having not left the ranch for fifteen years. Pulling Frank Swain out of ear-shot of the group, she hesitantly asked if picture shows in the outside world really talked?

Two miles beyond Crandall Ranch, the adventurers ran Rattlesnake Rapid (currently called Haystack), located at the head of Impassible Canyon. Here the river narrows and waves develop in the confines of the canyon. It was within the shaded depths of Impassible that the party chanced upon a hermit.

At Nugget Creek, they pulled in at a small log shack on the right bank, and stepped into the Middle Fork's version of Alice in Wonderland.

"Dear Oliver," said a note on the cabin door. "The cork came out of that bottle of Poison and a lot of it spilled in here all over stuff. I don't know if it would be safe to use it, but be careful. Better not monkey with it. Come on up, Parrot. You remember what the druggist said, a little of it would kill a horse. Be careful how you stir things up, you can breath enough to kill you."

Three members of the party carefully checked inside the shack while the others went down to the sandbar to look at some bear tracks. When they returned to the shack the three men who had stayed behind had disappeared. An investigation revealed the cabin contained a container of cornmeal, an iron frying pan, a gold pan and an old blanket.

Behind the shack was a faint trail that led to a hawthorn thicket. A wooden ladder reached up a steep rock wall to a ledge above. From that ledge, another ladder extended higher on the cliff face.

The three missing men called from above and the four below climbed up to join them. They then ascended several more ladders, eventually ending up in a small valley about 2,000 feet above the river.

Following a trail through the lush valley, the explorers eventually arrived at a small cottage with a fenced garden. The garden was irrigated by a small stream that cascaded down from the canyon rim. Corn, melons, strawberries, beans and potatoes were bordered by raspberries, colorful cosmos and sweet peas.

The man cautiously approached the cottage and read the note tacked to the door.

"Some of everything in the garden is poison," warned the note. "Nothing in the house is poison. Help yourself."

Smoke curled from the cottage chimney. Bus Hatch knocked on the door but there was no response. Swain called out but no one answered. None of the men dared to open the door. An eerie silence fell over the place with only the cry of a canyon wren breaking the stillness. The men sat down outside the cottage to await the owner's return. Thirty minutes into their vigil, they were startled by a voice from above.

"What do you men want down there?" the voice asked.

Squinting against the afternoon sun shining through the leaves of a tree, they spotted a camouflaged platform in the upper branches. A small man with piercing eyes peered down at them. Finally persuaded that the visitors meant him no harm, the man climbed down from his perch.

The hermit's name was Earl Parrot. The men learned Parrot would celebrate his seventy-first birthday the following day. So they invited him to their boats for a celebration dinner. Parrot was so excited, he raced down the ladders face out, beating the other members of the party to the bottom by twenty minutes.

The party lasted late into the night. The following morning, the Hermit of Impassible Canyon stood on the bank and waved farewell to his new friends as they floated away.

Reaching the main Salmon River by mid-afternoon, the group stopped to visit with Clyde Smith and his son, Don, who had a cabin and placer mine downriver from the mouth of the Middle Fork.

A couple of days later, the men spotted a mother bear and her cub foraging along the river bank. Swain and Mowrey decided to try to capture the cub and take it home as a souvenir. But as the men rowed toward shore the bears scampered along the bank, staying out of reach.

By the time they heard the roar of Big Mallard Rapid, it was too late to get to the left side of the river where there was a passage next to a big boulder. Swain managed to miss the rock but flipped when his boat hit a large hole below. He and Frazier were caught in the toilet bowl action of the hole, but managed to break free and swim to shore. Mowrey, following close behind, missed the passage entirely and his boat catapulted over the top of the boulder. In the churning hole below, Mowrey tangled with an empty five-gallon tar bucket and broke his leg.

Meanwhile, Mowrey's passenger, Bill Fahrni, bobbed off downriver. Frank Swain thought to himself, "There goes Bill to Riggins — the hard way."

Bus Hatch, seeing his friends in trouble, hurried to help. But *Lota Ve* caught her bow on the rock and capsized. Alt Hatch and his passenger had seen enough. They pulled *Who Cares* ashore and rushed downstream to help their companions. All the boats and the bobbing Bill Fahrni, were rescued and most of the gear was saved. Alt Hatch's boat was lined over the falls.

It was another two days before the party arrived at Riggins, where Mowrey received medical attention for his broken leg. Their journey down the Middle Fork was the first documented full-length run.

FORTY-NINE

Snake River — 1939

Edith Clegg: A River in Reverse

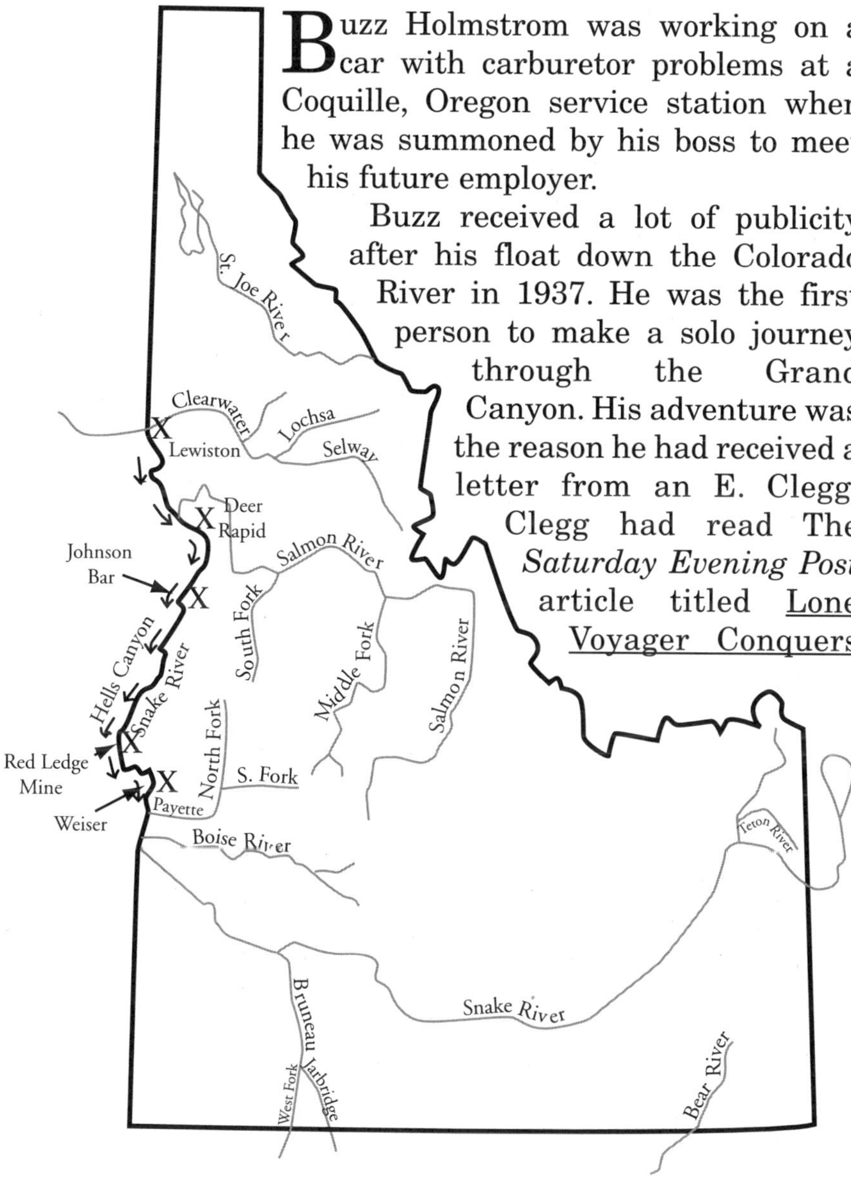

Buzz Holmstrom was working on a car with carburetor problems at a Coquille, Oregon service station when he was summoned by his boss to meet his future employer.

Buzz received a lot of publicity after his float down the Colorado River in 1937. He was the first person to make a solo journey through the Grand Canyon. His adventure was the reason he had received a letter from an E. Clegg. Clegg had read The *Saturday Evening Post* article titled Lone Voyager Conquers the Colorado. Clegg offered Buzz $150 a month to lead a river expedition that would cross the United States by water — from west to east. The money was too good for him to turn down.

When Holmstrom met his prospective employer, he gave Clegg a slack-jawed stare. Then with rude abruptness, he turned and went back to work on the carburetor.

Edith Clegg waited for the man to return. As a mother of four grown children and grandmother of nine more, the one thing the fifty-seven-year-old woman had in abundance was patience. The wealthy, widowed socialite from Vancouver, British Columbia, perched her petite, 100-pound frame on a stool and folded her manicured hands gracefully across her lap.

It had never occurred to Buzz Holmstrom that E. Clegg might be a woman. Once he recovered from the shock, he returned to the patiently-waiting Clegg and accepted the job.

Holmstrom designed two boats for the journey. Each fourteen-foot, flat-bottomed spruce hull was partially decked fore and amidships with watertight cargo compartments. Spare oars were lashed to the decks. Each boat was powered by a ten-horsepower Johnson outboard motor. The vessels were christened the *Mongoose* and the *St. George*.

The crew, hired by Holmstrom to handle the boats included "Doc" Hamilton, Clarence Bean, and Bill Johnson.

Doc Hamilton was a friend of Holmstrom's from Coquille. He had finished three years of college at Oregon State University and wanted to attend dental school in Portland. But he was short of tuition. The expedition money would finance his education. Doc's job was to maintain and repair the motors, hammer out bent props and operate one of the vessels.

Clarence Bean also was from Coquille. He was charming and entertaining, but reportedly lacked certain skills and common sense needed for river running. Rocks were hit and pins sheered when he took the throttle.

Bill Johnson was a coal miner from Thistle, Utah. He had accompanied Holmstrom on an earlier trip and proved himself useful. He did most of the cooking and kept everyone in high spirits with his entertaining stories and engaging sense of humor.

The adventure started on April 14, 1939, from Portland, Oregon. The group journeyed up the Columbia River to Lewiston. It was slow traveling as the two boats fought current and headwinds. The ten-horsepower motors were clearly too small for the *Mongoose* and *St. George*. Several hundred pounds of supplies were freighted ahead to Lewiston. Three members of the party walked along the bank to further lighten the load. Hamilton quickly developed serious blisters on his feet. He hobbled along with the aid of two walking sticks. He also was badly sunburned.

Five days into the adventure, Johnson injured his knee and had to ride in a boat.

Edith Clegg did more walking than any of the men. Holmstrom noted in his journal that Clegg "walks six to eight miles a day and none of us can outwalk her. She is tough as shoe leather and is a peach of a person."

It took sixteen days to reach Lewiston, plodding along at a snail's pace. The most challenging portion of the trip now lay ahead — the upstream assault on Hells Canyon. Perpetual Motion McKenzie had succeeded 120 years earlier with six men and a loaded barge. But local residents were skeptical. A common comment was, "The state border is the only thing that runs through that gorge without getting drowned."

Food and supplies were purchased in Lewiston. They were divided into four parcels and sent upriver on the *Idaho*, a twin-engine, gas-powered boat capable of carrying eight tons of cargo. The goods were unloaded at four strategic points between Lewiston and Johnson Bar.

The Clegg party departed for Hells Canyon on May 12, 1939, getting a late start and covering only eleven miles. The day was hot, with temperatures in the eighties. While Holmstrom and Hamilton ran the boats up Ten Mile Rapid, Clegg, Bean and Johnson walked.

The next day they were under way at 7 a.m., and made twenty-one miles before camping at Middle Creek Bar. Along the way they challenged the Buffalo, Lime Point and Grande Ronde rapids. They picked up their first supply cache at Grande Ronde.

The third day they fought upriver through McDuff, Wild Goose, Grotto Falls, Cache Creek, Cottonwood and Cook Creek rapids. The most difficult was McDuff, where groceries and gasoline were unloaded and carried around the falls. The hikers, including Clegg, had to scramble halfway up the hillside to get past the obstacle. The river was flanked by barren, rocky mountains. But there were several stretches where the stream grew calm — the sky, cliffs and yellow blooming cactus mirrored in the deep, dark water. Thirteen miles had been covered when the party made camp for the night just above Cook Creek.

They reached the Snake's junction with the Salmon River the next morning. They negotiated Mountain Sheep and Eureka rapids with little difficulty. At Deer Rapid, the boats were emptied and the supplies carried past the obstacle.

Holmstrom was running the *St. George* through the waves when one tossed the boat into the air, flipping him into the water. The current carried the boatman to a pool below the rapid. He wasn't wearing a life jacket. As he started swimming to shore he was sucked under in an eddy.

Hamilton dropped the supplies he was carrying past the falls and rushed to the *Mongoose*, tied to shore below the rapid. He ran the craft out to the eddy and fished the half-drowned man out of the water. Once Holmstrom was ashore, Hamilton retrieved the runaway *St. George* from downstream. Its engine was still running. After lunch the party proceeded up to Imnaha Bar and made camp.

On May 16, the boats had to be lined upstream to the Imnaha River. There had been a storm in the mountains and the Imnaha was running too high for the ground party to cross. One boat managed to make it to the far side pulling a rope. Once the rope was secured to both banks, the boats were used to ferry across equipment and supplies. Then the craft had to be lined through several rapids.

It rained all day, making everyone cold and miserable. Camp was made above White Horse Rapid late in the day. The exhausted party had only traveled three miles during the day.

Rain continued to fall on May 17. The boats had to go up six rapids, while the supplies were hauled along the steep, rain-slick banks. In some places, the men carrying the gear had to wade along the shore in water up to their chests.

On May 18 it rained. The Clegg party managed only nine miles, camping at Somers Creek.

The next day they made three and a half miles. Lewiston was seventy-four miles behind them and Kinney Creek — at the upper end of the canyon — was forty-two miles ahead. That evening the rain eased up and stars appeared.

May 20 dawned sunny and fresh. Mountain mahogany stood out gray-green against the freshly washed shale on the hillsides. Poison ivy leaves glistened a waxy green. Several homesteads dotted the surrounding hills, amid patches of spring grass.

The unloading and lining of the boats through the rapids, once an awkward chore, had become a expertly-choreographed routine. They moved nine more miles upstream.

Four rapids between Salt Creek and Johnson Bar were lined the morning of May 21. Camp was made just above the bar, where their last cache was located.

The next day, May 22, was the most difficult of the trip. Two major rapids — Rush Creek and Sluice Creek — pushed the explorers to their physical limits. The boats were lined through one rapid and portaged around the other. It drizzled all day, making the work even more difficult. Everyone, even the good natured Bill Johnson, sat silent and sullen that night in camp, thinking about the difficulties of the one and one half miles they had managed to cover that day.

On May 23, there was another difficult portage around Bill's Creek Rapid. Both the boats and gear had to be carried a long distance along the shore. The wind-driven rain added to the misery.

They met two sturgeon fishermen the next day. They had seven live fish tied to a log that they were floating downriver. The sun reappeared. Although much of the day was spent lining boats up through rapids, the improvement in the weather helped ease the frustrations of the previous days.

Granite Creek Rapid, the worst yet, was conquered on May 25. No one except the McKenzie party, had ever taken a boat upriver beyond that point. The boats had to be carried over huge granite boulders. Although they started early, they managed only three miles before making camp between Granite Creek Rapid and Granite Creek.

The rigors of lining, portaging and climbing had toned muscles and trimmed off pounds. Everyone in the party felt in top physical shape. Their clothing, however, had not fared as well. The soles of Clegg's and Johnson's shoes flapped when they walked. Holmstrom's shirt was in tatters and Hamilton's pants were ripped out in the knees. And those were their best clothes. All their other clothing had been reduced to rags.

"Night before last after supper, Doc and I sat in our sleeping bags with pants off sewing patches on," Holmstrom wrote in his journal. "Mine are badly torn in the crotch. It's about dark and I cut off a big piece of canvas and try to sew on and in the AM find the patch itself has a very big hole in it but it's smaller than the first one. Tomorrow maybe I'll patch the hole in the patch."

It was cloudy but warm on May 28. Lining and portaging continued. But everyone was pleased that they covered four and a half miles. They made camp just below Hells Canyon Creek.

The following day they labored through numerous unnamed rapids, making four miles before camping on a sandbar below Red Ledge Mine. The mine had been closed for years, but there were three tents at the site being used by a government geologist who was working in the area.

The days that followed were the same as those before — more lining and portaging. Near Steamboat Rapid they heard the sound of a vehicle somewhere above them. They discovered a road that led to the Red Ledge Mine. "How horrible," Clegg quipped. "A car in my canyon!"

They lined the boats through Thirty-two Point Rapid. Farther upstream, at Plummer's Rapid, they visited Plummer's Ranch and enjoyed fresh strawberries from the garden. After struggling through yet another "serious" rapid, they made camp. That evening, a truck delivered supplies to their camp above Black Point Rapid.

Edith Clegg rode in the truck the next day to their next campsite just above Kinney Creek, while the men worked the boats through the rapid of the same name. By the end of the day they were officially through Hell's Canyon. Hamilton's wife, parents and an assortment of friends brought dinner to the camp and spent the night. After their experience in the rugged and wild canyon, civilization felt more like an intrusion, than something to be embraced.

It took Edith Clegg's expedition eighteen days to travel from Lewiston to Kinney Creek. Hamilton, Bean and Johnson left the expedition at Weiser, since the worst part of the trip was behind them. Clegg and Holmstrom continued cross-country by water, reaching New York in time to attend the World's Fair.

Holmstrom said the upstream struggle through Hells Canyon was four times more difficult than his solo trip down the Colorado.

Clegg said the Hell's Canyon episode was the highlight of her 4,000-mile adventure. Throughout the remainder of the trip she often declared, "I want my canyon!"

Idaho's Lake Pend Oreille is forty-three miles long, six miles wide and more than 1,000 feet deep.

FIFTY

Boise River — 1943

The Flood

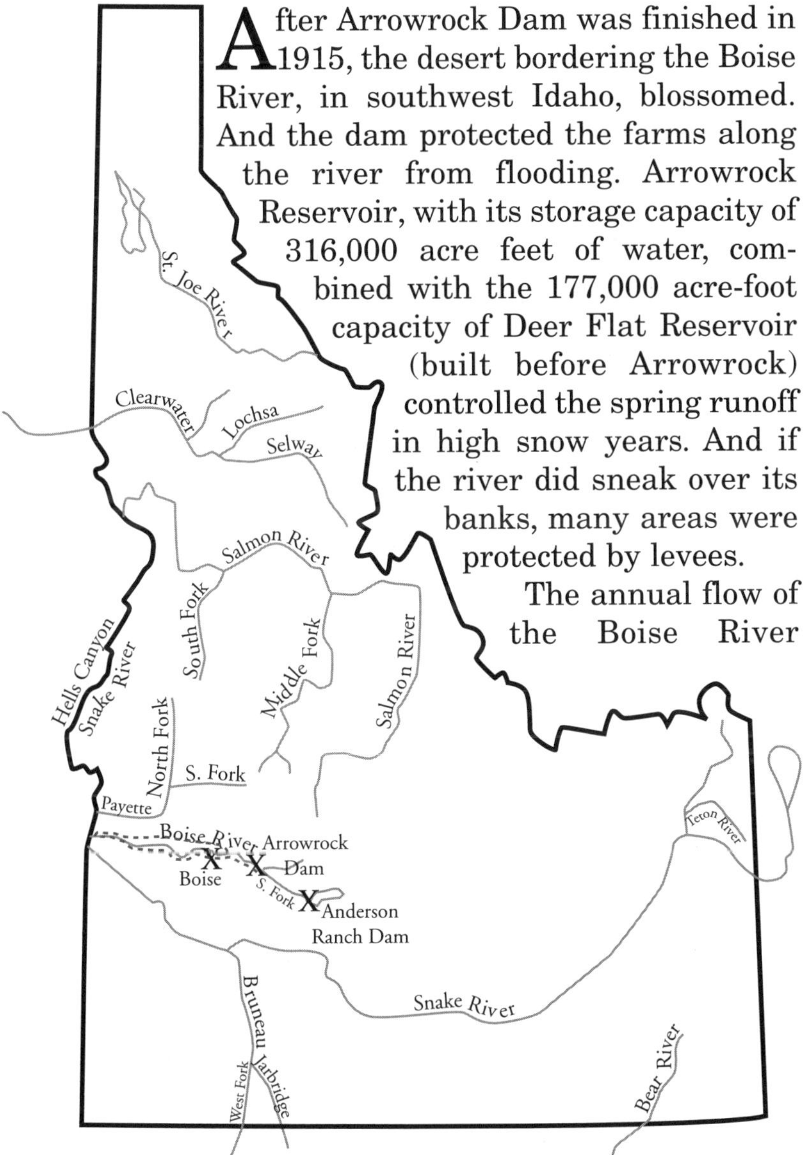

After Arrowrock Dam was finished in 1915, the desert bordering the Boise River, in southwest Idaho, blossomed. And the dam protected the farms along the river from flooding. Arrowrock Reservoir, with its storage capacity of 316,000 acre feet of water, combined with the 177,000 acre-foot capacity of Deer Flat Reservoir (built before Arrowrock) controlled the spring runoff in high snow years. And if the river did sneak over its banks, many areas were protected by levees.

The annual flow of the Boise River

ranged from 890,000 acre-feet in a low snow year, to a maximum of 3.57 million acre-feet in a high snow pack season. The average was 1.8 million acre-feet.

The combined capacity of the two reservoirs was about one-fourth of the average annual river flow. The Army Corps of Engineers estimated that between 1915 and 1943, the dams annually reduced high water in the spring by 3,443 cubic feet per second.

The reservoirs were a big help in 1917. That was the year high snowpack combined with two weeks of unseasonably warm weather. The dams managed to cut the river flow by 8,150 cubic feet per second.

Idaho suffered an agricultural depression in the 1920s. Despite the dams, extreme drought created an irrigation water shortage. Farmers lost money. Financial pressures forced some to abandon their farms. While the dams helped protect farms from flood damage, they were of little help when nature refused to supply enough water.

During the Great Depression of the 1930s, Civilian Conservation Corps programs and federal policy intensified flood control along the Boise River.

After severe flooding along the Ohio River, Congress declared flood control a national issue. The Army Corps of Engineers was given a flood control budget. The Idaho Legislature appropriated $10,000 to help confine the Boise River channel. The state highway department added more money for levee repair and labor. The Civilian Conservation Corps began filling lowlands and straightening the river's course to protect bridges and reduce erosion.

Flooding appeared to be a thing of the past. But farmers along the flood plain continued to back their bets. Instead of planting row crops that would be destroyed in a flood, many grew alfalfa, clover and timothy grass. Such plants resisted erosion and kept the land productive, although not very profitable.

By 1940, Boise was a small city of 26,130, with many of its residents living along the river. The urban growth was due primarily to agriculture that followed in the wake of irrigation.

Construction of Anderson Ranch Dam was approved to meet the increasing demand for water. The dam site was forty-two miles upstream from Arrowrock Dam, on the South Fork of the Boise River. When completed, Anderson Ranch would hold an additional 500,000 acre-feet of water, reducing the possibility of droughts of the kind experienced in the 1920s. The new project also provided additional flood control.

While the new dam was under construction, World War II began. The War Production Board ordered most of the equipment and labor for Anderson Ranch Dam transferred to war projects. Work on the dam slowed to a snail's pace.

Meanwhile, supplies of consumer goods decreased because of the war. Prices rose and rationing of sugar, canned fruits and vegetables began. Many farmers left the Boise Valley to fight for their country, leaving a shortage of labor to harvest crops already in the fields. Japanese-American internees helped bring in the sugar beet crop.

The government appealed to the remaining farmers to increase crop production. To do that they had to turn much of the land along the river into row crop ground. That increased the chance of problems if there was a flood. But most people felt the risk was worth it. Awards were offered for food production and patriotic farmers rallied to the cause. High prices added extra incentive.

Pastures yielded to hybrid sweet corn, potatoes, beans, onions and seed crops. For two years floodplain farmers produced bumper crops and huge profits.

Then the flood came.

In April 1943, an unseasonably warm spell quickly melted a heavy snowpack in nearby mountains. Boise River Watermaster William Welsh warned Idaho Governor C. A. Bottolfsen that without a drastic change in the weather, water would come over the dam emergency spillways within 15 days. He said the flooding would threaten more than 500 farms downriver.

Boise Valley landowners were notified of the approaching danger and began making preparations. Levees were repaired and strengthened. Junked automobiles were filled with rocks, then pushed into the river to fight erosion. The work came at a busy time, during the spring planting season.

Meanwhile, Watermaster Welsh organized area communities and put plans in motion to provide typhoid inoculations and evacuation of people and livestock. He divided the river into eight districts, each with a committee to deal with communication, evacuations and emergency loans. Flood information was broadcast on the radio every day at noon, when farmers were in from the fields eating lunch.

As Welsh predicted, the Boise came over its banks and many of the manmade levees. Farmers put aside their regular tasks to fight the river. Tractors were brought in from the fields to haul riprap to reinforce the riverbank.

But the efforts were futile. The river continued to rise. It spread out across newly planted fields; it flushed away emergency dikes; it dumped piles of debris into yards, barn yards and gardens. Worst of all, it defiled the land. At its peak, 20,000 cubic feet of water per second swirled down the river and across the adjacent countryside, carrying with it acres of topsoil.

Troops from the air base at Gowen Field, near Boise, reinforced fifteen highway bridges threatened by the flood. All but three were closed for five or more days, making it difficult for farmers to get milk to market before it spoiled in the heat.

The Army Corps of Engineers supervised levee construction but the river kept ahead of the effort.

The Idaho Volunteer Reserve helped more than 200 flood plain families evacuate, then stayed to guard the farms. Livestock was moved to higher ground. Feed for the animals was swept away by the churning water.

The flood of 1943 caused havoc in many parts of the Boise Valley. But given the situation in other parts of the world, residents didn't allow the situation to discourage them.

"In being prepared," said Paul Davis of the Ada County Flood Control Committee, "the old American individualism and ingenuity prevailed and our Boise Valley people took their misfortune in stride."

Marilyn Monroe gave the Salmon River international exposure in 1954, when she starred with Robert Mitchum and Rory Calhoun in The River of No Return. *The film was made on location in central Idaho.*

FIFTY-ONE

Bruneau River — 1950

Three Men in a Rubber Boat

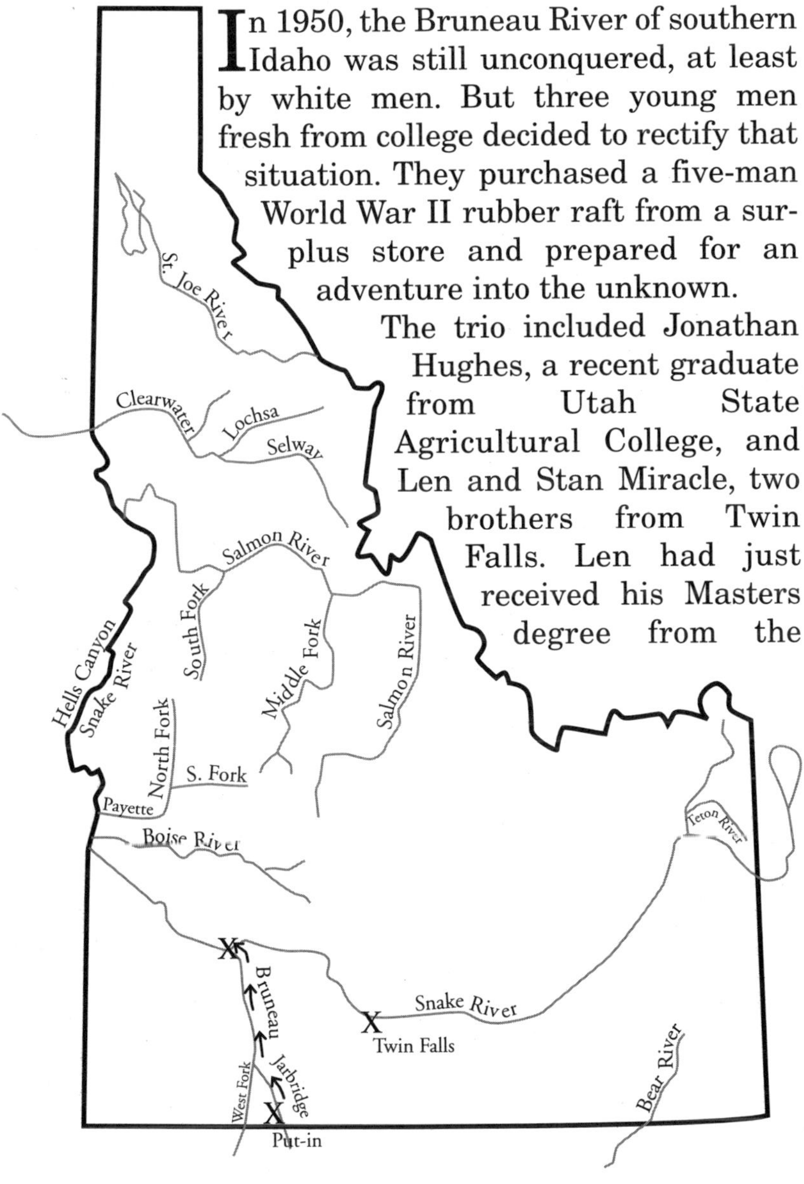

In 1950, the Bruneau River of southern Idaho was still unconquered, at least by white men. But three young men fresh from college decided to rectify that situation. They purchased a five-man World War II rubber raft from a surplus store and prepared for an adventure into the unknown.

The trio included Jonathan Hughes, a recent graduate from Utah State Agricultural College, and Len and Stan Miracle, two brothers from Twin Falls. Len had just received his Masters degree from the

University of Oregon and Stan was a graduate of Oregon's Linfield College.

The trip was the idea of Len Miracle, a journalist. He queried the editor of *Field and Stream* magazine about writing a story on a trip down the Bruneau. River float trips were common in Idaho. But no white man had ever made it all the way through the Bruneau River Canyon. There had been several attempts, but all had failed.

One thing that made the Bruneau trip hazardous was that in one seventy-five-mile stretch, there were only three points where the canyon rim could be reached on foot. That complicated rescue or escape.

The *Field and Stream* editor liked Len Miracle's idea and gave him a go ahead on the project.

Based on Stan Miracle's estimates, supplies were gathered for a four-day trip down the Bruneau. They included food (mainly canned goods), sleeping bags, fishing rods, pistols and ammunition, hunting knives, two snake-bite kits, a hatchet, miscellaneous cooking utensils and a camera with plenty of color and black and white film.

On the last Monday in June, 1950, the men made a hot, dusty drive across the sage-covered desert to their put-in point at Murphy Hot Springs on the Idaho-Nevada border. The Bruneau River begins where the Jarbridge branch, which flows north from the Jarbridge Mountains in Nevada, joins the waters from the springs. The combined stream then flows through a deep, narrow canyon. Along the way, the West Fork of the Bruneau, Sheep Creek and the East Fork of the Burneau flow into the main stream. The river eventually breaks out of the narrow canyon,

Jim Paxton

moseying across farmland before dumping into the Snake River near the small town of Bruneau.

There was enough water to float the rubber raft over some rapids near the launch site. At that point the canyon is wide and sparsely wooded with juniper.

After inflating and loading the rubber raft, the adventurers pushed off and gingerly made their way through the first rapid. Because they launched late in the afternoon, shadows soon darkened the deep canyon. They made camp after traveling for about an hour.

The second day began well. Stan Miracle caught a trout while still in his sleeping bag. But their luck on the water wasn't as good. The canyon narrowed and the river often was squeezed through boulder-strewn passages only a few yards wide. Steep banks often made it impossible to carry the raft around the obstacles in the water. Logs, submerged and on the surface, added to the hazards. Sometimes the river was frenzied whitewater as it shot through narrow gorges. At other times it flattened out and was only a few inches deep. The crew had to drag the boat through the shallows using ropes.

Paddles proved useless in maneuvering around hazards and were replaced with long, sturdy poles. Sometimes the boat had to be lined through rough water. Often, one of the men would swim ahead to catch the raft as it emerged from the whitewater. The men made camp on a sandbar in late afternoon. They were exhausted and had no idea how far they had traveled.

On the morning of day three, the Miracle brothers and Hughes were refreshed and ready to tackle the river again. The sun shimmered on the multicolored canyon walls. It was mostly play for the travelers until late afternoon. Ahead they spotted two giant rocks, forming a clamshell through which the entire river had to pass before dropping into a deep pool.

When the men tried to line the raft through the gap, the swirling water took control and forced the craft under a narrow overhang. Hughes nearly went under with the raft while trying to save it. The Miracles managed to pull him from the grip of the current.

The raft was finally freed by Hughes, who managed to open an air valve and partially deflate the craft. It sagged into a pool below.

All the cooking and eating gear and most of the food and toilet paper were lost in the mishap. All the kitchen matches were wet and there were only three waterproof matches. One was used to start a fire to dry out the sleeping bags.

When the gear was dried and the raft inflated, the men floated downstream to a sandbar and camped. Dinner consisted of a can of beans cooked over a campfire and eaten off the blades of their hunting knives.

The next morning, a second waterproof match was used to build a fire to cook some more beans. Gone were the carefree attitudes of young college graduates. They wondered what additional surprises awaited them downstream, and how many miles they would have to travel to reach Bruneau.

There were few stretches of easy water that morning. By noon, the men were soaked and chilled with little hope of a warm campfire or warm food. Their moods were as sour as the dock plants that grew in the seepage from springs along the shoreline.

Stan Miracle gathered dry grass and wadded it tightly. Then he pried the bullets out of two .22 cartridges, made a small pile of gunpowder and ignited it with a spark from a reluctant kitchen match. The fire raised their spirits as they warmed themselves and sipped hot soup from a can.

That afternoon they drifted past the ruins of an old gold mining sluice box. The canyon floor was about 100 yards wide. They spotted grazing sheep and immediately thought they were near the end of their journey. Then they noticed the sheep had long tails and realized the animals probably had been captives of the canyon for generations. Beyond the sheep the canyon narrowed again and a large hot spring flowed into the river, warming the water. That lessened their chances of catching any fish.

The channel narrowed even more and the water became deep, dark and still. The explorers poled their way through the eerie gorge. The echoes caused by their poles slapping the water seemed to scold them for violating the solitude of the place. Crouched in their rubber fortress, they sat silent and still.

Then they heard a more ominous echo — a roar of falling water that grew louder by the minute. The current picked up speed and the raft accelerated. The adventurers could do little but hold on tight and hope for the best. The raft raced through a long series of roller-coaster waves that made them feel like they were on an amusement park ride. At the bottom of the rapid, however, it was back to lining the boat through and around an assortment of obstacles. That night the exhausted and hungry men slept on a rocky sandbar, dreaming of the long-tailed lamb chops they had left free to roam.

On the fifth day, their luck improved when Jonathan Hughes shot a deer with one of the pistols. Len Miracle butchered it and they loaded the meat on the raft. They spent the rest of the day fighting their way through shallows, fallen logs, rocks and brush. That night they had trouble finding a place on the bank flat enough to camp. As they roasted the venison, the flames from the fire cast unearthly shadows on the sheer canyon walls.

Hunkered over chunks of dripping meat, the men looked primeval. Their morale was as tattered as their clothing. Gnawing on their unseasoned and undercooked meat, they speculated about their location and the distance to civilization.

On the sixth day of their "three to four day" journey, the raft hit a sharp rock about noon. The travelers were exhausted from two morning portages and frustrated from raft patching. They searched the canyon walls for an escape route, deciding it would be better to give up and flee across the desert than to endure another mile on the Bruneau. But there was no escape from their prison. As they waited for the patch to dry, they ate their last can of soup and some of the venison.

But when they returned to the river, the situation improved. The canyon grew wider and in the distance they spotted what appeared to be a road on the canyon wall! With spirits soaring they pushed on as the water grew deeper.

Suddenly they found themselves floating through a wheat field. A farmhouse came into view. They had reached the end of their historic journey.

Their return to the Miracle home in Twin Falls caused a celebration. Three days after their departure, Len and Stan's older brother, Ken, had flown the canyon and spotted a wrecked raft a few miles from the starting point. He dropped food and supplies. The raft belonged to another group. They feasted on their windfall from the sky before scaling the canyon walls. A search party had looked for the Miracle-Hughes party but had returned empty-handed.

Len Miracle's story appeared in the February 1951 edition of *Field and Stream*.

FIFTY-TWO

Snake River — 1958

The Drowning of Robinette

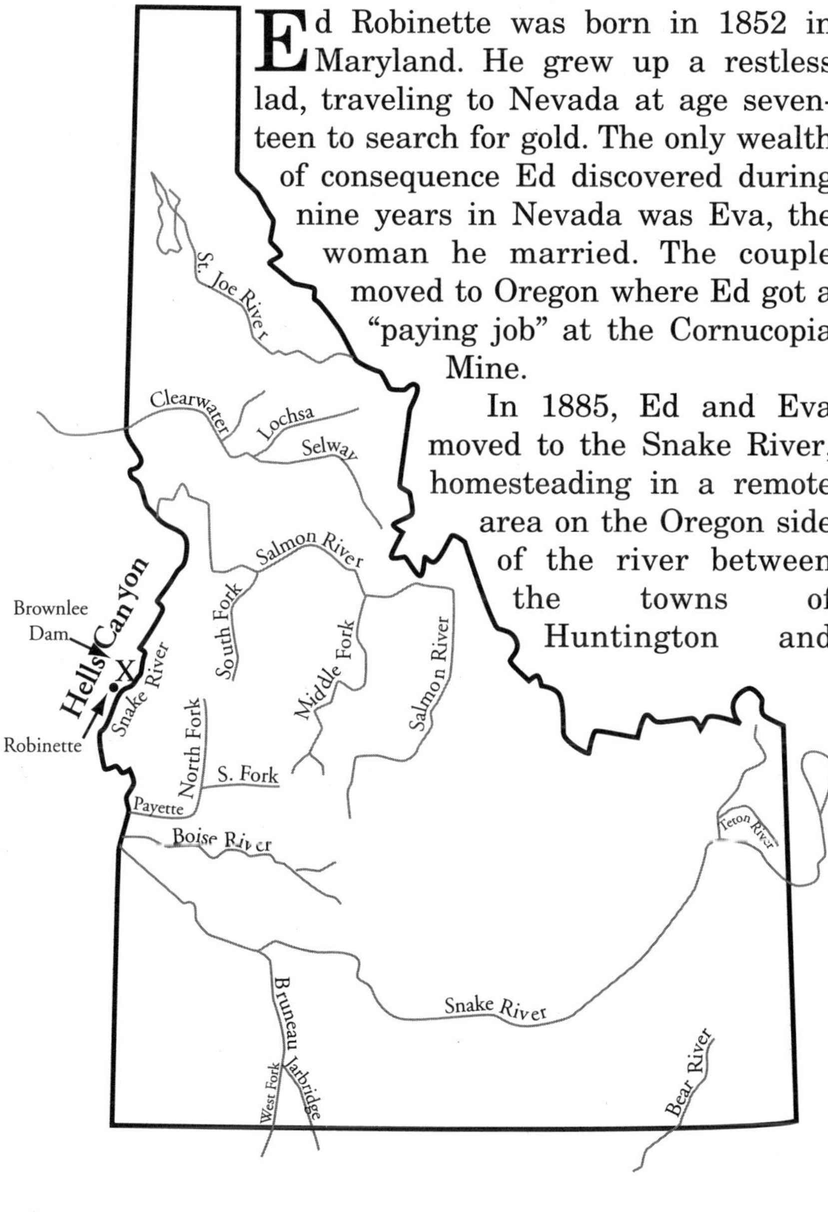

Ed Robinette was born in 1852 in Maryland. He grew up a restless lad, traveling to Nevada at age seventeen to search for gold. The only wealth of consequence Ed discovered during nine years in Nevada was Eva, the woman he married. The couple moved to Oregon where Ed got a "paying job" at the Cornucopia Mine.

In 1885, Ed and Eva moved to the Snake River, homesteading in a remote area on the Oregon side of the river between the towns of Huntington and

Homestead. Ed built a frame house on a knoll. They raised a garden, chickens and four children. Eva's husband made his living growing hay on a plateau above the river and doing a little placer mining for gold.

Ed's claim to fame wasn't panned out of the river. In 1910 he was contacted by representatives of the Oregon Short Line Railroad. Because of increased activity in Cornucpoia, Richland and Pine Valley, the O. S. L. wanted to build a spur so timber and cattle could be shipped out by rail. Soon the white-bearded Ed was working with surveyors platting the town of Robinette, and strutting around the place like a well-fed banty rooster.

When the spur was finished, the town of Robinette took hold and became the hub of the area. One of the first buildings, aside from the fancy train depot, was a general store and post office. Local homesteaders, lumberjacks and miners came there instead of going all the way to Baker City for their mail and supplies. A cable ferry carried people and supplies across the Snake River. A two-story hotel was built, followed by a tavern and a school.

The community thrived. A coal storage facility, a Standard Oil petroleum depot and an Idaho Power substation were built. By 1920, Robinette was home to nearly 100 people.

But 1920 also was the year fire destroyed the hotel. It never was rebuilt. Two years later the struggling mines stopped shipping ore. Hauling lumber and cattle wasn't profitable enough for the Oregon Short Line. The trains stopped coming to Robinette.

In 1936, a railroad crew came to town and took away the tracks.

On June 3, 1939, river adventuress Edith Clegg stopped in Robinette for gas and groceries. Clegg had traveled up the Snake through Hells Canyon on the first leg of a 4,000-mile cross-continent journey. The once grand railroad depot, an abandon railroad car at its side, stood with no track to or from it. Clegg took a photograph of the unusual scene.

The faded town slouched on the west bank of the Snake, humbled by its decaying buildings and growing uselessness until the spring of 1951. Things perked up when the Stillwell Lumber Company built a drying kiln and planer shed in town. The residents of Robinette celebrated their good fortune — but only briefly.

On May 10, 1953, the Idaho Power Company filed for a construction permit to build a huge earth-filled dam on the site of the old Brownlee Ferry, a short distance downriver from Robinette. Construction of Brownlee Dam began in July 1955. The project was to be completed in 1958.

The Brownlee Dam would have been of great economic importance to Robinette, except for one little problem. When the dam was complete and the flood control reservoir behind it filled, the town would be covered by one million acre feet of water.

The town of Robinette was disassembled. Idaho Power moved the substation to Homestead. The schoolhouse found its way to Homestead, too. Barney Edison sold his store to someone who moved it to Richland and remodeled it as a home.

Many of the buildings in Robinette were torn down and the lumber salvaged. Others were burned. On February 27, 1958 the town was pronounced dead. A few months later, Robinette disappeared under Brownlee Reservoir.

FIFTY-THREE

Snake River — 1958

Something Fishy at Oxbow

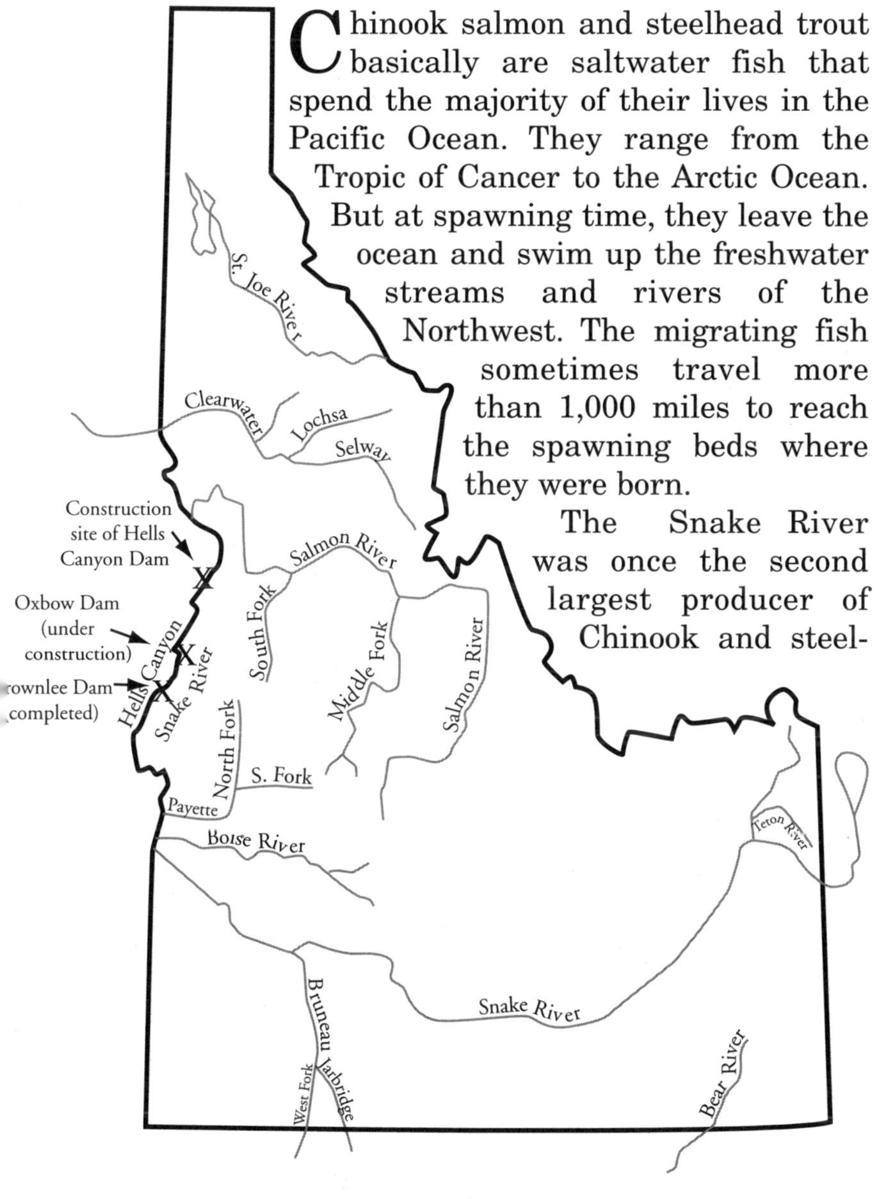

Chinook salmon and steelhead trout basically are saltwater fish that spend the majority of their lives in the Pacific Ocean. They range from the Tropic of Cancer to the Arctic Ocean. But at spawning time, they leave the ocean and swim up the freshwater streams and rivers of the Northwest. The migrating fish sometimes travel more than 1,000 miles to reach the spawning beds where they were born.

The Snake River was once the second largest producer of Chinook and steelhead in the world. Seventy percent of the annual salmon run branched off the Snake and headed up the Salmon River. Another five percent went up the Imnaha. The remaining twenty-five percent swam on up the Snake, some going as far as Swan Falls. In the 1950s the annual salmon run in the upper portion of the river ranged from 40,000 to 55,000 fish.

The Chinook appeared in the river in the spring and the steelhead arrived in the summer and winter.

Several months after the fish spawned, tiny salmonoids emerged from the gravel beds. They stayed near their birthplace for periods ranging from two months to two years. Then, following their instincts, millions of fingerlings (smolts) gathered in schools and began their journey to the ocean.

Beginning in 1958, ninety-five miles of the untamed Snake River was turned over to the Idaho Power Company to produce electricity. The Federal Power Commission grated a license to Idaho Power in 1955 to build three dams. The first, the 295-foot-high Brownlee Dam, impounding fifty-three miles of the river, was completed in 1958. Oxbow Dam, finished in 1961, was 140 feet high. The 318-foot-high Hells Canyon Dam came on line in 1967, creating 18,450 acres of slackwater. The dams buried five of the seven major rapids in Hells Canyon.

In granting the license to Idaho Power, the Federal Power Commission made provisions to protect salmon runs during construction and operation of the three dams. Articles thirty-four through thirty-six of the agreement clearly stated Idaho Power would spend a minimum of $250,000 studying the impact of the dams on anadromous fish habitat and seasonal runs. The power company was to construct "reasonable" fish passages that might be suggested by state of federal fish and game agencies. Idaho Power also was required to bear a fair portion of the cost of operating and maintaining the facilities.

There were two major problems in complying with the agreement — getting adult salmon swimming upstream through the dams and getting the young fish down to the ocean.

One solution for handling adult salmon was to lure the fish into a trap, then truck them around the man-made obstacles. Another proposal was to build a series of stair step pools fish could use to climb over the dams.

Idaho Power opted for traps to handle the adult fish. The trap, installed at the Oxbow construction site in May 1958, was a short, dead-end ladder topped with a weir and slatted hopper. Within a month, the trap began to malfunction. Water in the ladders began to stagnate and churning water developed in the area below the trap.

The system for catching the smolt coming downstream had problems, too. When fingerlings migrate, they travel tail first, drifting with the current. When they reached the reservoirs they lost the current and their sense of direction. Some of the small fish were swept over the dam spillway into the pool below. Many died from a condition called nitrogen narcosis, caused by improper aeration of water at the base of the dam. Other smolt were sucked through the power turbines, causing injury or death.

Idaho Power's solution to the downstream migration problem was to install a "skimmer" — the first and last of its kind to be built. The skimmer was a seven-acre net made of plastic with small holes. It was strung across the river about a mile above Brownlee and was held in place by a large boom. Floating barges rigged with minnow traps were stationed along the net.

The skimmer had problems from the beginning. Portions of the net sagged, allowing baby salmon to pass over the top. Some parts tore loose from the boom. Large sections became tangled and holes and rips began to develop. Scuba divers, sent to make repairs, found it hard to work in murky reservoirs at depths sometimes exceeding 100 feet.

On August 20, 1958, three representatives from the United States Bureau of Commercial Fisheries made a routine visit to the Oxbow adult fish trap. Water turbulence in front of the trap was pronounced. Upon closer examination, a large crack was found in the retaining wall behind the trap. The leak had flushed gravel and soil from under the salmon trap foundation. The entire contraption was ready to fall into the river!

The annual salmon migration already was under way. Idaho Power agreed to stop work on the dam, if necessary, to concentrate on repairing the trap. The work started on August 26 when the gates of Brownlee Dam were closed by Idaho Power without permission of the Army Corps of Engineers. The river flow dropped from about 14,000 cubic-feet-per-second to about 2,000 cfs. The drop in the river level concerned conservation groups, who feared for the safety of fish that had already migrated into the area. But the power company felt the reduction was necessary in order to make repairs.

On the following day, workers drove pilings made from corrugated sheet steel, behind the cracked wall. The effort was finished in three days and the flow was increased. Within hours the pilings washed out.

A temporary cofferdam was hastily built, completely drying up the river bed for seven hours while more pilings were pounded into place. When the water was again released, the surge tore out the new supports. It was obvious that temporary measures would not work. Morrison Knudsen engineers were brought in to help rebuild the damaged fish trap. It was a race against time. By September 9, 20,000 Chinook had been counted crossing Bonneville Dam on the Columbia, heading for Oxbow. By September 17, more than 1,000 Chinook Salmon had arrived at Oxbow and were leaping in the splash pool below the dam, frantically trying to get upstream. Because the permanent fish trap was a long way from completion, a dip net operation began near the Idaho shore of the Snake.

When the Chinook were netted, they were placed in plastic bags and floated downstream to a landing. The bagged fish then were tied to a rowboat and taken across the river to hopper trucks waiting on the Oregon shore to transport them past Oxbow to Brownlee.

Too many fish died because of prolonged stress, so a line was rigged across the river and the salmon were hauled across in a container filled with water, reducing the casualties. A temporary fish trap soon was in place. Within a week, 3,500 Chinook had been moved up to Brownlee reservoir. But many of them died from the stress. Thousands continued to arrive in the Oxbow Dam pool.

When the new fish trap was completed October 6, the temporary cofferdam had to be dismantled. Water flowing over the breach was reduced to a trickle, stranding the fish in the pool below the dam. No fresh aerated water reached the pool. The fish quickly used up all the oxygen.

"Shortly after 1:00 P.M. the water supply to the stranded fish failed," noted Robert T. Gunsolus, in a report, "and at 2:15 P.M. the first fish was observed to rise to the surface, turn belly up, and sink slowly from sight. This act, together with frantic dashes across the surface was evidence of the impending catastrophe. The request for pumped water was constantly pressed, but the rapidly receding water on the sloping upstream side of the breach made it necessary for the pipe fitters to continually re-rig the pump intake. Ten cfs of pumped water was finally obtained at 3:07 P.M. At 3:15 P.M. the water supply failed when the intake was once again stranded. Shortly thereafter, compressed air was introduced into the pool and within minutes the fish remaining alive responded to the increased oxygen. It was estimated that at least half of the fish in the pool were lost. When the success of the compressed air was obvious, attempts at pumping water ceased."

The dead Chinook numbered more than 4,000. The loss of that portion of the spawning run was one of the greatest anadromous fish disasters in history. The fish count at Oxbow before the loss showed a run of more than 20,000 fall Chinook. Five years later the magnitude of the loss was clear. Only 945 Chinook were counted at Oxbow.

FIFTY-FOUR

Snake River — 1965

Hells Canyon Dam

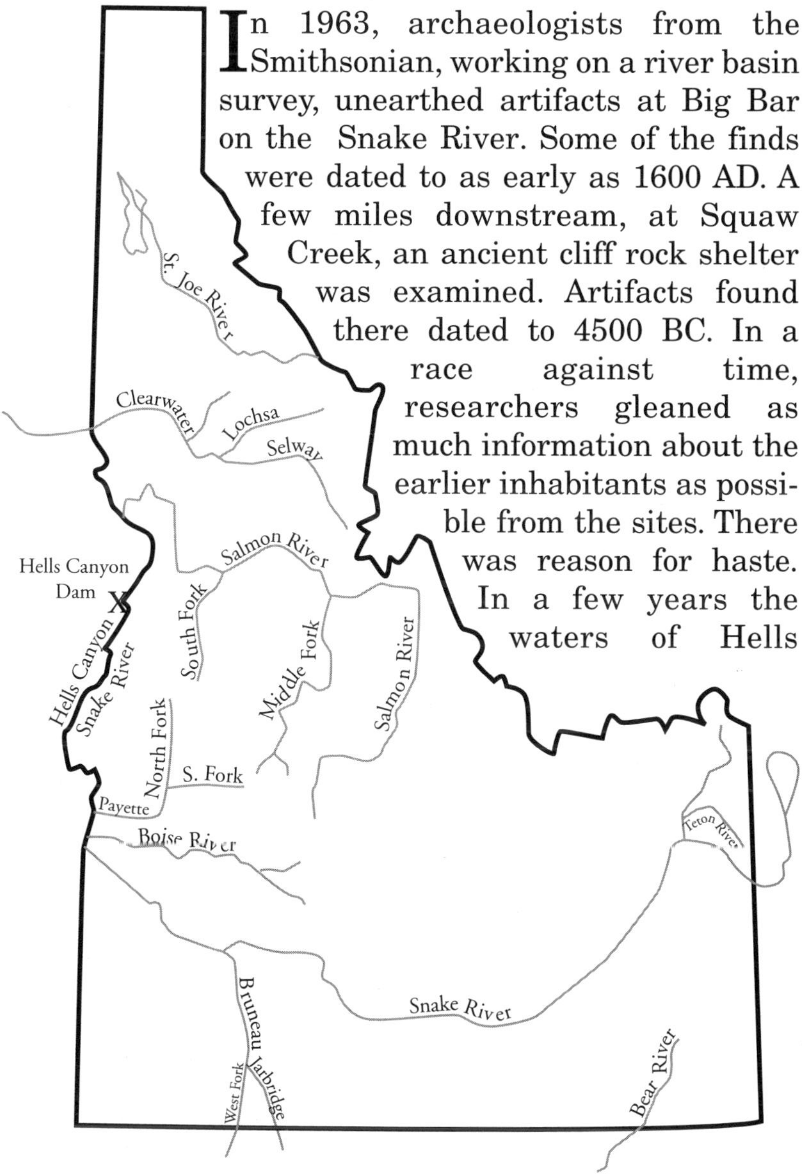

In 1963, archaeologists from the Smithsonian, working on a river basin survey, unearthed artifacts at Big Bar on the Snake River. Some of the finds were dated to as early as 1600 AD. A few miles downstream, at Squaw Creek, an ancient cliff rock shelter was examined. Artifacts found there dated to 4500 BC. In a race against time, researchers gleaned as much information about the earlier inhabitants as possible from the sites. There was reason for haste. In a few years the waters of Hells

Canyon Dam would cover the area, making further research impossible.

The Oxbow Bridge was completed and a twenty-three-mile access road cut along the cliffs above the river to Big Bar, near the Hells Canyon Dam construction site. By autumn 1965, heavy trucks growled along the road hauling in trailers to house 800 laborers hired by Idaho Power Company. Construction offices, tool shops and a first aid station were located near the Big Bar construction camp.

Just above Copper Ledge Falls, crews drilled and blasted a forty-five-foot diameter tunnel 1,800 feet through the mountainside. The interior of the tunnel was lined with concrete. Much of the aggregate used in the concrete was gouged out of the river's edge near Big Bar. Morrison-Knudsen Company's big crawler tractors and earth-moving Euclids moved earth and stone to form a weir across the river below the tunnel intake. The entire river was diverted through the tunnel, while temporary cofferdams were built upstream and downstream from the dam construction site. Concrete began replacing the earthen weir during the cold, windy March of 1966. Giant banks of lights were set up so crews could work around the clock. A quarter-mile-long conveyor belt brought aggregate to the mixing plant. The mixed buckets of concrete were hauled in engine-drawn shuttle cars to rail-mounted cranes hovering over the dam.

The bastion of concrete and steel grew. As spring turned into summer, the cramped working space in the narrow gorge recorded temperatures above 100 degrees. Aluminum tubing, controlled by temperature sensors, circulated water through the poured concrete to keep the curing temperature at seventy-five degrees Fahrenheit. Higher temperatures cause slips and cracks.

Nearly one million cubic yards of sand, gravel and earth were excavated to build the dam. More than 700,000 cubic yards of concrete were poured to create the 320-foot-high, 1,000-foot-long structure. Four men were killed during the sixteen-month project.

The gates and penstock can feed water through each of the three turbines at 10,000 cubic feet-per-second. This can cause fluctuations of the river level downstream by as much as one foot per hour.

When the river was returned to the channel after the dam was completed, the water backed up behind the new dam creating a twenty-three-mile-long reservoir. The dam itself blocked Copper Ledge Falls. As the water slowly rose, it swallowed the rocky obstacle known as Sawpit Rapid. The fiercest and most challenging cataract on the Snake, Buck Rapid, ceased to exist, as did the Squaw Creek and Kinney Creek Rapid. Archaeological sites, wild life habitat and fish spawning grounds also were lost.

The three-dam hydroelectric complex extends nearly 100 miles into the heart of America's deepest gorge, creating 19,000 acres of reservoir. Boat launching and docking facilities, picnic grounds, campsites, rest rooms and electric hook-ups for RVs replaced the natural habitat.

Portions of nine Idaho streams are protected by federal Wild and Scenic rivers legislation.

FIFTY-FIVE

Clearwater River — 1963

Dworshak, Idaho's White Elephant?

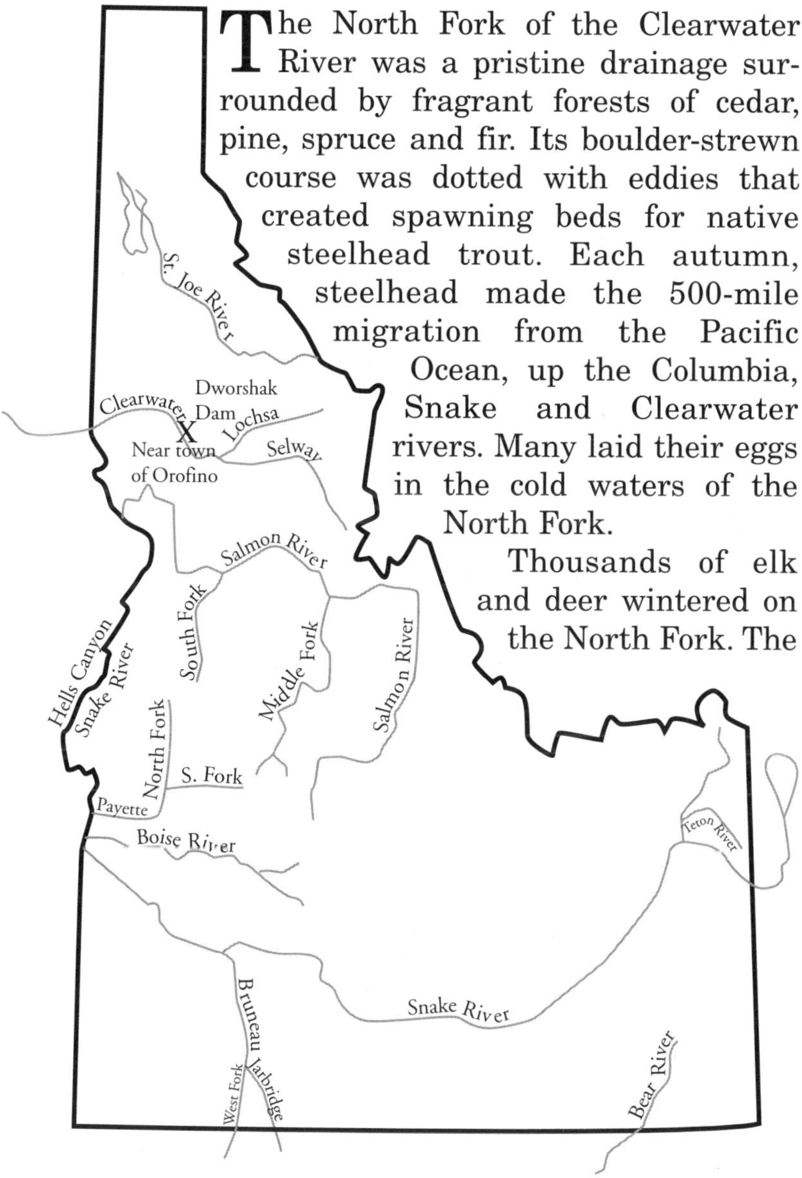

The North Fork of the Clearwater River was a pristine drainage surrounded by fragrant forests of cedar, pine, spruce and fir. Its boulder-strewn course was dotted with eddies that created spawning beds for native steelhead trout. Each autumn, steelhead made the 500-mile migration from the Pacific Ocean, up the Columbia, Snake and Clearwater rivers. Many laid their eggs in the cold waters of the North Fork.

Thousands of elk and deer wintered on the North Fork. The

meadows and forests along the stream offered plenty of food and shelter. For centuries, Nez Perce Indians roamed the area, hunting and fishing along the river. Their favorite fishing hole, a large eddy, was called Te-mee-mup.

Each autumn during the steelhead migration, a large Nez Perce camp was established at Te-mee-mup. The women wove cedar bark into panels that were placed in the river to trap the fish. The men speared the fish from platforms built out over the river. The women cleaned and boned the steelhead and hung the flesh on racks to dry. Dried fish was a valuable food source during the winter months.

Today, Te-mee-mup exists in name only. The site is under a 19,824-acre reservoir that stretches fifty-three miles into the mountains. The only Indian presence is the Big Eddy tourist concession, operated by the Nez Perce Tribal Council. Cigarettes can be purchased cheaply there.

In 1966, a mammoth concrete structure began to rise in the North Fork about a quarter mile from where the stream enters the main Clearwater River. The 717-foot-high, 3,000-foot-long dam is named for Henry C. Dworshak, an Idaho Republican Senator who served from 1949 to 1962. The massive memorial was built by the Army Corps of Engineers under the guise of flood control.

The $312 million Dworshak Dam was completed in 1973. It consumed 6,700,000 cubic yards of concrete. The reservoir creating the highest straight-axis, concrete gravity dam in the western world, slowly swallowed up acre after acre of forest and meadow land. Elk, deer and steelhead lost their wintering and breeding area.

The impact of Dworshak Dam was forseen. The public administrators were, after all, trained facilitators. An additional $21 million in federal tax money was used to build the Dworshak National Fish Hatchery, the largest steelhead trout factory in the world. The hatchery is located below the dam. Steelhead driven by instinct to return to the now non existent North Fork, are captured in traps. The females are stripped of their eggs and the males of their milt. The eggs are fertilized in sterilized trays, then incubated. Fry (baby steelhead) are raised in concrete tanks until they are old enough to be released to begin their journey to the sea. The hatchery, which costs more than one million dollars a year to operate, is managed by the Department of the Interior's Fish and Wildlife Service.

To replace some of the natural habitat destroyed by the dam and reservoir, 5,000 acres were set aside as an elk and wildlife refuge. Since the destruction of the natural steelhead spawning grounds, the reservoir is stocked with hatchery raised kokanee and rainbow trout.

Dworshak Lake is now surrounded by 47,000 acres of public-use land. However, in low water years the "lake" often turns into a reservoir with miles of muddy shoreline, unsuitable for most recreation.

Dworshak Dam hasn't lived up to its expectations. It generates less than half the power it was designed to produce. Operating at peak load would defeat the structures original purpose by causing flooding downstream.

The dam also has structural problems. In June 1980, a 236-foot-long crack was discovered in the reservoir side of the dam. The crack leaked an estimated 7,700 gallons of water per minute. Because the reservoir could not be drawn down due to a water shortage, a huge flume was built from sand bags and concrete barricades to channel the water past the powerhouse. Engineers drilled seventy holes in the face of the dam to intercept the creeping crack and relieve the pressure. A large plastic sheet was lowered into the water behind the dam. The sheet was sucked into the crack, reducing the water loss by half.

When the reservoir dropped, a patch was made from sawdust, cement and volcanic ash from the eruption of Mount St. Helens. The repairs cost more than one million dollars.

There is a visitor's center at the dam where tours are given every hour during the summer and twice during winter afternoons. Guests can see a half-hour film titled *The Construction of Dworshak Dam*. There also is a sign reminding them to "help protect this delicate environment for future generations."

FIFTY-SIX

Teton River — 1976

The Teton Dam Disaster

In 1964, Congress approved the construction of a dam on the Teton River in southeast Idaho. The dam was designed to control the chronic spring flooding that plagued prime potato and sugar beet growing farmland in the area.

Construction of the Teton Dam began in 1972. When complete, the dam was 305 feet high and nearly 1,700 feet thick at its base.

When the dam was finished, many homeowners, ranchers and farmers in the area canceled their flood

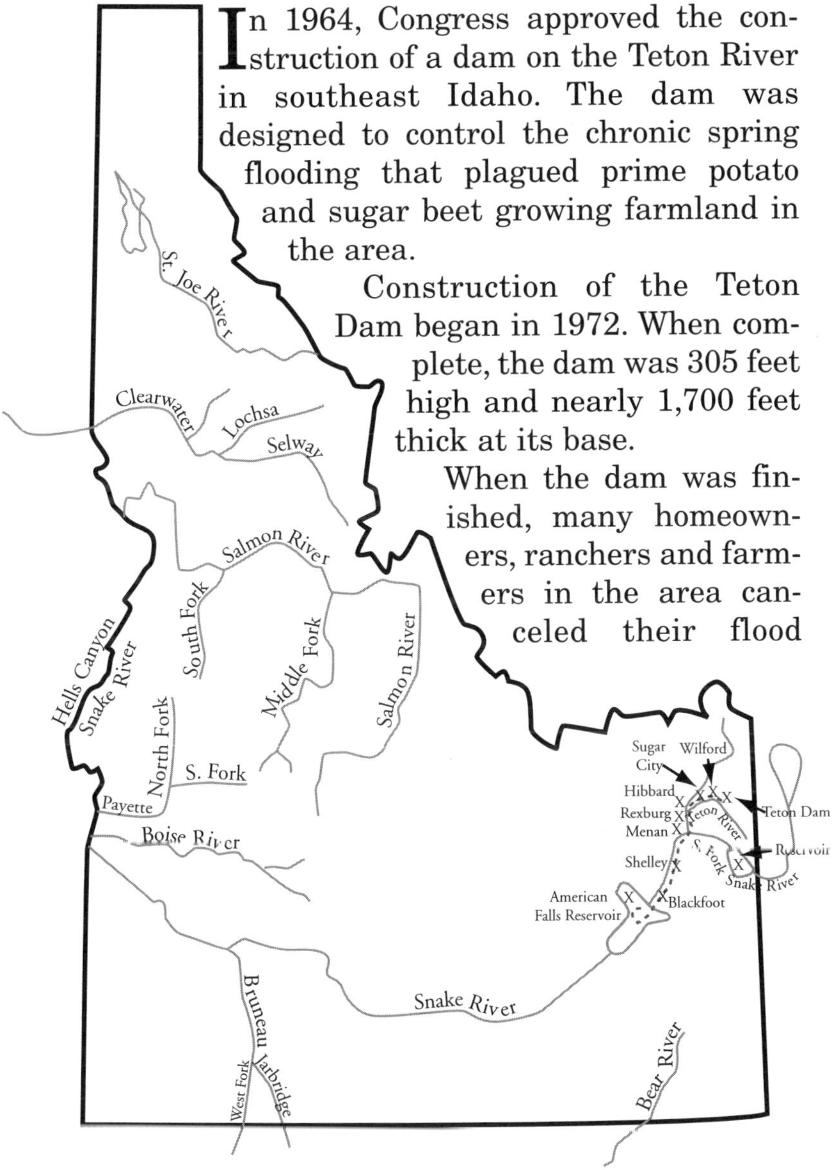

insurance, confident that the structure had eliminated that danger.

By June 1976, the reservoir behind the new Teton Dam was nearly full. Residents were excited by the irrigation and recreation potential. Those expectations were short-lived.

The morning of June 5, 1976 began with the skies the color of forget-me-nots and temperatures just warm enough to make Saturday outdoor chores a pleasure. About 8:30 A.M., a worker spotted two leaks in the Teton Dam — one along the right embankment approximately 130 feet from the top, and another on the downstream face near the base. An hour and a half later, the dam sprouted another large leak near the top.

While people downriver enjoyed the beautiful spring morning, workers at the dam used bulldozers to push earth into the rapidly widening gaps.

It was shortly before noon when the bulldozer operators realized that the leaks were out of control. They fled to safety as their machines were washed away by the flood. As workers watched from the canyon rim, the Teton Dam collapsed.

Officials at the dam quickly called the Madison and Fremont County sheriffs offices, warning them that the unthinkable had happened. Authorities had about an hour to spread the warning to residents of Wilford and Sugar City, communities directly in the path of the onrushing flood.

Many Wilford residents only had a few minutes warning. Others knew nothing until they saw the towering plume of dust that preceded the house-high wall of water down the valley. Six people drowned and

Jim Paxton

all but a few of Wilford's 154 houses were swept away or totally destroyed. The flood, now several miles wide, stripped away the topsoil down to bedrock as it rushed on.

Shortly after 1:00 P.M., the water, carrying hundreds of power and telephones poles and other debris, slammed into Sugar City. Moving at 15 miles per hour, the water shoved rock houses off their foundations and turned frame houses into rubble. Some buildings were carried down the valley. One four-year-old girl repeatedly told her aunt, "the house just was floating away — but soon it will come back, huh?"

The water level reached nearly ten feet in Sugar City.

The raging mass of debris moved through the tiny community of Hibbard and into the larger town of Rexburg. It gutted businesses, scattering merchandise across the countryside. It dumped tons of rubble, including dead livestock, into the lower section of town while residents watched from a nearby hill.

Near Menon, the floodwater poured into the Snake River.

Towns and cities downstream on the Snake had time to brace for the flood. They used the time to build sandbag dikes. Idaho Falls residents were able to keep most of the water in the river channel. But a few miles beyond, the water sneaked over the bank and swamped the west side of the town of Shelley. Farther on, it turned the Blackfoot shopping mall into a muddy swimming pool.

The rampage ended three days after it began. Officials at American Falls Dam released water for two days to make room in the reservoir for the coming flood. Another dam upstream on the South Fork of the Snake shut its gates to reduce the amount of water coming into the reservoir. The moves created a giant catch basin that absorbed the Teton flood with room to spare.

Hundreds of people lost their homes, businesses, prized possessions, treasured pets, and livestock. The area in the path of the flood lost valuable topsoil. It took years to rebuild. But a sense of humor is one of life's greatest assets and the victims of the Teton Dam Disaster kept a tight grip on their smiles.

When LaRee Howard began cleaning up the muddy mess that had engulfed her music box collection, she lifted one to wipe it off. It began playing, *How Dry I Am*.

The Trupp family home floated two miles and ended up on the Lusk farm. The table was neatly set for lunch and a pie was in the oven.

A woman grabbed a swimming suit and rushed out the door when she heard the flood was coming. When her neighbor asked her if that was all she was taking, she ran back into her house and grabbed another swimming suit.

One man began the long process of drying and cleaning out his house. He notice one wall was bulging. When the bulge continued to grow for several days he became concerned and tore the wall open. He discovered mice had stored a large quantity of dried beans on the wall cavity. The flood soaked the beans, which swelled up and pushed out the wall.

In the town of Hibbard, a woman found a dresser in her field. She took out the contents, washed and dried the clothing and linen, and returned the items to their owner in Sugar City. Another Hibbard resident walked around Sugar City looking for the owner of some false teeth he had found. But one Hibbard man's sense of humor was taxed when he found a dead cow "sleeping" in his bed.

The Teton Dam was not rebuilt.

FIFTY-SEVEN

Payette River — 1978

The South Fork Claims a Legend

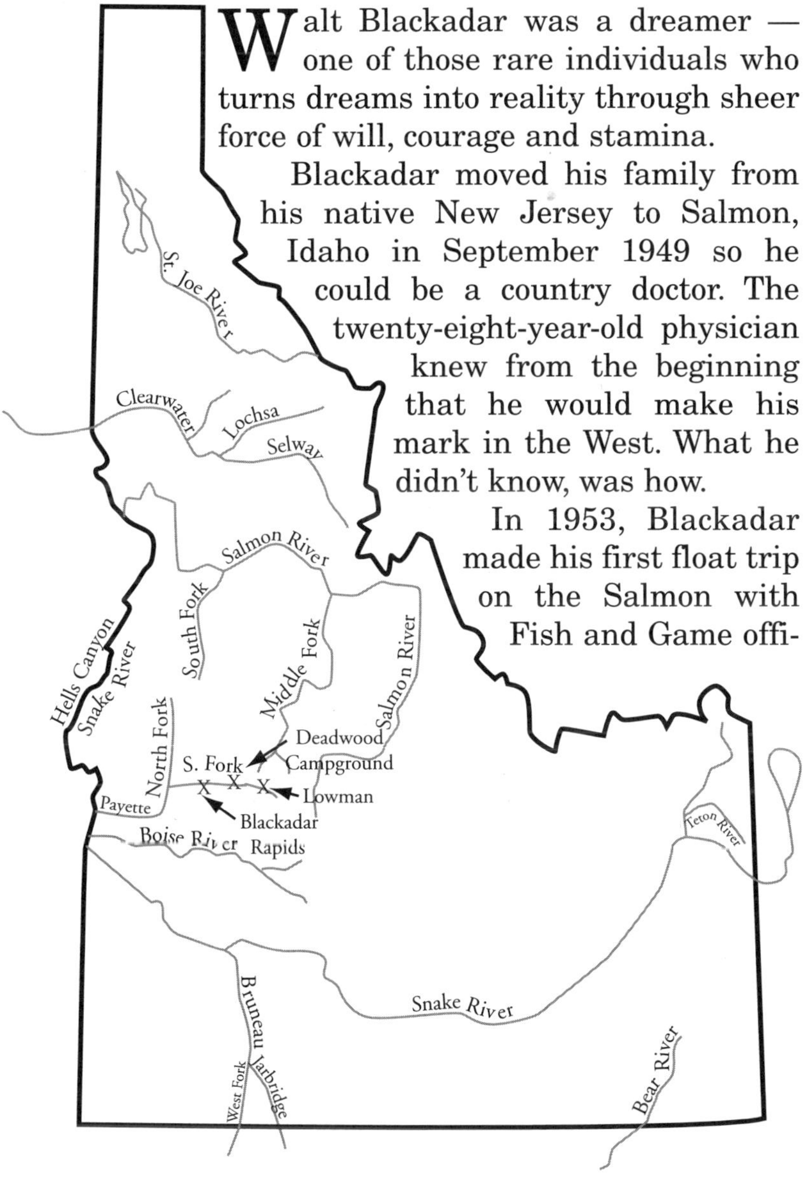

Walt Blackadar was a dreamer — one of those rare individuals who turns dreams into reality through sheer force of will, courage and stamina.

Blackadar moved his family from his native New Jersey to Salmon, Idaho in September 1949 so he could be a country doctor. The twenty-eight-year-old physician knew from the beginning that he would make his mark in the West. What he didn't know, was how.

In 1953, Blackadar made his first float trip on the Salmon with Fish and Game officer Eddie Linck. There was a wooden platform in the middle of their rubber raft with sweeps at each end to guide the craft. They put in at the mouth of the Middle Fork of the Salmon and floated downstream, portaging around Dagger Falls.

The Middle Fork is a challenge to all who float it. It was a voyage of one calamity after another for two men with little river experience. When rocks destroyed one of the sweeps, Blackadar tore to door off an abandoned cabin to make a new one. When the trip was over, the doctor was hooked on whitewater adrenaline.

Two years later, Blackadar again challenged the Middle Fork of the Salmon. He and three companions took a ten-man rubber raft through that stretch.

When the party reached Dagger Falls, Blackadar decided he didn't want to carry the heavy raft past the obstacle. Others had lined their craft through the falls and he decided to do the same. His plan was to swim out, towing a line to Dagger Rock, the boulder for which the falls is named. Then, with the help of the people on shore, the boat could be gently lowered down the four steps of the falls.

Blackadar was confident he could swim through the current to the rock if he was unencumbered by a life jacket. He reasoned that if he missed his mark, he could hold onto the rope until his friends pulled him to safety.

The current was stronger than expected. Blackadar was carried downstream, past the rock and over the first fall. He dangled there while his companions tried to free him from the force of the river. When his strength gave out, he let go of the rope and dropped into the pool below. He immediately popped to the surface and appeared to be safe. But an undertow sucked him back down, forcing him to come face-to-face with mortality. When the river finally spat him out, Blackadar felt elated. He had faced death and it didn't terrify him or make him panic. He had won.

In 1965, Blackadar became interested in kayaking. He was a pioneer in a sport that he enjoyed because he was one-on-one against the river. It wasn't until the 1970s that the sport became popular in Idaho. Until May, 1978, Blackadar was the most experienced kayaker in the state.

Blackadar decided in 1971 it was time for a man to paddle through Turnback Canyon on Alaska's Alsek River. No one ever had challenged a more intimidating stretch of whitewater. Blackadar was forty-nine years old, had a slight paunch and lacked an athlete's endurance. But he had plenty of nerve.

The problem was he couldn't find anyone else willing to take the challenge with him, because most people considered the idea insanity. Blackadar paddled through the canyon alone. After trying to power through a great roller wave that damaged his kayak, he managed to reach shore. In a drizzling rain, he sat beside his incapacitated craft and wrote a passage in his journal describing the adventure.

> "One huge horrendous mile of hair (the worst foamy rapids a kayaker can imagine), 30 feet wide, 50,000 cubic feet per second and a twenty degree downgrade going like hell. Incredible! I didn't flip in that mile or I would-

> n't be writing ... I'm not coming back. Not for $50,000, not for all the tea in China. Read my words well and don't be a fool. It's unpaddleable."

Perhaps his words were a warning to others who might try to run Turnback Canyon, a journey he completed in a patched kayak. But more likely it was a reminder to himself never to return, less he forget the intensity and danger of the experience.

Walt Blackadar became known throughout the kayaking and canoeing field. Numerous whitewater magazines and outdoor periodicals wrote of his experiences. Many of his daredevil runs were filmed. The doctor from Salmon became a legend in his own time.

No matter how dangerous or fearsome his journeys, Blackadar never seemed to get enough adventure or challenge. He continued to seek the ultimate whitewater thrill. Yet, it wasn't that ultimate challenge that brought him to his end. It wasn't the Alesek River, nor Alaska's treacherous Susitana River, which he ran twice between 1972 and 1974. It wasn't the Colorado, where he tackled Crystal and Lava Falls with tremendous courage. Blackadar wasn't known for his technique.

It was Mother's Day weekend 1978. The fifty-five-year-old Blackadar invited a group of friends from the Sun Valley area to join him in a run down the South Fork of the Payette River. Two of the friends, Keith Taylor and Tullio Celano, couldn't get away. But Taylor warned Blackadar about a big log spanning most of the river in the rapids below Big Falls. Such an obstacle is known to kayakers as a "sweeper."

Thin white jet vapor trails generated by transcontinental airline flights crisscrossed the powder blue sky above, as eight people unloaded their kayaks at Deadwood Campground that Saturday morning. Redwing blackbirds called out from a nearby cattail patch.

The first five-mile section of the South Fork run went smoothly, with all the members of the party easily pulling into the eddy above Big Falls. After portaging around the falls, everyone settled back in their kayaks. Two members of the group, John Petit and Jeff Bevan, headed downriver with Blackadar third in line.

Beyond the falls, the South Fork rushes into a series of Class IV rapids enclosed in a granite canyon. Spotting the submerged sweeper log just beyond the first drop, the two men pulled into small eddies. Blackadar drifted past. The men assumed he would line up at the drop and make a hard right turn to bypass the obstacle. But Blackadar hadn't seen any problem when he viewed the stretch from the road above. Ignoring the barely visible riffle, he maneuvered around the right side of a midstream boulder — the rock holding the submerged log in place.

His Lettman Mark IV kayak rammed head-on into the sweeper, jamming Blackadar under it. He reacted calmly, reaching up, out and down with broad sweeps of his paddle to keep his head above the water and his craft from slipping farther under the log. However the force of the current stood the kayak on end. It slipped below the surface where it remained pinned.

The other kayakers cleared the sweeper and eddied out below, unable to reach Blackadar. They bobbed in silence, helplessly waiting for their companion to surface. The doomed kayak was eerily visible below the surface.

Time passed. For Blackadar, the roaring of the rapids ceased. His empty life jacket bobbed to the surface while the river carried its prize down his last whitewater — now known as Blackadar Rapids.

And though you be done to death, what then?
If you battled the best you could;
If you played your part in the world of men,
Why, the Critic will call it good.
Death comes with a crawl, or comes with a pounce,
And whether he's slow or spry,
It isn't the fact that you're dead that counts,
But only, how did you die?

From *How Did You Die?* by Edmond Vance Cooke.

FIFTY-EIGHT

Salmon River — 1978

Incident at Devil's Slide

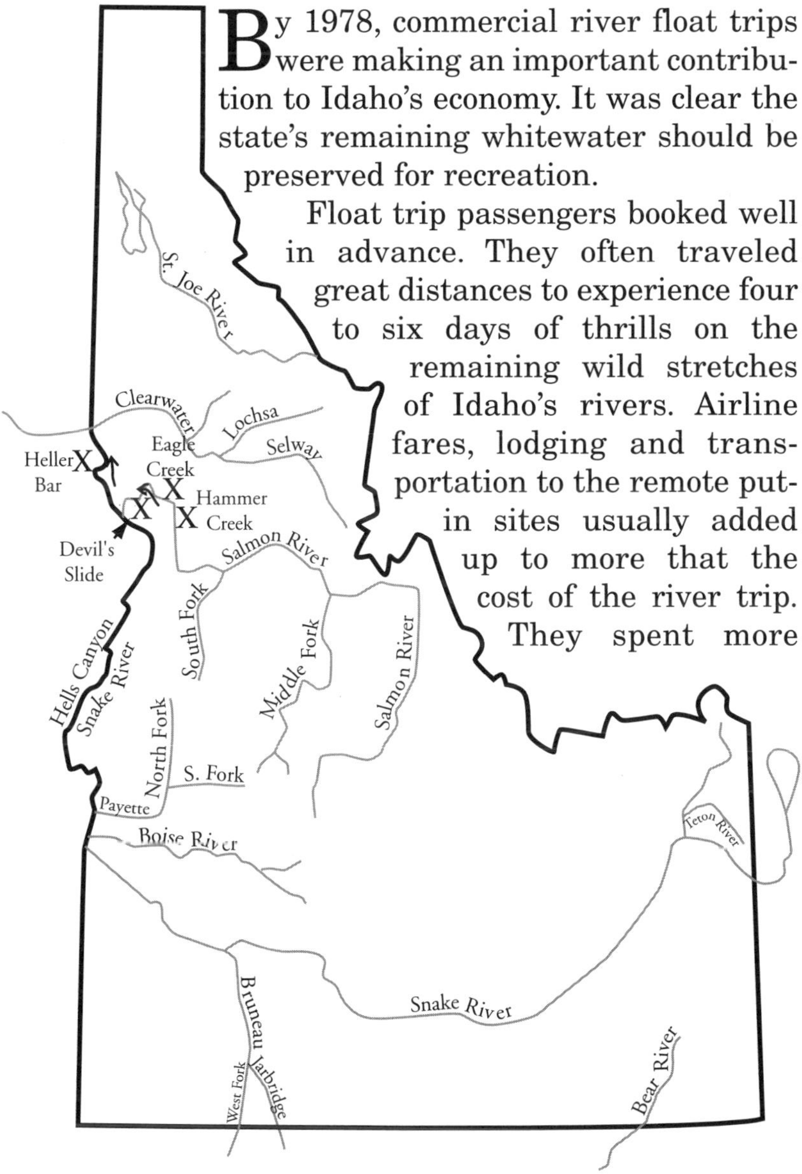

By 1978, commercial river float trips were making an important contribution to Idaho's economy. It was clear the state's remaining whitewater should be preserved for recreation.

Float trip passengers booked well in advance. They often traveled great distances to experience four to six days of thrills on the remaining wild stretches of Idaho's rivers. Airline fares, lodging and transportation to the remote put-in sites usually added up to more that the cost of the river trip. They spent more money for gear. After all, who would want to look like a "whitewater geek" or "river nerd?"

Many of the vacationers have never run a river before, and many never will have the electrifying experience again.

High water. Low water. Commercial river runners have little choice but to continue operations on schedule. They can't say "Sorry, folks, the water's too high (or low) this week. Go back home."

Nineteen seventy-eight was a high snowpack year, following a cold spring. A late June warming spell sent torrents of icy water down feeder streams, swelling the Salmon River. On June 29, when Grand Canyon Dories had scheduled its first trip of the season, the Lower Salmon was flowing at about 30,000 cubic feet per second — much higher than normal for that time of year.

Grand Canyon Dories, originally based in the southwest, had expanded into Idaho by 1974, running both the Salmon and Snake Rivers. The initial trip of 1978 was made up of one wood and two fiberglass dories — boats with narrow, flat bottoms, high ends and flaring sides. The campboat was an Avon Professional raft. Guides Clarence Reese and Gary Lane piloted the fiberglass boats. Barry Dow handled the wooden model and Chip Weber manned the raft.

Chip Weber, not a regular employee of Grand Canyon Dories, held a lead license for the Lower Salmon, and was hired to provide the qualifying commercial license for the June 29 trip.

The river flow caused some concern for the management as well as the guides. Most of the rapids were hidden under high water, along with most of the good campsites. The remaining rapids were massive, the largest being the Slide Rapid — Devil's Slide — fifty-one miles below the put-in. During high flow, the constriction formed by the slide on the left side, combined with the vertical walls of Blue Canyon, produces enormous breaking waves and dangerous hydraulics. The steep canyon walls make portage nearly impossible and the swift current prevents lining the boats through the rough water.

To minimize the danger at Devil's Slide, the support management team took several precautions. A small plane would fly over the slide on the day prior to the arrival of the dories. If the observers decided the run would be too risky, a take-out crew would be sent to Eagle Creek, the last place where it was possible to leave the river before reaching the slide. If it was decided that the run was possible, a jet boat would be hired to stand by at the bottom of the rapid to give assistance in the event of an upset.

Hammer Creek, just south of the town of White Bird was the put-in for the eighty-mile float trip to Heller Bar. Heller Bar is located at the junction of the Snake and Grande Ronde rivers, south of Asotin, Washington.

The first couple of days of the trip were uneventful, although Right Way Drop and Lorna's Lulu, normally insignificant areas, had developed into huge and challenging rapids. The skilled boatmen gave their passengers plenty of thrills, making the best use of the fast-flowing river.

The swift running water put the tour far ahead of schedule. The guides decided to lay over one day at White House Bar, usually a large, sandy beach on the right side of the river. The bar, however, was flooded back to a narrow strip of sand.

Barry Dow was the only member of the group to have previously seen Devil's Slide when the water was running so high. Discussions among the guides centered around Dow and his knowledge of the rapid. In hushed tones the men speculated on the river flow, which had been increasing daily, and their chances of successfully running the slide. The customers had seen little but smooth, fast-flowing water. Picking up bits and pieces of the conversation between the guides, the vacationers became convinced that the "huge rapid" was an elaborate myth concocted for their benefit.

On the morning of July 2, the layover camp was packed up more slowly than normal. Eagle Creek was fourteen miles downriver — a day's float at low water, but only a couple of hours away under existing conditions. The guides were fairly certain that the shuttle crew would meet them at Eagle Creek for an early take-out.

But there was no crew at Eagle Creek. The guides looked uneasy as the party floated past the point of no return. Their set jaws and sideways glances turned the melodrama into a class act play for passengers who began to believe their hosts should be in Hollywood instead of running rivers.

Near Flynn Creek, seven miles beyond Eagle Creek, the guides made lunch. Knowing what was ahead, they weren't hungry themselves. Seeing the guides' lack of enthusiasm for the meal, the passengers began to take the situation more seriously.

As they pushed off and headed through Blue Canyon, the skies darkened and a storm moved in. Thunder echoed down the gorge. They could hear the roar when they still were a half mile above Devil's Slide. When the slide appeared on the left in the distance, the guides pulled the boats to shore. Barry Dow described what happened.

> "After tying our boats we walked cautiously through the jagged rock of a land slide, making our way around bus-size boulders to get our first look at what lay below.
>
> "The first few minutes were silent as we all stared in shock at the violence below. I assumed that this water had risen to 40,000 cfs or more, given what I was looking at. Earlier in the spring a training trip had been through at 34,000 cfs and the rapid seemed to us to be pretty sketchy for safety, though we did not have problems at that level."

Chip Weber, convinced that the boats would flip regardless of the route taken, went back to the Avon raft. He was not carrying passengers in the camp boat and was responsible only for himself. He eased his feeling of impending doom with a couple of beers.

While Dow, Lane and Reese discussed possible maneuvers from their scouting point, Everett Spaulding, long-time river runner, arrived in his jet boat and positioned himself below the rapid. He was accompanied by a half-dozen Grand Canyon Dories personnel.

The guides couldn't decide on a route through the rapid. It was decided, however, to allow only two passengers in each dory. Their weight might be needed to help high-side a tipping boat. The remaining passengers would have to pick their way though the sharp, loose rocks of the slide. The dories would pick them up below the rapid.

Barry Dow volunteered to lead the way. He had been experiencing a rush of adrenaline since seeing the rapid and was ready to put an end to it. Having to hold back and watch the other boats would only prolong the anxiety. He was convinced that the only way through the torrent was to avoid the main vortex.

> "A left entry, pulling downstream through the left side of a huge V wave about twenty feet from the vortex, put me in a most violent eddy line and into the back footwell of my dory momentarily," Dow later wrote. "When I got back in the rowing seat, we were spinning wildly toward the wall on the left. I managed to get the boat straightened out and with the help of a favorable boil, stayed off the wall."

Dow parked his dory on a small sandbar a quarter mile below the rapid.

Gary Lane challenged the slide next, choosing to run down the vortex. He pushed hard into the center and disappeared into the maelstrom. About sixty yards downriver, his empty boat resurfaced. Everett Spaulding and the support crew plucked the swimmers from the churning river.

Clarence Reese powered his dory down the center, too. He and his passengers suffered the same outcome and the previous boat and were fished out of the river.

Chip Weber came last. The rubber raft floated into the rapid sideways, her foredoomed pilot never taking a stroke with the oars. Sixty yards downstream, the upside down Avon bobbed to the surface. Weber popped up nearby.

Due, in part, to the quick action of Spaulding and the support crew, no one was injured during the Devil's Slide challenge and little gear was lost.

Several years later, Barry Dow and Gary Lane hiked into the slide from Waphilla Creek when the Lower Salmon was flowing at approximately 70,000 cubic feet per second. They saw bubbles the size of basketballs rising up from the eddy to the right of the vortex. Logs up to 150 feet long, disappeared at the entry and exploded to the surface near the bottom of the rapid.

Although many boats run the lower Salmon each year, few venture into Blue Canyon and down Devil's Slide when the river is in its spring frenzy.

Author's note: On June 9, 1996, during a near record spring runoff, Clarence (Clancy) Reese drowned after his dory flipped at the base of Chittam Rapid on the main Salmon. His body was recovered at Spring Bar, nearly fifteen miles downriver.

At Spring Bar the following Saturday, an urn containing Clancy's ashes was placed in his dory. The craft was piled with driftwood and set ablaze. The dory drifted a short distance with the current, then sank.

Nearly 200 friends of the well-loved river-runner lined the banks of the Salmon to bid Clancy farewell.

River Time

J. C. Caccia, alias Johnny Buffalo, is a seasoned river guide. Once he sought employment during the "off-season." He asked his prospective employer if there might be a job that offered a schedule similar to "river time." The businessman asked the guide, "What exactly is river time?"

"River time," Johnny Buffalo explained, "is when you wake up in the morning and it's time for breakfast. Then before long it's time to make time, so down the river we go. It's just a matter of time before lunch and by that time it's time to spend time fishing. Of course you know how time flies when you're having fun, and before you have time to realize that you're practically running out of time, it's 'Happy Hour!', just in the nick of time, 'cause a person needs time to unwind from the time-filled day. Dinner gets served and eaten in a timely fashion and, not wanting to be pressed for time in the future, I like to bide my remaining time preparing for more good time come tomorrow. When you're on river time, time is always on time and there's no time like the present to sit around the campfire and talk about old times before bedtime."

The employer was impressed but said, "I'm sorry Johnny Buffalo, but I don't think we have a job that will fit your description."

"That's all right, sir," Johnny said. "I'm a professional river guide and I don't like to waste time working anyway."

Anyone who has ever run a river knows the "river time" that J. C. Caccia so sagaciously describes. Those who have yet to experience it are missing one of life's most enchanting reprieves from the clutches of the clock.

Bibliography

Ashworth, Williams; *Hells Canyon, the Deepest Gorge on Earth*; Hawthorn Book, Inc., N.Y., 1977.

Bailey, Robert G.; *Hell's Canyon*; Bailey Blake Printing Co., Lewiston, Idaho, 1947.

Bailey, Robert G.; *River of No Return*; Bailey Blake Printing Co., Lewiston, Idaho, 1947.

Beal, Merrill D.; *I Will Fight No More Forever*; Ballantine Books, N.Y., 1963.

Brown, Jennie Broughton; *Fort Hall on the Oregon Trail*; The Caxton Printers, Ltd., Caldwell, Idaho, 1932.

Carrey, John; Conley, Cort; *River of No Return*; Backeddy Books, Cambridge, Idaho, 1977.

Carrey, John; Conley, Cort and Barton, Ace; *Snake River of Hells Canyon*; Backeddy Books, Cambridge, Idaho, 1979.

Carrey, John; Conley, Cort; *The Middle Fork and the Sheepeater War*; Backeddy Books, Cambridge, Idaho, 1977.

Conley, Cort; *Idaho for the Curious*; Backeddy Books; Cambridge, Idaho, 1982.

Crowell, Sandra A.; Asleson, David O.; *Up the Swiftwater*, A Pictorial History of the Colorful Upper St. Joe River Country; Museum of North Idaho, 1995.

Dick, Everett; *Vanguards of the Frontier*; University of Nebraska Press.

Elsensohn, Sister M. Alfreda; *Pioneer Days in Idaho County* Volumes one and two; The Caxton Printers Ltd., Caldwell, Idaho, 1947 and 1951.

Gibbs, Rage; *Beckoning the Bold*; University of Idaho Press, Moscow, Idaho, 1976.

Gregg, Jacob Ray; *Pioneer Days in Malheur County;* Lorrin Morrison, Los Angeles, California, 1950.

Hanley, Mike; Ellis Lucia; *Owyhee Trails*; The Caxton Printers. Ltd., Caldwell, Idaho, 1988.

Hendrickson, Borg; Laughy, Linwood; *Clearwater Country*: Mountain Meadow Press; Kookia, Idaho, 1990.

Eloward, Helen Addison and McGarth, Dan; *War Chief Joseph*; The Caxton Printers, Ltd., Caldwell, Idaho, 1946

Huntley, James L.; *Ferry Boats in Idaho*; The Caxton Printers, Ltd., Caldwell, Idaho, 1979.

Jordan, Grace; *Home Below Hell's Canyon*; Thomas Cromwell Company, New York, 1954.

Lyon, Ruth B.; *The Village That Grew*; Ruth B. Lyon, Boise, Idaho, 1979.

Madsen, Brigham D.; *The Bannock of Idaho*; The Caxton Printers, Ltd., Caldwell, Idaho, 1958.

Madsen, Brigham D.; *The Northern Shoshone*; The Caxton Printers, Ltd., Caldwell, Idaho, 1980.

Mills, Nellie B.; *All Along The River Territorial and Pioneer days on the Payette*; Payette, 1963.

Monaghan, Jay; *The Overland Trail*; The Bobbs-Merrill Company, New York; 1947.

Moore, Greg; McClaran, Don; *Idaho Whitewater*; Classic VI Whitewater; McCall, Idaho, 1989.

Palmer, Tim; *The Snake River*; Island Press, Covelo, California, 1991.

Roberts, Edwards; *Shoshone and Other Western Wonders*; Harper and Brothers, N.Y., N.Y., 1988.

Robertson, Frank C.; *Fort Hall*; Hasting House, New York, 1963.

Rogers, F. B. *Soldiers of the Overland*; The Grabhorn Press, San Francisco, California, 1938.

Ricks College Press; *That Day in June Reflections on the Teton Dam Disaster*; Rexburg, Idaho, 1977.

Rhodenbaugh, Edward F.; *Sketches of Idaho Geology*; Boise, Idaho, 1961.

Stacy, Susan M.; *When The River Rises*; Boise State University, 1993.

Stuebner, Stephen; *Paddling the Payette*; Paddling the Payette Productions, 1995.

Tucker, Gerald J.; *The Story of Hells Canyon*; Gerald J. Tucker; 1977.

Watters, Ron; *Never Turn Back*; Great Rift Press, Pocatello, Idaho, 1994.

Williamson, Darcy; *Mountainmen of Idaho*; Maverick Publications, Bend, Oregon, 1988.

INDEX

Other Caxton Books by Darcy Williamson

Basque Cooking and Lore

ISBN 0-87004-346-3 175 pages comb binding $14.95

The Rocky Mountain Wild Foods Cookbook

ISBN 0-87004-367-6 251 pages comb binding $17.95

Other Caxton Idaho Titles

Southern Idaho Ghost Towns

by Wayne Sparling

ISBN 0-87004-229-7 135 pages paper $12.95

Gem Minerals of Idaho

by John A. Beckwith

ISBN 0-87004-228-9 129 pages paper $9.95

Tiger on the Road
The Life of Vardis Fisher

by Tim Woodword

ISBN 0-87004-333-1 269 pages paper $14.95

ISBN 0-87004-338-2 cloth $19.95

For a free catalog of Caxton books write to:

The Caxton Printers, Ltd.
Publishing Department
312 Main Street
Caldwell, ID 83605

or

Visit our Internet Website:

www.caxtonprinters.com